W9-BTO-947

PRAISE F[...]

Terror Incor[...]

"Utterly compelling, heroically [...]

"A fascinating and incisive catal[...]ng[...]ng of the known economic activities of organizations that, whether terrorist [...] or not, have [...] their aim the [...] transformation of the existing order in the Middle E[...] the broader Muslim world and [...] United States."
—*New York Times*

"A history of terror which extends far beyond the current Islamic threat . . . she ranges across the whole world to describe the terrible, entangled business of money and violence that she calls the 'new economy of terror' . . . to build a terrifying picture."
—*Literary Review*

"Economist Loretta Napoleoni comes up with a startling conclusion that the 'New Economy of Terror' is a fast growing international economic system, with a turnover of about $1.5 trillion, twice the GDP of the United Kingdom."
—*Wall Street Journal*

"Rather than look at terrorism from a political or religious standpoint, Napoleoni approaches it as an economist, which she was before becoming a writer. The business of terrorism is now so large and the financial networks supporting it so complex, she says, that if the flow of money to terrorists were suddenly cut off, the drop in liquidity could have a serious impact on the Western economies."
—*Newsweek*

"Napoleoni traces fifty years of Western economic and political dominance in developing Muslim countries—backing repressive, corrupt regimes, fighting the Cold War by Proxy and blocking the legitimate economic ascendancy of millions. 'As in the Crusades,' in which Napoleoni finds many modern parallels, 'religion is simply a recruitment tool; the real driving force is economics.'"
—*Publisher's Weekly*

"Most recent books on terrorism attempt to locate its motivation in history, culture, or religion. Napoleoni focuses on economics and therefore adds a useful new layer to the study of terrorism. The book's strength is its determination to 'follow the money,' highlighting the consequences of economic dependency and providing detailed accounts of how terrorist organizations are funded."
—*Choice*

INSURGENT IRAQ
Al Zarqawi and the New Generation

Loretta Napoleoni

Forewords by Jason Burke and Nick Fielding

SEVEN STORIES PRESS
New York

First North American edition, October 2005

Seven Stories Press
140 Watts Street
New York, NY 10013
www.sevenstories.com

In Canada:
Publishers Group Canada, 250A Carlton Street, Toronto, ON M5A 2L1

Library of Congress Cataloging-in-Publication Data

Napoleoni, Loretta.
    Insurgent Iraq : al-Zarqawi and the new generation / Loretta Napoleoni.— 1st North American ed.
        p. cm.
    Includes bibliographical references and index.
    ISBN-13: 978-1-58322-705-3 (pbk. : alk. paper)
    ISBN-10: 1-58322-705-9 (pbk. : alk. paper)
    1. Iraq War, 2003- 2. Insurgency—Iraq. 3. Zarqawi, Abu Mus'ab, 1966–   4. Terrorism—Iraq. 5. Qaida (Organization) I. Title.
    DS79.76.N36 2005
    956.7044'3—dc22   2005022959

College professors may order examination copies of Seven Stories Press titles for a free six-month trial period. To order, visit www.sevenstories.com/textbook, or fax on school letterhead to (212) 226-1411.

9 8 7 6 5 4 3 2 1

Printed in Canada

For Alexander, Andrew, Leigh and Julian—
to remind them to look for the truth.

Contents

Foreword

BY JASON BURKE

It was late 2001 and I was in Khost, in eastern Afghanistan. Kabul had fallen a few days earlier and the Taliban regime was crumbling. Osama bin Laden had vanished. American warplanes left a latticework of vapor trails across the blue sky. In Khost I found dozens of documents left by militants who had trained in the military camps around the city over the previous few years. They confirmed many of my previous ideas about al Qaeda.

Al Qaeda appeared to be more of an ideology than an organization, an idea or a cause rather than a structured group. Al Qaeda was a worldview.

Eight months later I was in northern Iraq, researching the group of Islamic militants who had carved out an enclave within the autonomous zone run by the Kurds. I spent days talking to former Ansar al Islam operatives and investigating the roots of the group. Like every other militant organization, Ansar al Islam was the result of the complex interplay of long-term and short-term factors in the Muslim world and in the interaction of the Muslim world with the West.

The first I heard of Abu Mos'ab al Zarqawi was when Colin Powell, the American secretary of state, mentioned him in his speech to the United Nations on 5 February 2003. Powell hoped to portray al Zarqawi as a link between Saddam Hussein and Osama bin Laden via Ansar al Islam, depicting him as the sophisticated mastermind behind what could be a wave of attacks with biological or chemical weapons. The speech linked Khost with Kurdistan.

Powell, I wrote at the time, was either misinformed or deliberately misleading. As Loretta Napoleoni shows in these pages, al Zarqawi was neither linked to Saddam Hussein nor capable of deploying hideous poisons through a global network.

However, al Zarqawi was—and is—significant in several ways. He is an example of how the West has created bogeymen. These figures of fanciful power (bin Laden is another one) are supposed to be the cause of the terrorist threat that confronts us. Al Zarqawi is also an example of how the bogeymen have a habit of, eventually, fulfilling the role we give them.

Al Zarqawi came to broad public notice with the videotaped kidnapping and killing of hostages in Iraq in 2004. To understand what led to these appalling atrocities, we need first to identify the intended audience for these statements. Islamic militant terrorism is primarily propaganda and not usually tied to specific political objectives. Though they served his purpose of frightening vital Western contractors out of Iraq and thus generating destabilizing discontent by slowing reconstruction, the videos fulfilled al Zarqawi's primary goal: to communicate. The videos were clever, professional, and laden with meanings that many in the West missed entirely.

This is not surprising, for al Zarqawi, like other Islamic militants, is not talking to the West. The hostages, the European and American publics, their leaders, and the 155,000 apparently impotent foreign troops in Iraq were all unwitting actors in his carefully scripted drama. The audience was the world's 1.3 billion Muslims.

Well aware of the fact that hacking people's heads off live on camera disgusts the vast majority of those he is addressing, al Zarqawi first set out to convince those watching that his actions were legitimate. To do so he picked the most emotive issues in the Islamic world. His execution of Ken Bigley, a hapless, elderly British engineer, was supposedly in response to the alleged imprisonment, and abuse, of Muslim women by non-Muslim men in Iraq and elsewhere.

The issue took al Zarqawi immediately into the realm of the myth. American jails did not actually contain thousands of such prisoners, as he claimed, but after Abu Ghraib most in the Middle East thought they did. The incarceration of women also tapped the profound sense of humiliation, disenfranchisement, and emasculation felt by hundreds of millions of young Muslim men faced with the apparent military, political, and, increasingly, cultural dominance by the West.

Al Zarqawi, whose thuggish demeanor belies his talent for exploiting modern media, then started to develop his themes, again appealing to the same basic belief with a series of videotaped kidnappings and executions. His message was simple: the United States is leading an aggressive attempt by the new "Crusaders" to subordinate the Islamic world. He deployed images of violent conflict, particularly the carnage of suicide bombings, and videotaped last testaments of "martyrs," stressing the power of faith, the crucial commodity possessed by the mujahedin and lacked by their enemies. His victims were dressed in orange jump-suits, like prisoners at Guantánamo.

The climactic act—the execution—was a ritualized slaughter. Militants actually kill with guns and bombs, not long knives. Al Zarqawi was deliberately trying to shock his audience. Though moderates may have been stunned by the brutality, he was gambling that those with any sympathy for the radical Islamic agenda might be impressed by how far he was prepared to go. Al Zarqawi has understood that violence affects not just victims, but witnesses too.

And there is another key audience. Though in very broad terms committed to a similar agenda, Islamic militants are a quarrelsome bunch, riven by personal jealousies and ambition. Al Zarqawi heads a new generation of younger, less-educated, less-political operators who now challenge senior leaders such as Osama bin Laden. Al Zarqawi, who grew up in a breezeblock house in a rough, poor city north of Jordan's capital, became involved in Islamic militancy in Afghanistan in the late 1990s, at about the time that forty-seven-year-old bin Laden started his "al Qaeda" project. As Loretta Napoleoni shows, the younger man, far from being an "affiliate," as the Americans say, has always resented the Saudi-born militant's preeminence and his wealthy upbringing. The executions, perhaps even by al Zarqawi's own hand, are a strong challenge to a man like bin Laden, who has, for fifteen years, sent others out to fight and die, and is confined to the mountains of eastern Afghanistan, far from the killing grounds of Falluja.

However, al Zarqawi does not share bin Laden's strategic intelligence. The Saudi's aim was to radicalize and mobilize the masses of the Middle East, and he has been careful not to alienate his core constituency by attacking only targets symbolic of the West's might. But al Zarqawi has misjudged his audience. Only the most extreme support his actions. Though numerous enough to do serious harm, they are vastly outnumbered by moderates. This offers hope of a sort.

In *The Secret Agent*, Joseph Conrad's superb and searching novel of anarchists in London a century ago, a terrorist mastermind dreams of "a band of men, absolute in their resolve to discard all scruples, strong enough to give themselves frankly the name of destroyers, and free from . . . pity for anything on earth." He would no doubt have approved of Abu Mos'ab al Zarqawi. But we need to remember that though the thirty-seven-year-old, Jordanian-born militant's actions may seem psychotic, there is method to his madness.

Foreword

BY NICK FIELDING

In December 2001, as he was on the run following the collapse of the Taliban regime in Afghanistan, Dr. Ayman al Zawahiri, the chief theoretician of al Qaeda and the man responsible for creating the myth of Osama bin Laden, decided to publish a book, *Knights Under the Prophet's Banner.*

As the emirate of Afghanistan, which for six years had been a haven and nursery for the rapidly expanding organization, crumbled around him, al Zawahiri—through the book and in speeches made since then—set out his strategy for the future.

For those of his followers who had just witnessed the 9/11 attacks on America and had heard his speeches extolling the importance of the global jihad, the book must have come as something of a shock. Instead of emphasizing the importance of what al Qaeda's followers have always thought of as the "far enemy," namely, the Western countries, al Zawahiri reasserted the importance of the return home from exile.

The argument that the road to the liberation of Jerusalem lay through Cairo had always been a strong theme amongst the members of the Egyptian Islamic jihad who made up the hardcore of al Qaeda's leadership, even though it ran in sharp contrast to the teachings of Abdallah Azzam, the spiritual mentor of Osama bin Laden and also of Abu Muhammad al Maqdisi, who fulfilled the same position in relation to the subject of this book, Abu Mos'ab al Zarqawi.

11

The "international" line had been strongly promoted by the Saudi faction within al Qaeda's leadership, who more and more were dominating the discussions within the organization. They argued that the global struggle should be aimed not at destroying Western civilization, but at driving the Americans in particular out of the Arab and Muslim world. Only then could the jihadists deal with their own rulers.

Al Zawahiri's book, in one sense, was a countercoup against the Saudi circle around bin Laden that argued solely for an international jihad. It would take several years for its ideas to sink into the movement. But it was to provide the basis for al Zarqawi to bring his organization into the fold of al Qaeda, an event sealed with an agreement on 17 October 2004.

The invasion of Iraq by America and its allies in March 2003 speeded up this process enormously. Clearly, there was no need to travel very far now to attack American forces. They were fighting on Arab soil. It gave the Islamists the perfect opportunity to focus once more on the Arab lands and to return from exile. That message has been taken to heart by a whole new generation of young Muslim fighters, who have streamed back to Iraq in their thousands for an opportunity to fight against the "Crusaders."

By mid-2005 hundreds of attacks were taking place against Coalition and Iraqi forces every day. More than one thousand policemen had been killed in the previous year. Al Qaeda was able to mount up to twelve suicide bomb attacks on a single day. More than thirty Iraqis were being killed in violent incidents every day. Nearly two thousand Coalition troops had been killed and thousands more severely injured.

Bin Laden himself was not slow to abandon his old ideas and those of the circle around him. More and more his speeches have concentrated on the conflict in Iraq and on the failures of the rulers of the Arab world. The aim now was to build jihad in Iraq and Egypt as a way of strengthening the struggle in Saudi Arabia. Next would come a move to unify the jihadists in Syria, Palestine, and Lebanon, followed by North Africa.

This was the basis for the rapprochement between bin Laden and al Zarqawi, bringing together the most charismatic and the most deadly leaders amongst the jihadists. Bin Laden, cut off from the world and apparently beleaguered, now had a new ambassador. The reflected glory of the continuous bombings and assassinations aimed against the Coalition forces in Iraq rejuvenated bin Laden. Doubtless he has not given a single instruction to his new disciple, but still he can feed on the battle honors of al Qaeda in the land of the Two Rivers.

In writing this book on Abu Mos'ab al Zarqawi, Loretta Napoleoni has produced the first comprehensive assessment of the man, his origins, and his politics. She shows how, in the course of just a few years, he has risen from obscurity to become the most hunted man in the world, more important in many ways than bin Laden himself. The book brims with detail and explanation and offers many insights into his phenomenal rise to power.

We find ourselves now in a situation where the war in Iraq (how quickly that phrase slipped into usage!) is now almost running out of control. In June 2005 a leaked classified CIA assessment stated that Iraqi and foreign fighters are developing a broad range of skills, from car bombings and assassinations to coordinated attacks. It said the insurgency in Iraq is creating a new type of Islamic militant who could go on to destabilize other countries and that has skills that make him more dangerous than the fighters from Afghanistan in the 1980s and 1990s. "Those jihadists who survive will leave Iraq experienced in and focused on acts of urban terrorism," said Porter Goss, head of the CIA. The threat may grow when these fighters begin to disperse, either back to other Muslim countries or, increasingly, back to Europe, where many of them have lived in exile or as the sons of migrants.

Nothing could prepare you better for understanding these developments and anticipating their likely consequences than reading this book.

—Oxford, July 2005

Acknowledgments

In January 2005, Seven Stories Press asked me if I was interested in writing a short book on the Iraqi insurgency and al Zarqawi for publication in 2005. At the time I was in the midst of writing a book on the economics of Islamist terror that had been commissioned by Constable & Robinson and Marco Tropea Editore, yet Seven Stories' offer was very tempting. I consulted with both publishers and not only did they consent to give priority to *Insurgent Iraq: Al Zarqawi and the New Generation*, but both also agreed to publish it. So my thanks go to Dan Hind, my editor at Constable & Robinson, who for months worked incessantly with me, updating the text almost in real time to meet the tight deadline. His professional advice has been invaluable. My gratitude goes also to Marco Tropea, who, more than a publisher, has become a special friend, and who for years has supported me. Yet again he has agreed to translate my English writings into my native Italian. A special thanks to Seven Stories Press for suggesting a topic that is so vital to understanding our world. I have learned a lot researching this book and this knowledge has helped me clarify important issues in the analysis of the ideology and economics of the jihadist movement. My gratitude to Ria Julien, my U.S. editor, who, while on holiday, has edited and copyedited with me the final version of the text. Without her valuable input this book would not have been published on time.

I must also thank Patrice Barrat and Najat Rizk, directors of the documentary *Zarkaoui: la Question Terroriste*, who provided me with unpublished material and interviews on al Zarqawi. Valuable insights have also come from Fouad Hussein's investigation and documentary on al Zarqawi and his new book published in Arabic called *Al Zarqawi: The Second Generation of al Qaida*. It is an outstanding analysis of the global jihadist movement and of al Zarqawi's personality. I hope this book will soon be translated into English and other European languages. Barrat, Rizk, and Hussein's investigations unveiled so many mysteries; without their contributions this book could not have been written. Special thanks go to Abdallah Anas, who shared his fascinating stories about the mujahedin, the origins of al Qaeda, the personality of Osama bin Laden, and last, but not least, the extraordinary life of Sheikh Azzam.

As always, my agents Roberta Oliva and Francesca Manzoni have done a superb job in keeping all my publishers updated and pleased with my work. A special thanks also to their subagents, who have sold rights to so many translations.

The list of terrorist experts, people with whom I share the burden of investigating such a complex and serious topic, is endless. A very special thanks goes to Nick Fielding, a friend and mentor, who wrote the preface; he has been, as always, an invaluable source of information. I must thank him for our Friday evening discussions on the jihadist movement, which sometimes lasted until the small hours of the morning. Without such exchanges my work would be much less accurate and original than it is. A special mention also for Jason Burke, who wrote the foreword while traveling from one war zone to another. Jason always has time to exchange ideas and information with me, even while away in Iraq, Afghanistan, and the Middle East. Thank you also to Ahmed Rashid, who read the book on a plane from London to Pakistan and sent me so many suggestions; to Noam Chomsky, my friend and mentor, who has constantly encouraged me to pursue my research and writing, and has always found time to discuss new ideas with me; to Yoram Khati, one of the leading experts on al Qaeda and the jihadist movement in Israel, who read and checked the text twice to make sure I did not make any mistakes. Thank you to Rico Carish, a sincere friend, who went through chapter after chapter and who is always at the other end of the phone line for me, and to John Cooley who read a first draft of this book while promoting his new book, *An Alliance Against Babylon: The U.S., Israel and Iraq,* in England.

Finally, a special mention for Grant Woods, who once again read my work and came up with interesting ideas and suggestions, and to my invaluable research assistants Orna Almog, Natalie Nicora, and Oliver Shykles—they have all met the deadlines and produced outstanding work. Without their contribution and suggestions I would not have been able to complete this book in such a short time. Thank you to my friends from Chapter One Bookstore in Hamilton, Montana, for looking after me, and to Russ Lawrence, Jean Matthews, Laura Wathen, and Shawn Wathen for reading the text and offering so many suggestions.

My friend and editor Elisabeth Richards once again held my hand, read and reread my writing, polishing my English; I could not have reviewed chapter after chapter without her gentle and professional advice. A special thank to Claudia Gerson for spending the last two days of her holidays proofreading this book.

A special thank you to all the journalists and war correspondents I have been in touch with over the last years, many of whom have become friends. It is an honor to share their remarkable stories and adventures. Thank you to all the sources which choose to remain anonymous. They have offered me the opportunity to write not only the life story of al Zarqawi, but also an exposition on the evolution of the jihadist movement. Any errors in this book are mine alone.

A special thanks to the staff of the Alexis Hotel in Seattle, where I twice edited this book during my endless peregrinations in North America, and to Colegio Mayor Cardenal Cisneros in Granada, where I completed the book.

My gratitude goes to all my friends who have put up with me

always being overworked and stressed: Giovanna Amato, Nick and Arlette Gerson, Cecilia Guastadisegni, Susan Johns, Noel Kirnon, Sabina de Luca, George Magnus, Simona Marazza, Venetia Morrison, Valerio Nobili, Michael Paley, Deb Thomson, Bart Stevens, Lesley Wakefield, Bob Wilkinson, and many others. Thank you to Silvia Marazza for looking after my family and me, as usual, and for being such a very special friend.

To my children, Alexander and Julian, and my stepchildren, Andrew and Leigh, who have to put up with my moods, working schedule, and constant traveling; to my family in Rome, who see me too rarely these days; and to my exceptional husband, who shares the same fate without complaint, thank you.

Introduction

In July 2005 a series of bomb attacks brought the violence of jihad to the streets of London in the worst terrorist attacks against the city since World War II. On 7 July, four British citizens blew themselves up during rush hour. At the time of writing, their intentions are still unclear, but it looks as though they were hoping to blow themselves up at the four points of the compass, drawing a cross in violence, inscribing the sign of Crusade and counter-Crusade across the slate of the city. If that was their intention they failed. The creaking public transport system frustrated their plans. A signal failure on the northern line forced one of the suicide bombers to try to reach his destination by bus. Two weeks later, a second attack, most likely an attempted replica of the previous one, took place. According to the confession of one of the perpetrators arrested in Rome, the aim was not to kill people but to terrorize Londoners.

In May 2004, Nicholas Berg was beheaded as the world watched in horror. Berg was the first of a series of hostages brutally executed in Iraq by armed Islamist groups. In the video, broadcast live on the Internet, a masked man flanked by three others read Berg's death sentence and warned Westerners to stay out of Iraq. He then proceeded to sever the head of the American hostage with a knife, proudly displaying it to the camera. Relentlessly, Western media showed those images to the world as proof of the jihadists' barbarism, of the inhuman nature of their fight in Iraq.

These awful events are manifestations of a new, little understood phenomenon: Islamist terror. In the words of those who claimed responsibility, their motivations and aims were identical: a protest against the presence of foreign troops—Coalition forces—in Iraq and a demand for their immediate evacuation.

The analysis of the jihadists' Web sites would suggest that the new global wave of terrorist attacks is not an isolated phenomenon, nor the insane manifestation of a small group of maniacal religious fanatics. The response of Western countries to the 9/11 attacks, especially Bush and Blair's "war on terror," has greatly contributed to the evolution of terror. In a series of propaganda campaigns directed at their populations, Western governments have hidden the truth, manipulated the facts, and vigorously published fictions to justify their policies. Their most extraordinary creation is the myth of al Zarqawi. The story of his life and legend reveals a great deal about Islamist terrorism and the West's ambiguous role in creating, defining, and sustaining it.

Was Abu Mos'ab al Zarqawi, the new leader of al Qaeda in Iraq, Nicholas Berg's executioner? The CIA and the White House insist that he was. To them, al Zarqawi is a barbarous psychopath, the leader of a ruthless group of terrorists. He is the ultimate villain, a foreigner who has hijacked with violence part of a country the West is trying to bring under control. He is a "consultant" to the London suicide bombers, the man who masterminded the Istanbul and Casablanca attacks, and who inspired the Madrid bombings. From New York to London, from Paris to Tokyo, al Zarqawi has come to symbolize the non-Iraqi nature of the insurgency and the new face of global Islamist terror.

This analysis clashes with the views of some people who met and knew him when he was much younger, in the city of Zarqa and later in Afghanistan, or as a prisoner in Jordan. None of them recognize, in the cold-blooded butcher of Nicholas Berg, the young man they have known, befriended, or even loved. Experts on Islamist terrorism, former mujahedin, and members of his group also cast serious doubts on the transnational nature of al Zarqawi's terror network; they seem skeptical of his purported role at the center of a worldwide web of cells and the idea that he is more important than dozens of other leaders of the insurgency. Many Iraqis also strongly deny that he is in control of the insurgency in their country.

Has al Zarqawi's profile been deliberately inflated by the U.S. administration to justify the war in Iraq, and subsequently to cover up the true nature of the Iraqi insurgency? Or have the Americans simply relied upon information provided by third parties such as the Kurdish secret service, the Jordanian authorities, and British intelligence? The first time the Bush administration heard of him was after 9/11, from the Kurdish secret service. Is the myth of al Zarqawi a product of neoconservative propaganda, the newest political merchandise, "Made in America" and sold to the public to promote the politics of fear? Or is his reputation the brainchild of Kurdish and Jordanian intelligence, eager to secure U.S. backing against the rising tide of Islamist movements in their countries? In retrospect, the Americans, the Kurds, and the Jordanians are among those who benefited most from the construction of his myth. How and why was he singled out from among hundreds of jihadists as early as October 2001? The myth of al Zarqawi has now taken on a nightmarish reality driven by brutal events in insurgent Iraq.

The first time the world heard about al Zarqawi was on 5 February 2003 when Colin Powell, U.S. secretary of state, went to the United Nations to justify the forthcoming war in Iraq. Powell claimed that bin Laden and Saddam Hussein were allies. Abu Mos'ab al Zarqawi was singled out as the link between them. "[W]hat I want to bring to your attention today is the potentially much more sinister nexus between Iraq and the al Qaeda terrorist network, a nexus that combines classic terrorist organizations and modern methods of murder," said Powell. "Iraq today harbors a deadly terrorist network, headed by Abu Mos'ab al Zarqawi, an associate and collaborator of Osama bin Laden and his al Qaeda lieutenants."[1] Today we know that there was no alliance between al Qaeda and Iraq, just as there were no weapons of mass destruction. But from Powell's fallacious claims sprung one of the most compelling myths of the "war of terror."

Throughout the "unofficial" Iraq war, begun as the U.S. president publicly declared a close to official hostilities, al Zarqawi's violent gestures have been manipulated by the Bush administration to personalize, demonize, and fictionalize the nature of the enemy in Iraq. At the same time, attacks conducted outside that country have been attributed to him. Thus, in the world's public opinion he has replaced in "liberated" Iraq the evil figure of Saddam Hussein. Elsewhere he now plays the role of Osama bin Laden. In the Arab world, his myth has encouraged foreign jihadists to travel to Iraq—a stream of Arab troublemakers exported as suicide bombers. This export reduced tension in neighboring countries, strengthened al Zarqawi's group inside Iraq, and consolidated his reputation. Suicide attacks have attracted media attention, shocked global public opinion, and relegated all other groups involved in the insurgency to a position subordinate to al Zarqawi's jihadists. The fact that foreign fighters are a very small minority—as little as 10 percent of the entire resistance—and that suicide attacks represent a fraction of the attacks in Iraq has been systematically obscured. The anti-Shi'ite aims of the suicide attacks masterminded by al Zarqawi have created a wedge between the Shi'ites and the Sunnis, a factor that has prevented the formation of a united Iraqi front, based on nationalist objectives, against Coalition forces. In a skilful power game, Shi'ite leaders have used these attacks to ally themselves and their militias with the United States against the Sunnis. Furthermore, the purposely inflated role of al Zarqawi and the excessive importance attached to the presence of foreigners in Iraq has allowed the United States to present the resistance as an insurgency manipulated by foreign forces.

The appeal of suicide missions is spreading among second-generation immigrants in Europe. These are young men from lower middle-class backgrounds, often well educated and acutely sensitive to the suffering of Muslims in occupied countries. The myth of al Zarqawi as the embodiment of the Islamist jihad has also been a decisive factor for young men in the Middle East who choose death as a manifestation of their political commitment. And the spread of jihadist ideology associated with him has prepared the ground for the recruitment of the European brigades of suicide bombers. In this, the links with bin Laden are important, providing a narrative of continuous resistance to Christian invaders beginning with the Soviet invasion of Afghanistan.

In the midst of propaganda wars fought by all sides and by all means of communication, it is difficult to keep track of the truth. Understanding the real nature of the Iraqi insurgency requires accuracy and objectivity. It also requires an investigation into the metamorphosis of al Qaeda from a small armed organization into a global anti-imperialist ideology, al Qaedism. This book is an attempt at a disciplined analysis of the roots of the armed jihadist groups, al Qaeda amongst them; of the rise of al Qaedism; and of the true nature of the Iraqi insurgency. These linked phenomena are comprehensible only in the wider context of Middle Eastern politics. At the end of this investigation, Abu Mos'ab al Zarqawi will appear for who he is: one of the anti-imperialist voices of al Qaedism, representing a part of the Iraqi insurgency and a section of the tapestry of political violence woven in the Middle East. A region plagued by poverty, deceit, tyranny, political betrayal, and religious radicalism, the Middle East is not lost to hope. It is a region still in transition from a traditional to a modern society, in search of a new identity. The tale of al Zarqawi's life is the tale of a Muslim world in deep turmoil and on the brink of dissolution. The construction of his myth is the latest manipulation of Arab politics, a screen to hide the real nature of the Iraqi insurgency.

The legends created around al Zarqawi are part of a strategy to present the Muslim world as a single culture and worldview on a dangerous collision course with the West. These legends have allowed the West and its allies, the Muslim ruling elites, to manipulate the perils posed by the jihadist movement and to justify the implementation of hegemonic and conservative policies both at home and abroad. America's decision to use war as a weapon against terrorism is a decision to reinvent the world through violent confrontation. Ironically, this is entirely consistent with the Islamist objective of forcing America and its allies into open confrontation. The objectives of the "war on terror" have been shifted away from Osama bin Laden and the perpetrators of 9/11 onto imaginary new enemies: Saddam Hussein in the Iraq of the past and al Zarqawi in the Iraq of today. This strategy has weakened counterterrorism measures, facilitated the rise of Abu Mos'ab al Zarqawi as an international leader, reignited an ethnic war between Sunni and Shi'ite Muslims, and facilitated the recruitment of jihadists in the West as well as in the East. Above all it has given birth to a new generation of jihadists in the West and opened a new sectarian front in Iraq.

Ironically, this strategy is a marked departure from the policies of old-style counterterrorism. Western European democracies previously fought the "propaganda by deeds" of armed organizations by stifling the broadcast of their ideology. In the United Kingdom, for example, Gerry Adams's voice was dubbed on all broadcasts, diminishing the power of his message. In Italy, likewise, statements by members of armed organizations were not publicized. These strategies, combined with appeals to the moderate majority, succeeded in reducing the effectiveness of political violence in Europe and undermining the legitimacy of armed groups. Islamist terrorism is a weak enemy. It can be defeated by the instruments of democracy. New technology makes it more difficult to suppress its propaganda, but meaningful engagement with moderate Muslims and continued commitment to the rule of law will greatly degrade the appeal of the Islamist jihad among European youth. To depart from these methods is to threaten our greatest achievement: societies ruled by justice and freedom.

Since 9/11, far too much weight has been given to the violent actions of al Zarqawi, contributing to the proliferation of legends about his life and boosting his popularity among jihadists. The myth of al Zarqawi is a creation of the politics of fear, a form of propaganda blossoming in the West and in the Muslim world. These politics feed on the collective memory of 9/11 and on the Madrid and London bombings, offering seemingly prescient visions of apocalyptic nightmares still to come.

The myth of al Zarqawi has fueled sectarian civil war in Iraq and encouraged terrorism in Europe. It belongs to a genre of political fantasy that may haunt the West and the Arab world for decades to come unless a concerted effort is made to understand both the appeal of heroic resistance and the uses made of youthful idealism by the jihadist leadership. If Iraq slips into civil war and ethnic cleansing, the fantasies of the jihadists and their enemies will come true. Ethnic violence between Sunnis and Shi'ites, or Kurds and Sunnis, Armenians, Turcomans, Maronites, and Jews, could sweep through the entire region, spilling sectarian tension and terrorism over into Europe. Our best hope is to reject the bad dream of a world transformed by violence. Understanding the origins of al Zarqawi the man and al Zarqawi the myth is crucial if we are to escape from what appears to be a deepening nightmare.

Prologue

THE CITY OF ZARQA

The city of Zarqa is a depressed industrial site north of Amman, the Jordanian capital. Unemployment, especially among the young, is rampant. Poverty is widespread and hope is a forgotten concept. Over the last forty years, the growth of the city has been marked by the proliferation of Palestinian refugee camps, a shanty belt of misery encircling its outskirts. For the residents of Zarqa, the Palestinian diaspora is like a tangible cancer, an uncontrollable growth that strangles the already weak local economy, reduces employment opportunities, and plagues their souls. Religious fundamentalism seems the sole cure for this terminal illness.

Through the years, the imams' sermons have become the heartbeat of the city; daily prayers mark the rhythm of life. Mosques are much more than places of worship; they are the core of Zarqa's sociopolitical identity, where people meet to discuss their bleak destiny and allow themselves to dream of a better future.

Religion and politics have met before in Zarqa. In the book of Genesis, we are told that Jacob, on his way home from Egypt, wrestled all night with a stranger at Jabbok, one of the crossings of the River Jordan. Jabbok was the ancient name of the city of Zarqa. At daybreak the stranger asked Jacob to release him. Jacob demanded the man's blessing in return. So the stranger gave Jacob his benediction and bestowed upon him a new name. He called Jacob Israel, "because you fought with God and men and won," he said.[1] Thus, the alliance between God and the Jewish people was sealed at Zarqa, the biblical birthplace of modern Israel.[2]

CHAPTER ONE

The Seeds of Religious Radicalism

Religion and State, spirituality and
action, Koran and sword.
—Hassan al Banna, founder of the
Muslim Brotherhood

Ahmed Fadel al Khalaylah, who would later become known as Abu Mos'ab al Zarqawi, was born at the end of October 1966 in Zarqa, a city of 800,000 people, about sixteen miles northeast of the Jordanian capital of Amman. His relatives still live in the shabby two-story family home at number 13 al Hasmi Street. Situated at the top of a hill, in the working-class Ma'sum neighborhood, the house overlooks an abandoned quarry. Like most of the local construction, it is built of cement blocks and borders a road strewn with trash. This is familiar scenery in a town renamed by its own inhabitants "the Chicago of the Middle East" for its poverty and crime.[1]

Ahmed Fadel's childhood was spent in this tough environment, rife with contradictions. Ma'sum is a place like many others in the Middle East, a miserable neighborhood where traditional and tribal values mix badly with the culture of Western consumerism and rapid modernization. Satellite dishes lie next to rows of clothes drying in the sunshine. Shop windows displaying electronic merchandise are framed with gigantic graffiti celebrating suicide bombers. Veiled women hurry down the streets holding the hands of young boys sporting brand new Nike sneakers. Just three decades ago, Ahmed Fadel was one of them. He attended the local school and used the neighborhood cemetery as a playground, an eerie yet exciting place for a child to wander about in. At school he was not a star pupil. According to his teachers, he was rebellious and unruly.

The family belonged to the al Khalaylah clan, a branch of the Banu Hassan, a large East Bank Bedouin tribe loyal to Jordan's Hashemite royal family. The tribe includes 200,000 people scattered across Jordan and its neighboring countries, including Iraq.[2] Ahmed Fadel had all the physical traits of his tribe: short and slim, with dark piercing eyes and black hair. He was agile in his movements but not athletic. His was the body of the men of the desert—thin and flexible—used to endless peregrinations.

For the members of Ahmed Fadel's family, their Bedouin heritage was a source of pride, even if the ancient Bedouin traditions had vanished before their eyes, wiped away by the greed and corruption of Arab consumerism. Part of the difficulty Ahmed Fadel faced in adjusting to Ma'sum's working-class environment and his family's low social status sprang from the speed with which the Palestinian diaspora tore into the Bedouin way of life. His father, Fadil Nazzal Mohammad al Khalaylah, a retired army officer, was very much a product of this changing reality. During the 1948 war, he participated in the Battle of Jerusalem, fighting to keep the Old City and eastern Jerusalem within Jordanian territory. Back in Zarqa, where he worked as a mediator in neighborhood problems, he witnessed the arrival of hundreds of thousands of Palestinian refugees from the Israeli-occupied territories.[3]

Ahmed Fadel's sense of security collapsed in 1984 when Fadil Nazzal died.[4] According to one of his sisters, Ahmed was "the apple of his father's eye"; they were very, very close. With their father gone, their mother, Um Sayel, a gentle and loving, but illiterate, woman, was left with a small pension on which to raise six daughters and four sons. Inevitably, mother and children sank deeper into poverty. According to a family friend, at times it was difficult to find enough to eat.[5] The adolescent Ahmed Fadel began acting out his anger and frustration.

He dropped out of secondary school, joined a local gang, began drinking, and turned into a bully. Soon he was arrested and charged for possession of drugs and sexual assault.[6] He was subsequently imprisoned.

Ahmed Fadel's initial entry into the community of "outlaws" was limited to interaction with petty criminals and child gangsters; he was too young and insufficiently politicized to know or understand that his birthplace was bursting with the work of intellectuals and activists engaged in reshaping the face of militant Islam. However, in Zarqa, as across the Arab world, the networks of petty crime and of revolutionary Islam constantly criss-crossed, especially in prison; both existed on the margins of Arab society, constituting a web of illegality that encircled Arab politics and progressively suffocated moderate voices. It is likely that this first encounter with Jordanian prisons triggered the long process of radicalization which transformed Ahmed Fadel, decades later, into Abu Mos'ab al Zarqawi, the new leader of al Qaeda in Iraq.

THE MUSLIM BROTHERHOOD

In the Middle East, the seeds of religious radicalism were sown in the early 1970s. Jordan, due to its geopolitical position and huge Palestinian refugee population, became a hothouse for revolt. An exceptional political event triggered this process. In September 1970, known as Black September, King Hussein of Jordan quashed an attempt by Palestinian organizations, mainly the Palestine Liberation organization (PLO), to overturn his monarchy. British-educated King Hussein was a man caught between two worlds on a collision course. He had welcomed Palestinian refugees into Jordan and backed their cause, but had undervalued the strategic genius of the leader of the PLO, Yasser Arafat. In less than a decade, the PLO had become a state within a state; it had penetrated the economic infrastructure of Jordan and gained control of most of its finances. At times, the king even borrowed money from the Arab Bank, which was the de facto central bank of the PLO.[7] Between mid-

1968 and the end of 1969, the military wing of the PLO repeatedly clashed with the Jordanian authorities (over this period there were no fewer than five hundred violent incidents).[8] In September 1970, in danger of losing his grip on the political situation, King Hussein expelled the PLO from the refugee camps in Amman and other Jordanian cities. The event was a watershed in the Middle East. Confused Jordanians watched endless caravans of Palestinians cross the border on their way to Lebanon, evicted for the second time from Arab soil.

After the exodus, King Hussein rewarded those who had backed his decision, including the Muslim Brotherhood,[9] an anti-Israeli, reformist Islamic movement which had rejected the PLO's use of violence and instead sought political change within existing institutions. The king offered the Brotherhood charge of the Ministry of Education. This shaped an entire generation of youngsters who became exposed in Jordanian classrooms to the reformist message. At the same time the Brotherhood's indoctrination prepared the ground for the proliferation, in the following decade, of radical Islamist groups as a disenfranchised generation was taught to think of reform along fundamentalist lines. Although in 1984 Ahmed Fadel was not conscious of these developments, he had already come under the psychological influence of religious radicalism. It had been working on him for years; from school to prison the message spread by the Brotherhood was to liberate the Palestinian Territories from Zionist occupation through direct political participation.

In the late 1970s, radical Salafi[10] preachers, representing a militant branch of Islam, had advanced their own message, which went well beyond the problem of Palestine and tackled the question of the legitimacy of Arab regimes. The central idea of radical Salafism was the purification of Islam from the Western contamination that caused corruption and stagnation in Arab countries. They blamed Arab states for the Palestinian fiasco, the 1967 defeat,[11] and the rise to power of Israel. Because of their reluctance to denounce the West for backing Israel, Salafi preachers claimed that Arab regimes had departed from the will of God. No loyalty was due to states that had forged alliances with the backers of Israel. In sharp contrast with the Brotherhood, the radical Salafi message was revolutionary and uncompromising; whoever followed it came into direct confrontation with the state and its laws.

Within this framework, criminality assumed a new dimension: it became a way to weaken the illegitimate state and to show political dissent. Thus, the "illegitimacy" of the Arab state blurred the boundaries between crime and insurrection. Political activists and petty criminals came to share a common enemy, a phenomenon which in the 1980s and 1990s facilitated the transition of thousands of people from perpetrators of crime to perpetrators of political violence, thereby turning prisons into recruitment centers. It was within this fast-changing environment that the first signs of the metamorphosis of Ahmed Fadel from a drunken, working-class bully into a mujahed and eventual global terror leader became visible.

Though Black September had evicted the PLO leadership, it did not interrupt the flow of Palestinian refugees to Jordan. Unable to escape being dragged deeper and deeper into the turmoil of the Palestinian diaspora, Jordan remained fertile terrain for religious radicalism. In the 1970s, 1980s, and part of the 1990s, anyone who was anyone in the fight for an independent Palestine passed through Jordan, which became a sort of gateway into radical Islamic ideology. During these decades, as several Arab regimes grew increasingly conciliatory towards the state of Israel, this steady stream of intellectuals, victims of the Palestinian diaspora, came to reject the revisionism and moderate views of the Brotherhood and progressively embraced a revolutionary ideology. Among them was Abdallah Azzam, Osama bin Laden's spiritual mentor and the cofounder of al Qaeda.[12]

ABDHALLAH AZZAM

Born in Jenin in 1941 to a religious peasant family, Azzam was drawn early on to the Brotherhood and became one of its strongest supporters in Palestine. In 1966 he graduated from the Faculty of Sharia at the University of Damascus, where he studied Muslim religious law. The following year he moved to Jordan after Israeli troops occupied the West Bank and the Gaza Strip. In Jordan, he began to reflect on the possibility of staging an armed struggle against Israel. Between 1969 and 1970 he participated in several attacks against the Israeli army. This ended after Black September because the border between Jordan and Palestine was closed.

Azzam was a man of the diaspora. Exiled for his entire life, he moved from one Muslim host to another. Unlike Hassan al Banna, the founder of the Muslim Brotherhood, and Sayyed Qutb,[13] its revolutionary voice, Abdallah Azzam had limited contact with the West.[14] He belonged to the second generation of Islamic leaders, forged predominantly inside the Arab world. The boundaries of Azzam's world were strictly defined by Islam. Like the future terror leader Abu Mos'ab al Zarqawi, Azzam was essentially the offspring of Middle Eastern, postcolonial contradictions, shaped by complex political events, such as Black September.

Like al Zarqawi, he sought a solution, a way out of the stalemate of Arab politics. Also like al Zarqawi, his universe was confined to only one language, Arabic; his knowledge and understanding of nineteenth- and twentieth-century European revolutionary movements was strictly filtered through the writings of the Brotherhood. It was the voice of leaders like Azzam that, in the 1970s and 1980s, spread across the Middle East.

In 1971 Azzam moved to Egypt to study Islamic jurisprudence at the University of al Azhar. After graduating in 1973, he returned to Jordan where he worked for the Department of Information in the Ministry of Religious Donations, al Awqaf, in charge of distributing charitable funds. From this official position, he succeeded in creating and activating the mosque network, a web of radical religious preachers who spread revolutionary messages to the masses of Palestinian refugees residing in Jordan. He also supervised the publication of several religious magazines that were distributed throughout the Middle East.

The idea was to reach out to Palestinian refugees and Arab youth—a vast reservoir of unemployed and disenfranchised people who were to be mobilized in the fight against Israel. Azzam's voice also appealed to the better educated and to intellectuals. From 1973 to 1980 he taught at the Faculty of Sharia at the University of Amman, also delivering lectures in Zarqa. At the same time he continued to be one of the leaders of the Muslim Brotherhood of Jordan.

In 1980, the Jordanian government expelled Azzam by military decree. The administration feared his growing popularity inside and outside the university; more than anything, the regime was afraid of his "revolutionary rhetoric," which seemed to mesmerize young people. Convinced that those involved in the Palestinian fight were too remote from "true Islam," Azzam decided to move to Saudi Arabia, where he obtained a teaching position at King Abdul Aziz University in Jedda. A fortuitous meeting in Mecca with Kamal al Senaniri, a member of the Muslim Brotherhood, prompted his subsequent relocation to Pakistan. Al Senaniri, who had just returned from Afghanistan, told Azzam about his work among the Arab fighters engaged in the war against the Soviets. The Palestinian was enthralled by his friend's tales of the mujahedin. Through the intercession of the dean of the university in Jedda, Azzam was appointed to the Islamic University of Islamabad. Towards the end of 1981 he arrived in Pakistan. He was one of the very first religious leaders to reach the mujahedin.

In Afghanistan Azzam found what he had been looking for all his life: the international army of the mujahedin. He soon became their spiritual leader and financial backer, via the Maktab al Khidamat, the Arab-Afghan Bureau, which he founded in 1984 to take charge of the influx of Arab fighters wanting to participate in the anti-Soviet jihad.[15]

IS THERE ONLY ONE JIHAD?

The 1979 Soviet invasion of Afghanistan prompted a civil war. Backed financially by the CIA and the Saudis, an international army of Arab warriors flocked to the country to help the Afghans fight the Soviet invaders. The solidarity generated by the event was reminiscent of the international support at the outbreak of the Spanish civil war in the 1930s, when socialist volunteers from Europe and the United States rushed to support the republicans. In both cases the call to arms had a global appeal because there was much more at stake than the politics of one country; these were conflicts fought on international issues, struggles between two opposing visions of the world.

In 1981, when Azzam reached Afghanistan, the conflict was already beginning to be known in the Arab world as the anti-Soviet jihad. This terminology symbolized the struggle of the Muslim alliance—the Afghans and the international Arab brigades—against communism. Jihad is a Muslim concept that is often misused and its true meaning easily escapes understanding. In 2003, an American Muslim asked me if I knew what the jihad was. I explained that jihad means "striving in the name of God." This effort can be spiritual, a fight against the daily temptations of life—the greater jihad—or physical, against an enemy—the smaller jihad. He smiled and shook his head. "There are many more interpretations of the smaller jihad," he said, "indeed too many. It is the most manipulated concept in our religion."

The lives of generations of Islamic political activists of the twentieth century—mujahedin, jihadists, and their leaders, among them Azzam, bin Laden, and al Zarqawi—were shaped by the heated debate over the meaning of the smaller jihad, the modern jihad. Any attempt to reconstruct the life history of these men must include an overview of this debate. In the early 1980s, Ahmed Fadel was not yet conscious of the nuances of this argument, but, as we shall see, the interpretation of the modern jihad was to forge his destiny.

Developed after the death of the Prophet Muhammad by the *ulema* (religious scholars), the jihad was an elaboration of both the Koran and the teachings of the Prophet. Formulated when Islam was already a superpower, the idea of the smaller jihad reflected the imperial spirit of the time.[16] It was essentially a tool to protect the community of believers. The religious scholars of imperial Islam distinguished between two forms: the defensive and the offensive jihad. The defensive jihad was the obligation of all members of the community to take up arms against the enemy to safeguard Islam. The offensive jihad, on the other hand, could be called only by the emir, the caliph, the ruler of the community. Its task was to spread Islam, not protect it. As long as the emir had sufficient warriors ready for combat, the community was exempt from joining in.[17] This is a crucial concept in understanding the appeal that Osama bin Laden and other leaders of Islamist armed organizations, including al Zarqawi, exercise over radical Muslims. These leaders claim that they are emirs and that it is thus the duty of all Muslims to join them.

As the years passed and imperial Islam faded, the greater jihad remained unchanged while the smaller jihad assumed new meanings, being adapted to the needs of the time. Faced with the uncompromising violence of the Frankish Crusaders, Saladin renovated the concept of the jihad as a response to the First Crusade.[18] The radical spiritual resources of Islam animated his followers in their successful campaign of reconquest. It was an aggressive jihad; the war had been lost and a peace treaty agreed. However, it became known as the counter-Crusade, a defensive war against an invading power that was alien to Muslims in culture and religion. Saladin blurred forever the boundaries between the defensive and offensive jihad, and the Second Crusade became the benchmark for the smaller jihad.

At the beginning of the twentieth century, the reinvigoration of Saladin's jihad was part of the Middle Eastern struggle for deliverance from colonization. During the British domination of Egypt,[19] Hassan al Banna, the founder of the Muslim Brotherhood, reshaped it into the anticolonial jihad, the fight for full independence from the British. A few decades later, Sayyed Qutb, an Egyptian intellectual, transformed it into a revolution—a vehicle for regime change. Because the revolutionary jihad was the brainchild of a man imprisoned, tortured, and eventually hanged by the Nasser regime, Qutb became the voice of the victims of repressive Arab regimes.

Since the late 1950s, the debate over the true meaning of the modern jihad has revolved around three main concepts: counter-Crusade, anticolonial struggle, and revolution. Today, the boundaries of the modern jihad are defined by these interpretations. The 7 July London suicide bombers sought to draw a cross on the city's map to emphasize their fight against the new crusaders. Investigation into the lives of the perpetrators of the bombing has shown that their indoctrination included watching videos of Muslims being killed by Israeli and Western soldiers. "The film images clicking by in rapid-fire sequence to a soundtrack of pounding drums [showed] dead Iraqi children, Palestinians under siege, Guantánamo prisoners [and] snippets of President Bush repeating the word 'crusade.'"[20] The Sunni resistance in Iraq has a distinct anti-imperialist matrix vis-à-vis the new colonizers, the Coalition forces. Al Zarqawi is seeking to ignite a *fitna*, a civil war or a revolution, against the predominantly Shi'ite government, regarded as the supporters of Western powers.

Against this background, the nature of the modern jihad appears ambiguous. Is it a counter-Crusade, an anticolonial fight, or a revolution? This dilemma of definition is at the heart of modern Islam and at the core of the ideological differences that characterized the relationship between Osama bin Laden and Abu Mos'ab al Zarqawi until the end of 2004 when, as we shall see, they entered into partnership.

In recent years, the West has been confronted by an identical dilemma at home and abroad. What is the meaning of the Madrid and London bombings? Is the insurgency in Iraq a national resistance against a foreign occupying power or a revolution led by a small and violent vanguard of foreign Arab forces, masterminded by Abu Mos'ab al Zarqawi? Is it a counter-Crusade, a national liberation movement, or a civil war? Above all, are the motivations of the modern jihad a manifestation of a global anti-imperialist ideology, of al Qaedism in the West as well as in the East? Thus, the answer to the dilemma presented by the jihadist movement at home, as well as abroad, must be sought in an exploration of the true meaning of the modern jihad.

THE MAKING OF A MUJAHED

The anti-Soviet jihad can be described as the classic counter-Crusade jihad with a twist; it incorporated anticolonial elements into Saladin's jihad. This cocktail, a creation of Sheikh Abdallah Azzam, made it possible, even desirable, for Arab regimes to support the war in Afghanistan. As long as the jihad was directed against godless communists, their own states were largely left alone.

In the 1980s, Azzam's preaching in Pakistan centered upon the urgency of returning to the root of Islam, of purifying the religion from Western contamination in order to develop a fighting strategy. The jihad became a sort of cleansing process. Such exhortations carried the echo of the heroic battles of the mujahedin. In Jordan they fueled heated discussions among supporters and sympathizers of the Muslim Brotherhood. Eventually, Azzam's radical message produced an ideological split inside the organization: his followers accused the Brotherhood of being a proestablishment group and disassociated themselves from it.

Azzam's preaching was welcomed by Jordanian radical imams of the mosque network that he had developed a decade earlier. The anti-Soviet jihad became daily news. Preachers encouraged the mujahedin who returned to Jordan to address the faithful; they raised money among the *umma*, the community of the faithful, to fund the distant war. Funds soon reached the Maktab al Khidamat, the Arab-Afghan Bureau created by Sheikh Azzam. Money was allocated to support the mujahedin in Afghanistan and to raise new recruits across the Middle East. Mosques soon became recruiting centers for the anti-Soviet jihad.

It was against this fertile religious and ideological background that, in the late 1980s, Ahmed Fadel, the future al Zarqawi, began frequenting al Hussein Ben Ali Mosque in Zarqa. Out of prison and now married to a cousin, he was still too young and naive to grasp the true meaning of the anti-Soviet jihad. He clearly did not understand that the mujahedin were fighting a war by proxy, the last of the Cold War, nor did he realize the role that the Americans and the Saudis were playing in the conflict. Most likely he was instinctively drawn to the Muslim warriors' revolutionary role because they fought for a cause he could relate to.

In the mosque, he was fascinated by the stories of the Jordanian mujahedin who returned from Afghanistan, and captivated by the heroic image and romantic status of the mujahedin. Thus, like many other Arab youths, bursting with energy, Ahmed Fadel's decision to become a mujahed was taken without a true understanding of the politics involved. He was motivated by the desire to be part of a major initiative, to abandon the marginalization of his life. What could be better than joining an army of Islamic warriors?

Ahmed Fadel's transition from petty criminal to Arab warrior was facilitated by the fact that the anti-Soviet jihad was yet another dimension of the underworld of Arab "outlaws," an underground web that had grown in the shadow of corrupt, tyrannical, and repressive Arab politics. The Arab brigades were composed of informal soldiers, mostly people who had passed through the experience of Arab prisons; yet for Ahmed Fadel the status of mujahed represented a step up on the social ladder of the "outlaws." In the Arab world nobody likes a drunken bully, but everybody respects the mujahedin. "During the days of the jihad in Afghanistan the men used to leave their countries respected and praised."[21] Ahmed Fadel was one of the thousands of Arab youths eager to gain respect through the jihad.

For many young men, joining the distant fight to free fellow Muslims from the hegemony of the Soviet superpower also sublimated the memory of the struggle at home, enabling them to put aside the frustrations of daily life in the poor suburbs of the Arab world. "Jihad in Afghanistan was the same as anywhere else, same as in Eritrea or elsewhere on God's earth. Jihad in Afghanistan was about reinstating the value of Islam in people's minds [. . .] so when the opportunity arose, Muslims flocked to Afghanistan to spread the teaching of God's liturgy which was banned by the Soviet-installed government."[22] In the 1980s, this was the message that radical preachers and former mujahedin proselytized across the Arab world, a formula that succeeded in widening the horizons of a generation of disenfranchised, young petty criminals like Ahmed Fadel.

In post-9/11 Europe, a similar message spread among a new generation of Muslims. Two of the 7 July London bombers—eighteen-year-old Hasib Hussein and twenty-two-year-old Shehzad Tanweer—were as young as al Zarqawi when they were recruited. Like him, they sought the deliverance of fellow Muslims from the humiliation of occupation by a superpower. Al Zarqawi wanted to join the anti-Soviet jihad to free Afghans from the Soviet Union, while Hussein and Tanweer joined an army of suicide bombers to liberate Iraqis from American and British occupation. In both circumstances, indoctrination and recruitment took place via a network of radical mosques, preachers, and recruiters—in the case of the two London bombers, a web of informal places of worship, prayer rooms in private homes, and universities.

However, while for the young Jordanian bully the al Hussein Ben Ali Mosque became a gateway into a new life in Afghanistan, for the four London suicide bombers the network of informal places of worship was a gateway to death. Thus, radical preachers and recruiters have gone underground, and the call is no longer to arms but to suicide missions. These are the fundamental differences between the indoctrination of al Zarqawi and of the new generation of jihadists.

Back in Zarqa, the Jordanian government, eager to export troublemakers such as Ahmed Fadel, facilitated the crossing. The necessary arrangements and expenses for traveling to Afghanistan were handled by a recruiter, Sheikh Abd al Majeed al Majaali, better known as Abu Qutayba, the Jordanian representative of the Arab-Afghan Bureau.[23] Today, the role of the recruiter is still paramount. A recruiter is is believed to have bankrolled three of the 7 July London suicide bombers' trips to Pakistan.

In the spring of 1989, Ahmed Fadel left Jordan. The young man who stepped into the Afghan adventure lacked the background to comprehend his novel environment, but his instinct compensated for the absence of culture, knowledge, and understanding of world politics, religion, and war. He sensed that major changes were about to take place in his life. This was the first of several metamorphoses leading to the emergence of Abu Mos'ab al Zarqawi, the representative of al Qaeda in Iraq. Before departing from Zarqa, Ahmed Fadel buried his identity. The young man who boarded the plane to Pakistan was called Abu Muhammad al Gharib, the Stranger.

CHAPTER TWO

Stranger Among Warriors

[P]aradise is for alGhurabaa [the stranger].
—The Prophet

Former mujahedin say that Afghanistan is a deeply spiritual, almost magical place.[1] Set at the foot of the highest mountains in the world, the country breathes the air of the Himalayas. Many mujahedin describe the emptiness of the land as liberating compared to the overcrowding of Arab cities.

Upon al Gharib's arrival, in the spring of 1989, he went to the city of Khost. An ancient, dusty town, Khost, at the time, was teeming with former mujahedin; Arab Afghans from all corners of Afghanistan wandered along its streets, waiting for events to unfold. With the Russians' recent retreat, the city was in turmoil.

Al Gharib's first impression of Afghanistan was very different from the romantic images projected by the tales of former mujahedin delivered inside al Hussein Ben Ali Mosque. A frontline city, Khost was mired in the chaos that always follows a long and bloody war. Far from being united in the spiritual reawakening of the jihad, the mujahedin were plagued by deep infighting, split into several ideological groups, often along lines of ethnicity. Egyptian, Palestinian, Kuwaiti, and Saudi spiritual leaders skillfully manipulated their own groups as pawns in a power game conducted in the dilapidated streets of Afghanistan. This tough sociopolitical landscape did not intimidate the Stranger; on the contrary, he seemed eager to explore it. Raised in a similarly hostile environment, he instinctively knew the rules of the game. Lacking connections, however, and a proper understanding of the politics pursued by the various groups, he remained an outsider, drifting from one group to another.

Al Gharib's late arrival, at the very end of the war, reinforced his status as Stranger among warriors. Throughout his stay in Afghanistan, he would remain an outsider; he would not join any group and would not become a member of al Qaeda.

It does not seem possible that al Gharib participated in the legendary siege of Khost;[2] by the time he reached the city, the Soviets had gone and the only remaining enemies were those loyal to the Afghan government of Najibullah. Failure to show his courage and determination in battle was for the Stranger a constant source of frustration. If only he were given a chance to prove himself! Attempting to blend into the tapestry of the Arab-Afghan war, he began in Khost to develop personal relationships within the community of Jordanian mujahedin.

Between 1989 and 1990 he befriended Saleh al Hami, a Jordanian mujahed journalist who had lost a leg in battle. "I got to know him while I was wounded and covered in blood," recalls al Hami. Al Gharib visited him regularly in the hospital. "Then one day he offered me to marry his sister. Actually I admired his noble character and courage. He reminded me of the noble characters of the Prophet's companions, may God be pleased with them, when one of them would offer his sister or daughter to another companion as a wife."[3] Adrift in a world expansive beyond his comprehension and more complex than he had ever before known, the Stranger followed a well-known script, the only one he was acquainted with: he relied on his Bedouin instinct and used the teachings of Islam and the life of the Prophet as a guide.

Though al Gharib made this promise to an unknown man in a distant land, his family backed him fully. When his sister learned of the promise he had made to Saleh al Hami, she rejoiced and said, "God honors the handicapped or the mujahedin."[4] Unlike many Arab troublemakers shipped by governments and relatives to Afghanistan, the Stranger never lost touch with his family, especially the women, who often visited him in Pakistan and Afghanistan. This closeness to his family is another important aspect of his personality, linked to his Bedouin background. At the time, the maintenance of family contacts was facilitated by the ease with which mujahedin family members could buy tickets and travel to Afghanistan and Pakistan. Arab regimes, charities, and the Arab-Afghan Bureau provided loans and financial help. It was during one of these family visits that al Hami met and married his wife.

In the video of the wedding, the Stranger hands his sister over to the disabled mujahed. Gone is the drunken bully who left Zarqa months earlier; the new man is a respected brother and son. "Abu Mos'ab [al Zarqawi] was a very simple person, normal, looking for truth in his own way, conducting jihad spontaneously, he was simple amongst people," remarked Hamdi Murad, one of the spiritual leaders of the mujahedin. Hamdi, who was present at the wedding, is today a professor of Sharia at the Jordanian university of al Balqa. He believes that the young man who smiles in the video of the wedding is far removed from al Zarqawi, the terror leader, as portrayed by America. "You would never have thought that he would perhaps turn out to be a military leader one day, if ever."[5] Similar comments have been made by people who knew Mohammad Sidique Khan, one of the 7 July London suicide bombers. Khan worked for four years as a learning mentor, an assistant who helped students, particularly children of immigrants, adapt to new school environments. Parents and colleagues confirm that "he was invaluable, a friendly and trusted person who loved children."[6]

Those who met al Zarqawi in Pakistan and Afghanistan concur with Hamid Murad's analysis. "I remember Abu Muhammad [al Gharib], he was a short, polite young man," said Abdallah Anas, son-in-law of Sheikh Abdallah Azzam and then head of the Arab-Afghan

Bureau in Peshawar, Pakistan. "He always addressed me as 'Uncle Abdallah.' This was a sign of respect. He worked for us for quite some time, maybe over a year. He was a hard-working man, religious and rather quiet."[7] In the tales of the mujahedin who met al Gharib, there are no traces of Ahmed Fadel, the bully of Zarqa, nor of al Zarqawi, the leader of al Qaeda in Iraq. The metamorphosis from a bully had already taken place. The metamorphosis into a terror leader would take place later. As we shall see, this latest transformation would be triggered by personal trauma, as well as by the transition of a generation of mujahedin from warriors to terrorists. However, were these factors sufficient to turn a modest young man into the butcher of Nicholas Berg and terror's new global leader? Or has his myth contributed to this radical transformation? Many who met al Zarqawi are convinced that all of these factors played a role.

In 1990, al Gharib could not have envisaged such a destiny when he moved to Peshawar from Khost. This city, close to the Afghan border, was the first stop for the mujahedin on their way to battle and the main shelter town for their families. The city was rife with young and old warriors, and their wives and children. Night and day the mujahedin roamed the streets like orphans. It was an amazingly cosmopolitan human landscape, crisscrossed by several ideological undercurrents, which fascinated the Stranger. Only a very small group of people, however, were aware that for some time Peshawar had been at the core of a fierce ideological battle for the control of al Qaeda.[8] Al Gharib was not one of them.

THE BATTLE TO TAKE CONTROL OF AL QAEDA

Originally shaped around the preaching of Azzam, al Qaeda was born as the military arm of a global Muslim insurgency, part of the army of Arab Afghans. "Every revolutionary ideology needs a rugged, elite cadre to protect it, inspire it and lead it to ultimate victory," wrote Azzam in *al Jihad*, the official magazine of the Arab-Afghan Bureau.[9]

This Leninist-style vanguard had the task of spreading the jihad to liberate the oppressed across the Muslim world.

As far back as 1986 Azzam had openly denounced the tough conditions in which Muslims lived in Yugoslavia, Bulgaria, and Uganda, declaring it the duty of all Muslims to defend and protect such populations. In Jedda, while teaching at King Abdul Aziz University, Azzam had described the jihad as a form of Muslim solidarity. This idea mesmerized and inspired a young Saudi, Osama bin Laden, who would soon join Azzam in Afghanistan. "Sometimes you are looking for justice in this life or something more to give to Muslims all over the world and when you see the world slipping from the Muslims everywhere, you wake up, the jihad wakes up inside of you." This is how a former student and friend of Azzam's summarized Azzam's message in Jedda. "You see them in Bosnia, Sudan, Somalia, Kashmir, Afghanistan, Albania, Egypt, Syria. . . . You think about these things and if you don't get together and if you don't hold hands and believe in the same cause, then others will destroy you without you knowing it. You have to do something. . . . Jihad is the only saviour."[10]

Towards the end of the anti-Soviet jihad, Azzam began envisaging Soviet-ridden Afghanistan as a safe haven for the future international army of mujahedin, a place to train new generations of Islamic warriors, who would then go out to defend the rights of Muslims around the globe. Essentially, Azzam saw the victory over the Soviets as the first step towards a new Muslim world order. As Trotsky had rejected the concept of a communist takeover of a single country—wanting the Soviet Union to be the engine of a permanent revolution—Azzam saw Afghanistan as the core of a global jihad. Al Qaeda was the vanguard of armies of Saladin's Muslim warriors engaged in wars of liberation across the Muslim world. Thus the jihad became a global counter-Crusade against alien, oppressive cultures, enemies of Muslims.

Conscious that the anti-Soviet jihad had been a war by proxy, Azzam wanted to end the dependency of the mujahedin on Pakistan's secret service, the Inter-Services Intelligence (ISI), and on the main sponsors of the war: the Unites States and Saudi Arabia. Therefore, towards the end of the war, he urged the mujahedin to consolidate their power in Afghanistan. It was at this point that Osama bin Laden, the de facto representative of Saudi interests in Afghanistan, clashed with Sheikh Abdallah Azzam. Until then the two had worked closely together.

At the root of the dispute was a difference of opinion about the future of the mujahedin and of al Qaeda. Bin Laden was not interested in the consolidation of power inside Afghanistan. Clearly, bin Laden was conditioned by his Saudi sponsors who wanted to continue to influence and manipulate the future of the Arab brigades and of their vanguard, al Qaeda. According to Egyptian investigator Abderrahim Ali,[11] bin Laden was also greatly influenced by the Egyptian faction inside the Arab-Afghan Bureau, guided by Ayman al Zawahiri.[12] Al Zawahiri's followers sought to involve al Qaeda in terrorist tactics and to transform it into an armed organization. At the end of the anti-Soviet jihad, their idea was to use al Qaeda to prompt terrorist activity in Egypt in order to trigger a regime change via civil war.

Osama bin Laden's former personal bodyguard, Nasir Ahmad Nasir Abdallah al Bahari, confirms that there were plans and discussions to unify the Egyptian jihad and al Qaeda. "I remember that these contacts and meetings began in 1997 and even before that. There were coordination of operations, logistical support, and joint implementation of some operations in and outside of Afghanistan. There were al Qaeda Organization elements fighting within the ranks of the Jihad Organization and members of the Jihad Organization were fighting in the al Qaeda Organization ranks," he recalled.[13]

"Al Zawahiri was a newcomer," explains Abdallah Anas, who was at the time in charge of the Arab-Afghan Bureau. "He arrived in Afghanistan at the end of the war. He was not part of the inner circle of the Arab-Afghan Bureau. He had his own agenda, his fight was in Egypt; Afghanistan was only a vehicle to return to Egypt."[14] Osama bin Laden was very much part of his plan; the Saudi had the finances to make it work. According to Anas and several other sources, the Egyptians won over bin Laden by offering him the title of emir, or prince, of the group.[15] This recognition flattered bin Laden and gained al Zawahiri access to the Saudi's fortune.

Sheikh Abdallah Azzam strongly rejected the idea of using al Qaeda as a terrorist group and warned against the diversion of mujahedin funds to causes outside Afghanistan. He even issued a fatwa, stating that channeling money earmarked for the jihad to terrorist activities was a violation of the Sharia.[16] The feud ended on 24 November 1989 with the assassination of Sheikh Azzam.[17] From that moment onwards Osama bin Laden and al Zawahiri progressively took control of the Arab-Afghan Bureau and transformed al Qaeda into the terrorist vanguard of revolutionary forces operating inside Arab countries.

The death of Sheikh Azzam was a major watershed in the evolution of al Qaeda, leading to the reformulation of its final objective. By taking control of al Qaeda and the Arab-Afghan Bureau, Osama bin Laden and al Zawahiri framed the jihad within the armed struggle.

The assassination was the first of a series of murders among al Qaeda's leadership, similar to Joseph Stalin's purges of top-ranking Bolsheviks, that transformed the organization and prepared the ground for the first bombing of the World Trade Center. In March 1991, Mustafa Shalabi, a supporter of Azzam, was also assassinated. He was in charge of the al Kifah Refugee Center on Atlantic Avenue in Brooklyn, New York, and was replaced by the Egyptian Sheikh Omar Abd al Rahman,[18] better known as the Blind Sheikh.[19] In 1993, when Ramzi Youssef arrived in New York to plan and execute the first bombing of the World Trade Center, he met the Blind Sheikh and took refuge in the al Kifah center.[20]

According to Muhammad Sadeq Awda, an imprisoned former member of al Qaeda, Osama bin Laden ordered the assassination of Azzam because he suspected that Azzam had links with the CIA.[21] Many sources, however, believe that al Zawahiri, not bin Laden, ordered the purges. The death of Sheikh Abdallah Azzam and the subsequent assassination of people close to him in the inner circle of the mujahedin movement, in fact, benefited the Egyptian faction, which gained full control of bin Laden's finances and of al Qaeda.

THE MEETING WITH AL MAQDISI

When al Gharib joined the Arab-Afghan Bureau, Sheikh Abdallah Azzam was already dead, and the struggle for power was hidden and removed from people like him. He was unaware of the changes which were taking place. His future path, as that of thousands of young people like him, would be marked by these struggles.

In 1991, in Peshawar, al Gharib was still in search of his destiny. In the chaos of the city, he sought refuge in Zayd Bin Harithah Mosque, a popular place among Arab worshippers. The familiarity of the mosque appealed to him; prayer was therapeutic. "Many Arab brothers used to come and pray alongside us, including Abu Mos'ab [al Zarqawi]," recalls the preacher of the Zayd Bin Harithah. "I learned that he had come from Jordan for the purpose of jihad. He used to pray alongside us and he was a learned man. He even prayed alongside us in the evenings, especially during the last ten days of the month of Ramadan, together with the other Arab brothers."

In Peshawar, the Stranger refined his religious affiliation and seemed eager to perfect his role of believer. "Once, before I went on pilgrimage, after Ramadan," continues the imam, "[al Zarqawi] said to me: if you go on pilgrimage, pray and say may God forgive me."[22]

During this period of intense religious fervor al Gharib met and befriended Issam Muhammad Taher al Barqawi, better known as Abu Muhammad al Maqdisi, a distinguished radical Salafi thinker. Of Palestinian origins, al Maqdisi had been brought up in Kuwait, where he studied theology.[23] In the 1980s he had moved to Afghanistan with the Palestinian sheikh Omar Mahmoud Abu Omar, known by the nickname Abu Qatadah, who later found refuge in London. These two figures became the main source of authority for the Salafi jihadist ideology in Jordan, which established its stronghold in the city of Zarqa.

The Stranger and al Maqdisi were two completely different characters, yet they immediately became close friends. Al Maqdisi was a well-known scholar; he came from the inner circle of radical Salafism and had gone through the mujahedin training camps. Though he never actively participated in the fight, he was an insider. The meeting and their friendship was a crucial turning point for the Stranger and, as we shall see, for the development of his leadership. It is likely that, initially, their common ground was Jordan and Zarqa (where, after 1967, al Maqdisi had taken refuge with his family before moving to Kuwait)²⁴ and the milieu of radical Salafism which blossomed in the Palestinian refugees' shanty towns. Though the Stranger had no links with this movement, he was a child of that environment, someone who had grown up in the shadow of the Palestinian diaspora, who had gone through, even if only as a petty gangster, the harshness of Jordanian prisons. It is reasonable to believe that the two had acquaintances in common, since the worlds of Jordanian outlaws and that of radical Salafi jihadists were deeply intertwined.

In Peshawar, al Gharib and al Maqdisi began weaving a symbiotic relationship that was to last for a decade. The former became the pupil of the latter, absorbing his teachings. They were an odd pair who must have caught people's eye. Al Maqdisi was tall, with blond hair and blue eyes, a strikingly good-looking man, while al Gharib had all the physical characteristics of his Bedouin blood.

Around the beginning of 1992, the Stranger, possibly thanks to al Maqdisi, began his training in al Sada, one of the camps set up by Sheikh Azzam. Training in the camps was the mujahedin equivalent of baptism, a sort of initiation for Muslim warriors; the Stranger could not have left Afghanistan without experiencing it.

AL SADA TRAINING CAMP

Sheikh Azzam had to battle for permission to run al Sada. Until 1985, his role had been confined to funding and facilitating the jihad, not to forging its soldiers and commanders. Wael Hamza Jalaidan, a Saudi activist and fundraiser who became one of the top aides to Azzam, summarized the vision behind the camps as follows: "We wished that everyone coming after us should pass through the same method of preparation—by participating and sharing [. . .] after morning prayers we would get together for Koran recitation, while after the afternoon prayer, we would get together to read some *hadith* [religious narratives attributed to the Prophet Muhammad] and benefit from them. After that, if there were any military operations, we would participate in them."25 Thus the idea was not only to indoctrinate the volunteers in combat tactics, but to teach them unity of religious thought and by so doing, create a brotherhood that would neutralize ethnic and regional distinctions. After the death of Azzam and the purges, the camps came under the control of Osama bin Laden and his Egyptian followers. More emphasis was put on military and guerrilla preparation.

Osama bin Laden's former personal body guard, Nasir Ahmad Nasir Abdallah al Bahari, describes life in the camps as a strenuous and disciplined regimen:

> There are three phases in the Al-Qa'ida Organization military camps. The first is the testing period. It is called the days of experimentation. The second phase is the military preparation period. It is called the drilling period. It lasts forty-five days. The third phase is called the guerrilla war tactics course. It also lasts forty-five days. During the experimentation period we used to experience all forms of exhaustion, including psychological exhaustion, as well as moral exhaustion. The training was extremely hard. Sometimes we hardly slept for four hours in two days at various times. The experimentation period is just over fifteen days. At the end of this period, when we were extremely tired, the instructor would come and say with extreme coolness: "Today is the last day of experimentation. You must now walk for thirty kilometers."

Only very few individuals lasted until the end of the experimentation. Yet, each one of us used to urge his exhausted comrades, to encourage them to remain steadfast and continue. This phase teaches recruits to withstand difficulties.

Indeed, because of the exhaustion and fatigue during the experimentation period, some of them said that they could take no more, that they no longer wanted jihad.

During the second phase, the drilling period, the new recruits take all military courses, deeply studying all kinds of weapons, beginning with light machineguns, through antiaircraft guns, and ending with shoulder-borne missiles, like SAM-7 and Stinger missiles, in addition to explosives and all kinds of guns, like the recoil and recoilless guns and the bow guns (madafi' qawsiyah). They are trained on surveys, maps and how to draw them, as well as sand maps, and other things. The trainee in this phase is given an integrated military education just like any graduate from the best regular military colleges.

Then comes the third phase, which is called the tactics and guerrilla warfare course. It also lasts forty-five days. This course was compulsory for all because the irregular warfare is based on guerrilla warfare. In this course, theoretical military skills are learned. Practical applications are carried out using all kinds of weapons that had been studied in the previous course, and employing military skills that have been gained. Indeed, this is a period of testing to measure what a man can absorb during previous courses.[26]

Al Sada is near the border between Afghanistan and Pakistan; several of those who participated in both attacks on the World Trade Center, including Ramzi Youssef, who was responsible for the first bombing, and Khaled Sheikh Mohammed, one of the people who masterminded the destruction of the Twin Towers, trained in this camp.

AL TAWHID

In Peshawar, al Maqdisi introduced his young Jordanian friend to modern Salafism.[27] Ironically, at its outset in the second half of the nineteenth century, Salafism was not an anti-Western ideology. On the contrary, it was Arab admiration for the modernized West that prompted the movement. Fascinated by European development, Arab countries began to compare their socioeconomic and political conditions with those of Europe. This evaluation triggered deep reflection on the crisis of the Ottoman Empire, the political power that controlled the Arab world at the time, and stimulated great interest in Western civilization. In the Arab world this process is known as *al Nahda*, literally, the "awakening" or "renaissance." Produced by the interaction of Arab thinkers with Western revolutionary ideals, al Nahda marked the beginning of Arab modernization or, rather, of the will to modernize. In essence, the Arab world acknowledged the socioeconomic and political superiority of the parliamentary European states. Looking to the achievements of the Old Continent, Arabs wanted to create a Muslim modernity in the new Arab states emerging from the disintegration of the Ottoman Empire.[28]

Salafism identified the Ottoman Empire as the primary cause of the Arab failure to modernize. To overcome this obstacle, the doctrine called for all Muslims to go back to the purity of religion, to the origins of Islam and the teachings of the Prophet. Reconnecting with their roots would provide them with the necessary strength to gain independence from the Ottoman Empire and a way to create an Arab identity. This was essentially a process of spiritual purification, of cleansing from centuries of political and economic domination.

Thus, Salafism envisaged the regeneration of Islam along lines compatible with the political, economic, and technological conquests of the West. According to Muhammad Abduh (1849–1905), founder of the political Salafiyya movement, "properly understood, Islam is perfectly in sync with the liberal, democratic and scientific values of the modern world."[29] To achieve this symbiosis, the core principles of Sharia law had to be adapted to the process of Western modernization.

Towards the end of the nineteenth century, the betrayal of Europe, which, far from freeing the Arab world, colonized it, contributed to the transformation of Salafism into the xenophobic, conservative, and puritanical revivalist movement of today. The central idea of modern Salafism is still the purification of Islam, but this time from the contamination of corruption and stagnation produced by Western colonization. Foreign European powers, not the Ottoman Empire, are blamed for the decadence of the Arab world.

Against this background, in the 1950s, Sayyed Qutb reformulated the concept of *al Tawhid*,[30] the divine and absolute unity of God, giving it a distinct political identity. "God is the source of power," wrote Qutb from the Egyptian jail where Nasser had imprisoned him, "not the people, not the party neither any human being."[31] This notion, known as *al hakimiyya lil-llah* (the principle of the government of God), projects Islam to the core of the political arena, the boundaries of which are strictly defined by the interpretation of the Prophet's teachings. Qutb's message is one of total severance from the Western-style politics embraced by Nasser and, at the same time, an exhortation to cleanse Islam of any external influence, including that of men. Any departure from the principle of the government of God, he affirms, is an act of apostasy (*kufr*).

Although the accusation of apostasy (*takfir*) is a religious concept, it has, from the outset of Islam, been molded into a powerful political weapon. The first war of apostasy was fought soon after the death of the Prophet, during the reign of Caliph Abu Bakr (632–34).[32] Through the centuries, both Shi'ites and Sunnis have used the concept of takfir to exclude each other from power.[33]

AL TAKFIR

In insurgent Iraq, al Zarqawi accuses secular and moderate Iraqi Muslims (especially those with liberal and democratic tendencies) as well as Shi'ites (whom he characterizes as the allies of the Coalition forces) of apostasy. They are heretics, he says, and as such they should be killed. One can draw dangerous parallels with the Spanish Inquisition in the fifteenth century.[34] Religion in Europe at that time was essentially a political weapon. The sin of apostasy was a crime punishable by a gruesome death by fire. Europe was alight with the auto-da-fé, as bodies burned in the name of God. The Iraq envisaged by al Zarqawi would be forced into this apocalyptic path.

The great danger faced by fifteenth-century Europe was the outbreak of civil war between Catholics and Protestants, a war fought along religious divides, with its roots in the Continent's vicious power struggles. Today, al Zarqawi's accusation of apostasy against the Shi'ite population aims at triggering just such a civil war (fitna)—that is, a war of religion in which political and economic interests are obscured.

Fitna in Iraq takes a characteristic form. At its root is the battle for power between the Shi'ite majority and the Sunni minority, who have succeeded in imposing their hegemony on the country for centuries. The feud between Shi'ites and Sunnis is almost as ancient as the Muslim religion. It was ignited in 655, a year before the assassination of Caliph Uthman, when the followers of Muhammad fought the Great Fitna over the issue of succession. Uthman was charged with apostasy by the supporters of Ali, considered the direct descendent of the Prophet. The Great Fitna gave birth to the schism between the Sunnis, the followers of Uthman, and the Shi'ites, the followers of Ali. The hostility between them remains virulent to this day.

From those early days, the concept of takfir remains solidly anchored to political and economic issues. It is essentially an instrument to challenge existing powers. In the eighteenth century, Abd al Wahhab, a Saudi preacher and founder of the Wahhabi movement, accused the Ottoman Empire of apostasy on the basis of heresy; he claimed that it had departed from the true source of legitimacy, the word of God. The alliance between the House of Saud and Wahhab was forged around the takfir of the Turks, a sin and a crime which allowed the population of the Arabian Peninsula to take up arms against its rulers.[35] For the following two centuries, the war of conquest conducted by these two powerful allies was fought with economic and political weaponry, but dressed up as a war against apostasy.

The final aim of the takfir is not the exclusion of the heretics from the *spiritual* community, but their eviction from the *material* community: removing them from the system of social rights and privileges and from the economy. The heretics are pushed outside the boundaries of political legitimacy. Defining the takfir is as slippery as defining terrorism. In the 1970s, when the Red Brigades accused the Italian state of terrorism, the government promptly returned the favor. In the mid-1990s, Ramzi Youssef, while on trial in the United States for the first bombing of the World Trade Center, accused the American government of engaging in terrorism.

In the 1950s and 1960s, members of the Muslim Brotherhood redefined the takfir to justify their opposition to Nasser, who they claimed had pushed them into the underworld of illegality. Again the question centered upon the legitimacy of the state. In response to tough government repression, Sayyed Qutb accused the Arab ruler of being an infidel, stating, "God is the sole source of power." The return to the legitimacy of God, to al Tawhid, to the acceptance of an absolute, supernatural power, allowed Qutb's followers to condemn the injustice done in the name of Arab nationalism. This move crippled Arab secularism. Against the bleak political landscape of the Cold War, rife with corruption, injustice, and treason, al Tawhid became the voice of God, the deliverance of the oppressed Arab people; for the new Arab generations of unemployed and dispossessed, it became the only hope to change the world they lived in.

These are the concepts that al Maqdisi unveiled to al Gharib in

Peshawar, the pillars of the radical Salafi jihadist movement. What al Zarqawi learned from al Maqdisi was the fundamentalist way of thinking; he learned to reject all those who do not believe in al Tawhid ideology, and to reject all those who do not join in condemning all tyrants, including Muslims and Arabs. Listening to his tutor, al Gharib began to understand his own past. Al Maqdisi's teachings projected him further into the fringe, into the Salafi jihadist movement, which shuns both Western and Arab socioeconomic and political environments. Takfir became the answer to al Gharib's many questions; it wiped away the deep contradictions of his upbringing. Takfir was his response to the consumerism and rapid modernization that had destroyed the Bedouin way of life, and to the Jordanian government, which had imprisoned him. Takfir was how he attacked those who had forced upon him a life of misery, of socioeconomic marginalization, of endless humiliation.

The radicalization of modern Salafism appealed to al Gharib and to the thousands of his peers who had completed the journey from petty criminal to mujahed. "The Salafist ideology is primarily a movement of violent rupture with the environment," explains Nadine Picaudou, professor at the National Institute for Oriental Language and Civilization (INALCO), Paris.[36] While the Muslim Brotherhood exists within the political space (its members participated in the elections in Egypt, Jordan, and Kuwait), modern Salafism not only rejects such a space, but seeks its destruction. The former are associative and legitimate, the latter are disruptive and illegal. What appealed to the Stranger in Peshawar was precisely the uncompromising, destructive nature of modern Salafism. In Europe, the same violent ideology draws a new generation of jihadist to suicide missions.

Modern Salafism also offers a way forward, a future vision. From the ashes of the disintegrating infidel regimes will rise al Tawhid, the ideal society. Thus, for al Zarqawi, to build the true Muslim state, the Iraq of Saddam, as well as the Iraq of Allawi and of those who follow him, must be demolished.

However, in 1993, al Zarqawi was not thinking of Iraq, but of his homeland. Together with al Maqdisi he began gathering Jordanian mujahedin to convince them to return home to begin the destruction of the Jordanian regime. Before the year's end, they were both back in Zarqa.

CHAPTER THREE

The Imprisonment

*The personality of al Zarqawi changed
completely in prison.*
—Member of al Zarqawi's training camp in Herat

In 1993, when al Gharib and al Maqdisi arrived in Jordan, they were welcomed as mujahedin, as victorious Arab warriors. However, neither of them had participated in any battle nor killed a single individual. Their experience was limited to the basic training received in the camps in Afghanistan. Nor did they possess specialized weapons knowledge; for example, neither was an expert on explosives. These facts, however, did not stop the pair from using the status of mujahedin to promote their revolutionary ideas in Jordan's new, hostile political landscape.

Major political changes had taken place in Jordan during the time al Gharib and al Maqdisi had spent in Afghanistan. In October 1991, the Jordanian government had backed a peace conference for the Middle East that was held in Madrid. This decision had created a wedge between the Muslim Brotherhood, who strongly opposed it, and the government. Then, at the beginning of 1993, King Hussein had passed repressive legislation to weaken the power of the Islamic Action Front, the party representing the Muslim Brotherhood. As a result, political propaganda was prohibited inside mosques; during the electoral campaigns, public meetings were forbidden; and electoral legislation was modified to penalize the Brotherhood. These measures were essen-

tially aimed at curbing the popularity of the Islamic reformist movement and its involvement in Jordanian politics. Therefore, in the 1993
election, the Islamic Action Front won only sixteen seats, down from
the thirty-four it had obtained in the November 1989 elections.
Finally, on 13 September 1993, just weeks before al Gharib and al Maqdisi returned to Jordan, the signing in Washington of the Oslo Peace
Agreement between Israel and the PLO cemented the hostility
between the Brotherhood and the Jordanian government.

Back in Zarqa, al Gharib and al Maqdisi began their propaganda
activity amidst a growing milieu of religious outlaws, fueled by the
progressive marginalization of moderate and reformist movements
such as the Muslim Brotherhood.[1] Initially they gravitated towards the
city's belt of Palestinian refugee camps, starting at al Ruseifah. Soon,
however, they traveled to other Jordanian cities. According to local
jihadists, al Maqdisi and al Gharib preached *al Dawa*, the Islamic mission, door to door, teaching their followers to regard Arab regimes as
infidels guilty of apostasy. They visited people's homes and talked with
whomever was willing to listen. They encouraged people to embrace
their vision, at the same time carefully distancing themselves from the
Muslim Brotherhood.[2] According to Layth Shubaylat, leader of the
Islamic Action Front and former member of the Jordanian parliament,
who met both al Gharib and al Maqdisi in al Suwaqah prison, they
regarded the Brotherhood as part of the infidel Jordanian regime
because it was a reformist movement. For example, they condemned
its acceptance of legislative councils, which they renamed "infidel
councils." "They labeled the police as infidels," explained Shubaylat,
"they labeled us [members of the Muslim Brotherhood] as infidels
and they labeled everyone who cooperated with the regime as infidels. They do not believe in the reformist trend."[3]

On 26 October 1994, the signature of the peace agreement between
the Jordanian government and Israel triggered the birth of a new wave
of clandestine Salafi jihadist groups. These organizations were similar
to the one founded in 1993 by the Stranger and al Maqdisi, al Tawhid,

which the Jordanian authorities soon renamed Bayaat al Imam (the Pledge of Alliance). Al Tawhid was a carbon copy of other radical jihadist groups founded in the early 1990s by veterans of the anti-Soviet jihad across the Arab world, groups such as the Groupe Islamique Armé (GIA) in Algeria and the Aden-Abyan Islamic Army in Yemen. Essentially, they were armed organizations whose task was to ignite a revolutionary jihad. The fitna, the civil war, they hoped, would evict the existing Arab regimes, which they regarded as *tagut* (not pious) and composed of infidels.[4] Thus, al Gharib's final aim—to trigger a civil war in Jordan in order to purify its corrupted political landscape—was already clear; Jordan became the stage where the future al Zarqawi rehearsed the role he would play a decade later in Iraq.

Al Maqdisi's message did not shun the use of terrorist tactics; on the contrary, in 1994 he even issued a fatwa to legitimize the recourse to armed attacks, including the use of explosives, against the Israeli army in Palestine. Al Maqdisi's thoughts were along the same lines as those of al Zawahiri, whom he had met in Afghanistan; both wanted to transform the mujahedin into the vanguard of the Muslim armed struggle. Al Maqdisi, who considered al Zawahiri one of the most important leaders of the Salafi jihadist movement, justified the recourse to terror tactics as the natural evolution of the mujahedin revolution.[5]

In the early 1990s, in many Arab countries, this message gained new momentum thanks to the eviction of moderate Islamic parties from the political arena. "Followers of the history of violence and Islamic extremism in Jordan can see that they first emerged in the early 1990s, when the Muslim Brotherhood [had] five of its members as cabinet ministers and twenty-two in parliament, including the Speaker of the House. It was capable of rallying a majority in parliament in many cases and on many issues. [From 1991 onwards] the Islamic movement of Jordan was forced out of its real [political] arena and entered a field unknown and strange to it and for which it had no tools."[6] Across the Middle East, people, especially young people, regarded the shunning of Islamic movements and parties from politics as the failure of the reformist strategy to bring about change, and flocked to join the radical jihadist groups.

The popularity of Bayaat al Imam, coupled with the radical preaching of its spiritual leader, drew the attention of the Jordanian secret service (Mukhabarat). In March 1994, both al Gharib and al Maqdisi were arrested. Al Gharib was charged with possession of arms and explosives, which he had hidden in the cellar of the family home. When interrogated, he claimed that he had found them in the street.[7]

The arrest and the accusations are emblematic of the radical change in the degree of tolerance of the Jordanian state towards modern Salafism. "Following the signing of the Jordanian-Israeli peace accord in 1994, cases of violence and extremism before the State Security Court mounted and continued."[8] Al Maqdisi understood and capitalized on this shift in policy. During the trial, he publicly denied that he had been part of Bayaat al Imam. "We do not have an Imam to whom we have pledged our loyalty," he said and stressed that both he and al Gharib belonged to the community of Muslims who recognized the absolute and divine unity of God, al Tawhid.[9] Cleverly globalizing their radicalism and at the same time attacking the motives behind the accusation that he had created an illegal terrorist cell, al Gharib argued that the case was part of the government's campaign to persecute Muslims like him and his companion on the basis of their religious beliefs.

THE GUERRILLA TRIAL

The trial of al Gharib and al Maqdisi soon turned into a replica of the "Guerrilla Trial" staged against colonial France by members of the Algerian independence movement. The defendants became the prosecutors and charged both the court and the king of Jordan with treason. "What was strange is that the Pledge of Allegiance (Bayaat al Imam) accused the judiciary and the head of state," explained Judge

Hafez Amin, who presided at the trial. "They submitted a letter of accusation in which they claimed that we were acting against the teachings of the Holy Koran."[10] Judge Hafez Amin was even given the task of informing the king of his crime against the law of God.

In a similar fashion, in the late 1970s, the founding members of the Red Brigades, on trial in Turin, accused the Italian court and the state of treason. The defendants claimed that they were "prisoners of war," discharged their lawyers, and refused to be part of a trial staged by the state, whose authority they did not recognize. This tactic created a stalemate that lasted for several months, as, according to Italian legislation, a trial could not take place without the participation of the defendants. In the end the legislation had to be modified.

The purpose of the Guerrilla Trial, however, was never to create a legal stalemate, but to transform the courts into an open stage for the armed struggle, to extend guerrilla tactics to institutions such as the judiciary. For members of the Algerian independence movement as well as for the Red Brigades, the courts became the official platform from which to publicize the violent actions conducted by comrades still at large. During the Red Brigades trial the defendants regularly claimed responsibility for all the attacks carried out outside the courts. As a propaganda tool, the Guerrilla Trial of al Maqdisi was extremely effective; during the trial the traffic on his Web site increased.

Al Maqdisi was clearly familiar with this technique and used it to boost his proselytism. In 1993 Bayaat al Imam was not yet an operative armed group, but only a vehicle for the creation of one. Its leaders' main activity was limited to mobilizing young people, without having yet reached the stage of planning and implementing any attack. The armed struggle was still to come. Thus, the trial was used exclusively to expose the Jordanian government's infidel policies and its repressive treatment of religious Muslims. It became a propaganda tool.

In court, al Gharib played an insignificant role, as he was still living in the shadow of his mentor. A celebrated scholar throughout the Arab world, al Maqdisi was the undisputed charismatic leader of the group during the trial. In sharp contrast, the Stranger was unknown, a former petty criminal, transformed in the fires of Afghanistan's war into the companion of a jihadist leader.

THE PRISON

In 1995, two years after being arrested, al Gharib and al Maqdisi were sentenced to fifteen years in prison for creating illegal jihadist cell—which in Jordan was considered a crime; they were not convicted of any terrorist attacks. They spent the next five years in captivity. It was during this period that another extraordinary metamorphosis of Abu Muhammad al Gharib took place.

Arab prisons have reshaped the lives of several generations of Muslims and transformed myriad personalities. Torture and the systematic use of solitary confinement are common features. In liberated Iraq, under American supervision, these practices are still in place. Sheikh Ali Bapir, leader of the Komala Islami Kurdistan (Kurdistan Islamic Group), was jailed in a U.S.-run detention center near Baghdad's airport for twenty-two months on the basis of false accusations. He was tortured and kept inside a cell 2.5 meters square. "It had a bed, a blanket, a big strong door and no windows," he told a *Guardian* correspondent in Iraq. "Much of the time there was no electricity, no lights. At the beginning I spent 23 hours inside my cell."[11] During the first ten days of captivity Sheikh Ali Bapir lost fifteen kilograms and his heartbeat rose significantly.

Before the war, Sheikh Ali commanded a thousand-strong militia that controlled a mountainous area in northeastern Iraq. He had about three thousand followers and was actively engaged in the resistance against Saddam's regime. Yet he was imprisoned with Saddam's henchmen, including Ali Hassan al Majid, better known as Chemical Ali, the man accused of masterminding the gas attacks against the Kurds. Initially, Sheikh Ali was enraged by the presence of these men, which included Saddam Hussein, though the former dictator was kept apart from the others. But as they shared the harshness of the prison, Sheikh Ali and his unlikely cellmates grew closer. "What they did to my people and the Iraqi people in general was not to be forgiven," he said. "But they were also in prison and in a weak position. It was my duty under Islam to show mercy." Sheikh Ali introduced his former enemies to the teachings of the Koran and taught them to find comfort in Islam.[12] Religion is often a great consolation for Arab inmates.

Al Gharib's experience in the al Suwaqah prison was similar to Sheikh Ali's ordeal, but harsher. When he arrived he "was a simple young man with limited cognitive and personal skills," recalls journalist Abdallah Abu Rumman, chief editor of the Jordanian weekly newspaper *al Mira'ah*, who met al Gharib in jail.[13] What turned this simple young man, in thrall to the charisma of al Maqdisi, into the emir of al Tawhid, the leader of a large group of inmates? Many believe that the traumas suffered in captivity altered his character. "I think that seven years in jail are more than enough to reshape the personality of anybody," explained a former inmate. "Reflecting has helped him . . . I think that he came to the conclusion that a strong leadership is indispensable for Islam."[14]

Undoubtedly, the need for strong leadership was also prompted by the experience of physical suffering. Al Gharib was brutally tortured. He was often placed in solitary confinement. At one time he spent eight-and-a-half months in the baking heat of the Jordanian desert, locked inside a cell that resembled, in size and comfort, an animal cage.

The harshness of prison also demanded great physical exertion. Inmates remember al Gharib exercising constantly, lifting whatever he could use as weights, including buckets of rocks. "Sports items were not available," recalls a prisoner, "but he used primitive exercises, like push-ups and sit-ups, to keep himself in shape."[15] Was he conditioning his body, preparing it for the role of the emir, for a life-long battle? Whatever his intentions, he soon lost his slender figure and his body became massive, solid. Those who had met him in Pakistan and Afghanistan did not recognize him in his new shape. "When my old deputy at the Afghan-Arab Bureau asked me if I remembered al Zarqawi, I said no, I really do not," said Abdallah Anas, who had met him in Afghanistan. "He reminded me that he had worked as a junior at the bureau, in Peshawar and that he used to call me Uncle Abdallah, yet I could not see any resemblance. Then one day I saw a picture of Abu Mos'ab when he was young on al Jazeera and suddenly I remembered him. He was much thinner and he even looked shorter."[16]

In prison the relationship between al Gharib and al Maqdisi evolved. Though al Maqdisi never ceased to be al Gharib's mentor, it was clear to everybody that al Gharib would eventually go his own way. He was destined to lead. "Abu Mos'ab was always very independent and remained so; he was very independent from Maqdisi. Although they agreed in principle on everything, they were still totally different human beings."[17]

Unlike al Maqdisi, a sophisticated intellectual, al Gharib acted on instinct; like the leader of a pack of wolves inside a cage, he was aggressive, constantly bordering on physical confrontation with his captors. He maintained some of the character traits of the young bully who had roamed the streets of Zarqa, and his relations with the prison authorities and guards were strained. In the eyes of his followers, however, his behavior was not disruptive, but heroic, justified by his mission to spread the word of God. For al Gharib, the prison guards were takfir, infidels guilty of apostasy, a sin punishable by death. Years later, in Iraq, he would use the same argument to justify the killing of Iraqi policemen. Besides seeing them as the tools of tyrants, he claimed that they were shields protecting the Americans: "As for you soldiers and policemen, if you are Muslims and believers, how can you serve as soldiers of that cross, policemen for those apostates? We will not let you destroy our hopes in this blessed jihad."[18]

Today as a decade ago, al Zarqawi's rhetoric is strong and straightforward, calling for immediate action and therefore very appealing to his followers. "The youth surrounding him in prison were actual jihadist fighters," explains an inmate; "they rejected the command of Abu Muhammad al Maqdisi, preferring Abu Mos'ab al Zarqawi because of his strength and determination."[19] The Stranger's organizational skills impressed inmates. According to Abu Rumman, al Gharib possessed strong organizational leadership, a quality that al Maqdisi lacked. He was able to control everyone and organize the relationships within the group; he was a true leader. According to Khaled Abu Duma, a Palestinian who had met al Gharib in al Suwaqah,[20] the Stranger "rapidly and almost naturally became the leader of the section where he was imprisoned. He did not have important ideas, yet people obeyed him because they feared him."[21] Behind bars, the ability to instill fear and respect is more powerful than eloquence.

Al Gharib was familiar with the prison environment and understood the rules of the game. Unlike al Maqdisi, he had grown up in the slums of the Middle East and had already experienced the social milieu of Jordanian prisons. His working-class background earned him considerable sympathy from the predominantly Palestinian prisoners because he embodied all the contradictions of his generation. "This young man, for strange reasons, came to resemble, to my fear, the stereotypical Jordanian young man who, ever since the economic reform policies and privatization, fell prey to unemployment, depression, and lack of confidence in the future," explains Abu Rumman, "constantly searching for the good city up in the sky and working towards it on the ground."[22]

One of the major contradictions sprang from his Bedouin background. "Al Zarqawi's personality was to me," admits Abu Rumman, "worth observing and analyzing for many reasons, at the top of which is that this simple and modest young man is a member of the Banu Hassan tribe and cannot be an extremist in his attitude towards the Jordanian government and society considering the number of his relatives employed by the army, police, and other institutions which his group, Bayaat al Imam, indiscriminately accuses of unbelief."[23] Yet al Gharib was able to turn his Bedouin origins into an asset. According to Abu Othman, an inmate at al Suwaqah, "his tribal background made it possible for [Abu Mos'ab] to obtain oaths of allegiance from other inmates."[24] Among them there were common criminals, including drug addicts, whom he defined "victims of society."[25] Thanks partly to their common background, he gained their respect and their trust. They joined his group and embraced his religious ideas because they believed he would protect them.

There is no doubt that al Gharib was fully committed and devoted to his followers. "On one occasion, he flew into a rage and attacked a guard who had been beating one of his disciples."[26] Leadership also demands humility and humanity, and while in prison al Gharib proved to possess these qualities. "He was well known for loving his brothers in God more than his relatives."[27] Once he personally bathed and took care of a new inmate, a jihadist who had lost both legs in a terrorist attack.[28] He was also easily moved to tears, a quality which generates respect in the Muslim world. "One day, I was with him in Zarqa driving the car," remembers Sheikh Jarrah al Qaddah. "In Zarqa the streets are normally so crowded that no one would even think of crying. You may cry when you are on your own, when you are lonely in the middle of the night, or when you are praying, but he was crying in the streets of Zarqa, in the crowded streets, during the day. I was talking to him about fraternity in God and I mentioned one of our brothers in God. The next thing I knew, I saw his tears pouring down. I swear to you this is what happened."[29]

Abu Rumman admits that he finds a gulf between the man he knew in 1996 and the Abu Mos'ab al Zarqawi as portrayed by the U.S. media. "Despite the halo surrounding him, he seemed gentle, extremely well-mannered, romantic, idealistic in his life and thoughts, and always striving to be worthy of the trust of his colleagues. . . . He is, in brief, a man from the first hegira century in terms of his manners, looks and hopes, but who was thrown by history into the twenty-first century with all its abnormalities, sins, and depressants."[30]

Members of his group in al Suwaqah concur with the above description. "He had a tendency to remain alone to the degree that people would call him the Stranger and he liked that. He was very, very quiet. Many times, he wouldn't talk and if you didn't talk to him, he wouldn't talk to you. He was silent for long periods."[31]

There are other aspects of his personality which appear to clash with the image of the ruthless, barbarous terror leader and serial killer of Western hostages. One was the love and respect he showed for his mother. "He loved her so much that he was always sure to write letters and cards on religious occasions and sign them 'the Stranger.' He cried when mentioning her name and when she visited him in jail he wore his best clothes. When others asked why, he would respond: because she is my mother."[32] Seven years in a Jordanian prison contributed to a radical change in his personality, but as we shall see in the following chapters, other factors, not related to his life but linked to world events and policies, played an equally big role.

In al Suwaqah, inmates also admired al Gharib's intellectual effort when he set out to memorize the entire Koran. This was a monumental task for anybody, let alone for an uneducated man. There is no doubt that in prison the Stranger came across as a rather simple individual. He spoke the Jordanian dialect and did not understand classic Arabic. He wrote using simple sentences, with almost a childish style. "He did not have a good grasp of politics either," explains Khaled Abu Duma, "for example, he always said that he loved the Americans because they were Christians and believers."[33] However, after the 1998 bombing of the U.S. embassies in Kenya and Tanzania, he changed his mind. According to Youssef Rababa, another prison mate, al Gharib lacked the vision of leaders such as Osama bin Laden.[34]

Determination and willpower, however, compensated for the absence of formal education. "His primary concern was to learn the Holy Koran by heart," says Faiq al Shawish, a cell mate. "I helped him; he used to recite at least ten verses a day to me. Al Zarqawi was relentless when it came to jihad and learning. If he had devoted himself to learning, he would have outdone his teachers by far. He had the patience to stay up all night, studying a single issue.[35]

In al Suwaqah, inmates were mesmerized by the complexity and contradictions of his personality, by his innate abilities as a leader and his emotional nature. He was one of them, born and raised among the unemployed, a working-class boy, and yet he was special, different. Captivity in his own country offered al Gharib the opportunity to show his true nature to his peers, to put his courage to the test and to become a leader—a chance he had never had in Afghanistan.

THE EMIR OF AL TAWHID

By 1996, the simple man who had gone to Afghanistan dreaming of becoming a mujahed was only the pale shadow of the man described by prison inmates. In jail al Gharib acquired a magical aura of respect that overshadowed that of his mentor, al Maqdisi.

Captivity reversed the roles between the two friends. Was the teacher conscious of the great appeal that his companion enjoyed inside al Suwaqah? Did he willingly step aside, letting his pupil become the emir, the prince, of their group, al Tawhid? In a letter written in September 2004, al Maqdisi admitted that he had encouraged his followers to elect al Gharib as their emir.[36] According to several inmates, "al Zarqawi used religious texts to become the head of the al Tawhid group, to become the successor of Maqdisi, of whom all group members had been students."[37] Al Madqisi encouraged and promoted his pupil and soon a division of tasks emerged between the two. "People thought that if al Zarqawi was their emir, Abu Muhammad al Maqdisi would have spare time for engaging in independent judicial ruling and religious study."[38] Thus, while the Stranger performed the role of emir, al Madqisi was in charge of "the Friday's and holy days' prayers and of teaching the youngsters."[39]

The reversal of roles between al Gharib and al Maqdisi should not be undervalued. The issue of the emirate is central to Islam; the role of the emir refers to the fundamentals of Islam. "The prophet is said to have proclaimed that in a group of two, one should always lead," explains Fouad Hussein, a Jordanian journalist who met al Zarqawi in prison. "Decisions should always be taken by one person. Just as they say, 'a ship only has one captain.' On this basis, if in prison or anywhere else, an Islamic grouping always has an emir."[40] Becoming an emir takes time. It is a process through which the members of the group come to recognize and accept the leadership qualities of one individual and then choose him as their leader. Taking the lead for al Gharib was a remarkable achievement, which showed his determination and managerial skills, qualities that would serve him well in the Iraqi insurgency.

In 1996, when Abu Rumman was imprisoned, there were several "emirates" in al Suwaqah. "They were organizations and groups which shared the prison cells and had huge differences of opinions. Al Zarqawi's emirate was among the strongest and most influential within those groups for organizational reasons, because it extended to all prison quarters and attracted a large number of inmates."[41]

According to Layth Shubaylat, who met him in prison, al Gharib was a stubborn, firm man who believed in his principles, "a real man." Shubaylat understood the power that a man like al Gharib could accumulate inside the prisons and the damage that, in the long run, the propagation of the Salafi jihadist ideology would do to the reformist movement he supported, the Muslim Brotherhood. When Shubaylat left prison, thanks to a special pardon from the late King Hussein, he sought, unsuccessfully, to secure the release of members of al Gharib's group and other jihadist groups. He directly approached the king. "I told him: Let me give them the good news. He said: Who do you mean? I said: The prisoners, or let me say the political prisoners, or let me say the Islamists, or let me say the Afghans. He [the king] was taken by surprise. I said: Sir, let me tell you that you and I are responsible for these people. He said: How? I said: For fifty years you have been teaching them to stand against Zionism and you want them to change overnight?

But . . . you also failed me. You did not allow me or those who think like me [the moderates] to implement any part of my program. So, Sir, you should expect people worse than me who will label you as infidel. They will not only label you, they will label you and me as infidels."[42]

Layth Shubaylat's analysis proved correct; during the second half of the 1990s, against the repressive background of Jordanian politics, the Salafi jihadist movement blossomed. Al Maqdisi and Abu al Gharib used their new position as leaders inside the prison to build up al Tawhid, their jihadist group. It was during their captivity that they gathered a considerable number of activists, many of whom were common criminals. Arab prisons are the most common recruiting ground for jihadists. Indoctrination is facilitated by the torture, humiliation, and inhumane treatment of prisoners imposed by their state captors.

While in captivity, al Gharib and al Maqdisi continued to proselytize outside the prison. "Supporters never stopped visiting the two, bringing and delivering letters to and from them. The number of essays and books on issuing fatwas and Islamic heritage written by al Maqdisi in prison reached about one hundred, and his supporters reiterated their titles with pride. It also appears that in prison Abu Mos'ab [al Zarqawi] set up a network of connections that would help him when he left prison in 1999, and made months-long preparations to return to Afghanistan accompanied by a dozen of his men who were in the Jordanian prison and by others who waited for him to leave prison."[43]

As the prince, the emir of his group, the Stranger ruled over the lives of his followers in captivity and became the man with whom the prison authorities had to engage. "He was tough, difficult to deal with," admits Sami al Majaali, former head of the prison authority in Jordan. "We were always careful in approaching him especially because he was a real leader, a prince as the inmates called him. All the dealings with any of those convicts had to go through him. He was our primary concern; if he cooperated, the others would follow suit."[44] As the emir, al Gharib could impose his own rules on his followers. He ordered inmates to wear Afghan clothes; he also decided what they could watch on television and which books they were allowed to read. "One day, I was reading *Crime and Punishment* by Dostoyevsky when Abu Mos'ab approached me," remembers Khaled Abu Duma. "'Why are you reading the book of an infidel?' he asked. I suggested he should also read it but he did not reply." When, on another occasion, Abu Duma expressed interest in learning the poetry of an author blacklisted by the Stranger, suddenly everybody stopped talking to him.[45]

Nobody could challenge the authority of the emir; any attempt was punished and the perpetrator was isolated. "In strictly religious terms, in the way most of those people [the inmates] saw the prince, i.e., the emir, his authority was sacred, you would not doubt his word," explained Fouad Hussein. "Added to which, anyone who would defy his prince would be defying God, so there is a religious authority which rules everything else."[46]

In 1996, Fouad Hussein was imprisoned in the cell next to al Maqdisi and al Gharib. "When I first met al Zarqawi in prison, he was fairly distant. . . . A week later, the prison authorities ordered him to solitary confinement, after a verbal spat with one of the guards. His followers tried to bring him back, but the prison authorities would not give in. In those days I was the spokesperson for all the 360 political prisoners. Al Maqdisi asked me to join in a protest action, along with the rest of us. We did just that, the protest was effective, the prison director promised to release al Zarqawi. When he was released and heard of what I had done for him, he warmed more to me."[47]

Although al Gharib considered Fouad Hussein a nonbeliever, he was a fellow inmate, someone with whom he shared the harshness of the prison. As a true leader, the Stranger used this common ground as a bridge towards him. "Once, al Zarqawi asked me whether I had ever been harmed physically during interrogation. I told him what happened to me. He sighed [and] then told me what he had been subjected to in solitary confinement over eight and a half months. After this, I knew that when al Zarqawi would eventually be released, he would not want to remain in Jordan."[48]

Torture, solitary confinement, the instruments of repression, all molded the emir and thousands like him. Thus, while in captivity and because of it, his transition from an ordinary individual, who was not conscious of his inner leadership qualities, to a leader took place. The appeal he exercised among his peers derived from the common background he shared with them. "We are talking about drifters, the lost children of the revolution, people marginalized by society," explains Nadine Picaudou. "These are people who have been traumatized by repression, by the prison experience. This factor must be remembered and must be taken into consideration, without, of course, justifying their violent actions."[49] Prison instructed Arab Islamists in the importance of discipline and hierarchy. Psychological respite could only be found in obedience to an unquestioned emir.

Far from being a psychopath, a serial killer of hostages, or a sadist, the emir of al Tawhid, in the second half of the 1990s, was a lost soul, a victim as much as a perpetrator of a culture of violence and poverty, an inhabitant of the jungle that had grown in the shadow of the politics of corrupt, short-sighted Arab elites.

CHAPTER FOUR

The Road to 9/11

*Martyrs write the history of nations because the history
of nations can only be written with sweat and blood.*
—Sheikh Abdallah Azzam

Throughout the 1990s, while the Stranger and al Maqdisi were imprisoned, the Salafi jihadist movement was greatly influenced by Ayman al Zawahiri.

Born into an elite Egyptian family, al Zawahiri studied medicine and became a pediatrician. Like Osama bin Laden, he grew up in a sophisticated and wealthy environment; he originated from a world completely alien to al Gharib. In the Middle East, the socioeconomic divide is an ocean that cannot be easily bridged. Politics was a daily topic of conversation in the al Zawahiri household and a matter in which members of the family were directly engaged. University classrooms were another forum where the young Ayman could exchange political ideas with other equally privileged students. Yet, unlike Osama bin Laden, al Zawahiri was imprisoned; he entered the murky world of Arab "outlaws" and was confronted with the violence and repression of the Arab penal system.

Al Zawahiri's prison experience radicalized him, leaving him determined to use the jihad as a political tool to strike back at his captors. This was a common phenomenon among those who had experienced torture inside Arab prisons. According to Osama bin Laden's former personal bodyguard, al Bahari, the bombing of the Egyptian embassy in Islamabad in 1995 was a "retaliatory attack because of what the Egyptian Government had done to [the perpetrators of the bombing], in terms of the dishonor and torture to which they had been subjected in Egyptian jails."[1]

Applying the principle of takfir, that is, the accusation of apostasy, al Zawahiri reelaborated Sayyed Qutb's concept of revolutionary jihad. Both Arab and Islamic governments were guilty of apostasy for their collusion with Christian and Jewish governments; regimes such as Egypt's, that had enslaved its own people, became his targets. Against this backdrop, the duty of any good Muslim was to rebel, not only against the corrupt regimes, but against the institutions which supported them: the army, the police, the intelligence services, even the ulemas (religious scholars). Thus al Zawahiri went much further than Qutb; he legitimized the jihad against all fellow Muslims who did not join the fight, including imams and religious figures. This is a key issue. Years later in Iraq, Abu Mos'ab al Zarqawi would use the Shi'ites' support for the Coalition forces and the new regime to justify his terror campaign against Shi'ite mullahs.

Al Zawahiri's denunciation of the endemic corruption of Arab regimes, of their responsibility for the Palestinian diaspora, and of the role they played in the rise of Israel as the hegemonic power in the region, were and still are powerful arguments in the Muslim world. They evoke painful, shameful memories. "As you know, all the Arab regimes act as guards for the state of Israel. Israel would not have existed thus far had it not been for the role played by the Arab regimes," Fouad Hussein explained during a program on al Zarqawi on Lebanese television. The question of Palestine is a constant source of humiliation, a reminder of the failure of Arab regimes to protect their own brothers. "The young mujahedin in Jordan went to Afghanistan when they could not fight the Jews in Palestine. They then went to Iraq. The political aim of Abu Mos'ab al Zarqawi and other jihadist groups in Iraq is liberating the country from the U.S. occupation, so that Iraq can be used as a launching pad for the liberation of Palestine. Thus, we cannot ignore the impact that the U.S. occupation of Iraq will play in the future of the Palestinian question."[2]

Sheikh Abdallah Azzam, one of the victims of the diaspora, also sought to free his own land from Israeli occupation. However, back in 1988, he was not interested in attacking Arab regimes, which had been funding and sponsoring the mujahedin in Afghanistan; he was determined to keep the fight on the international level. The road to Jerusalem was an international highway. As long as Jerusalem was the final destination, it was irrelevant whether one arrived via Bosnia or Uganda. For al Zawahiri, however, the road to Jerusalem was a desert trail that necessarily passed through Cairo and other Arab capitals. "Jerusalem will not be opened until the battles in Egypt and Algeria have been won and until Cairo has been opened."[3] Thus, the sole acceptable form of jihad was the armed struggle.

From the outset, the dilemma of the Islamist insurgency is strategic. It boils down to the question of how to fight two enemies: one near and the other remote. The former is represented by the Muslim regimes, illegitimate because they originate from military coups or because they are takfir, corrupt, and repressive. The distant enemy is the West, which is represented in the Middle East by the state of Israel, the occupying power in Palestine and the holy sites. Today, for al Zarqawi and the jihadist movement, the distant enemy includes Coalition forces in Iraq. Western countries, the United States in particular, are equally responsible for backing infidel Arab and Muslim regimes, such as Mubarak's Egypt, the House of Saud, and democratic Iraq.[4] As we shall see, this dilemma is to plague the jihadist movement until 2003, when the international and domestic fronts merged in Iraq. In Iraq, Abu Mos'ab al Zarqawi would find himself fighting both fronts simultaneously: a war against the distant enemy, represented by the Coalition forces, and a fitna, a civil war against the near enemy, the U.S.-backed Shi'ite majority government.

Back in the 1990s, however, the end of the war in Afghanistan, coupled with the purges and the assassination of Azzam, had shifted the jihad front away from the international arena to the domestic one. Inevitably, this phenomenon altered the nature of the conflict and triggered major tactical changes. While the mujahedin fought a war against an occupying foreign power, bin Laden and al Zawahiri's al Qaeda, as well as the Salafi jihadist movement, were engaged in domestic armed struggles against Arab regimes. Against this background, military techniques were replaced by terror tactics, amongst which the most effective were suicide missions.

SUICIDE MISSIONS

The impact of suicide missions goes well beyond the immediate damage caused by the terrorist act itself. On 25 April 2004 one of al Zarqawi's suicide bombers crashed his vessel into an oil export facility in the southern port of Basra. As the news of the attack spread, oil prices shot up in trading rooms around the globe; dealers were frantic; speculators rushed to the futures markets to profit from the price surge. For more than twenty-four hours there was nothing but chaos in the oil market. Did the young man who blew himself up anticipate these events? It is doubtful.

In a video shot a few hours before the attack by members of al Zarqawi's group, the soon-to-be suicide bomber looks relaxed and happy. Lying in the bottom of a small boat, he chats with the cameraman, smiles, and laughs. It is difficult to believe that in a few hours he will be dead, that parts of his body will be scattered all over the estuary of the Tigris and Euphrates. "Praise to God and to Muhammad, the commander of the mujahedin, and to his family," he says to the camera. "To my parents, to my wife, and to my brothers, peace be on you. I will not forget you."[5] The video ends with the celebrations of his martyrdom.

Suicide missions are a new phenomenon for the jihadist movement. They were not part of the anti-Soviet jihad. Sheikh Abdallah Azzam had envisaged a completely different future for the members of al

Qaeda. As a vanguard of Muslim warriors, he thought that they would embrace sacrifice, including death, for their fellow brothers, not that they would commit suicide to kill the enemy.

The celebration of death in battle—essentially an apocalyptic concept—was very dear to the mujahedin. It constituted the core of their great psychological and emotional strength. The mujahedin were the protectors of their religion, who in death became martyrs. "Martyrs are those who safeguard the tree of this religion," wrote Azzam in the 1980s, "its maintenance or disappearance is up to them, because this religion is irrigated with blood." Like the early Christian martyrs,[6] the mujahedin are drenched in spirituality; their destiny goes well beyond the boundaries of life, and will be fulfilled only in the afterlife. "I am not afraid of death," admits Abdallah Anas. "I was a mujahedin. I saw many of my brothers dying in battle. Death does not scare me."[7] Death is part of the mujahed's destiny; it is an ineluctable fate because it constitutes the will of God. Death is seen as one of life's essential transitions, like getting married or having children.

This vision of death is remarkably similar to that of the early Christian martyrs. "As Christ had endured martyrdom on the cross to save humanity, so Christians welcomed their destiny, which was to cross the threshold of salvation to the promised afterlife."[8] However, unlike the Christian martyrs, who were not conscious of their political role in the destruction of the Roman Empire, the mujahedin had a clear idea of their political impact. "Martyrs write the history of nations because the history of nations can only be written with sweat and blood," wrote Azzam. The life of the Prophet, modernity, and two thousand years of history shaped Azzam's vision of the role of the mujahedin.[9] Their primary motivation was to defend their brothers from oppressive foreign powers, not to reach Paradise. Thus, before becoming martyrs, the mujahedin of Sheikh Abdallah Azzam were warriors and heroes whose task it was to fight.

Throughout the anti-Soviet jihad the concept of suicide remained distinct from martyrdom. Suicide was accepted only in very special circumstances, for example, in captivity in order to protect vital secrets.[10] Therefore, those who commit suicide are considered martyrs, motivated by the will to protect fellow Muslims and Islam. The conditions required are very strict: the secret that the martyr is taking to the grave must be very important, and he must be a prisoner of the enemy and unable to resist torture.[11]

It was Ayman al Zawahiri who merged the concepts of martyrdom and suicide into a terrorist technique.[12] At the end of the 1980s, he stated that in order to avoid a direct confrontation with the enemy, which can be dangerous for the cause, jihad must be conducted with "trick and deceit." One of the tactics of the art of deceit is the recourse to suicide missions. As we shall see, al Zarqawi's current terror campaign in insurgent Iraq centers on this type of action.

The legitimacy of suicide missions is a source of great debate in the Muslim world. Al Zawahiri justifies them using various arguments: it is permitted to commit suicide to consolidate and proselytize Islam; religious scholars agree that people can expose themselves to dangerous situations during the jihad; one person can attack a large number of enemies, knowing that by doing so he will die; suicide is permitted to avoid revealing secrets under torture. Although these arguments are backed by several religious authorities, in the ultimate analysis the justification of suicide missions is essentially political and strategic.

To make martyrdom more appealing to the masses, al Zawahiri celebrated the rewards of suicide missions. "Their [the martyrs'] sins are forgiven and they have a special place in Paradise . . . they have 72 virgins and can intercede for 70 relatives."[13] Ironically, a thousand years ago Pope Urban II offered the crusaders a similar package when he launched the First Crusade in his famous speech in the cathedral of Clermont, France. The Pope guaranteed eternal salvation to those who joined the armies of the Crusades. By doing so, he introduced the notion of salvation gained through an act of violence: by killing Muslims.[14] "Killing infidels is not murder, it is the path to heaven," says a preacher in the Hollywood blockbuster *Kingdom of Heaven*.

Even suicide martyrs' intercession on their relatives' behalf is a Christian concept, introduced in the early centuries of the Catholic Church, when martyrs were canonized and the faithful began praying to them for intercession.

As the boundaries of the revolutionary jihad become regional, it follows that innocent Muslims can easily fall victim to suicide missions, which use the tactics of terror (explosives, car bombs, etc.) with the objective of igniting the fitna, the civil war. This is an important issue, which alienated support for Islamist armed groups across the Muslim world, including in insurgent Iraq. Islamist radical intellectuals and scholars are divided upon this issue. Al Maqdisi, for example, has condemned suicide missions because they end up killing fellow Muslims.[15] Al Zawahiri counterargues that the slaughtering of fellow Muslims is necessary, justified, and permitted in pursuit of jihad, but concedes that Muslim victims of terror attacks are also martyrs. In insurgent Iraq, al Zarqawi uses identical concepts to justify the random killing of innocent Iraqis. "God ordered us to attack the infidels by all means . . . even if armed infidels and unintended victims—women and children—are killed together. The priority is for jihad so anything that slows down jihad should be overcome," said al Zarqawi in May 2005, justifying the killing of hundreds of innocent Muslims during a wave of suicide attacks launched by his followers in Iraq.[16]

Al Zarqawi and al Zawahiri have much in common: they both experienced torture and the harshness of Arab prisons; each had broken down under torture, each provided information, and each confessed to their torturers; both were emotionally and psychologically scarred by their own people.

THE NEW GENERATION OF SUICIDE BOMBERS

The most famous soap opera broadcast by Iraqi television, *Love and War*, ended in spring 2005 with the tragic death of one of the two lovers in a suicide bombing. The program, which had kept the entire nation and several million other Arab viewers in the Middle East glued to their television screens for months, shows the extent to which this type of attack has become part of the daily life of Iraqis. "This is really a story about ordinary people," said Hassan Dixon, the scriptwriter. "It is about love under this American occupation. It shows how life goes on despite all the things we are living through."[17]

In insurgent Iraq, the jihadists guided by al Zarqawi have perfected the use of suicide missions. Most of them cross the border ready to die. The majority do not even communicate to their parents what they are about to do, and in fact, they hide their intentions. A former kung fu champion in Jordan, for example, told his family that he was going to participate in a martial arts tournament, only to blow himself up in a Baghdad marketplace.[18] Unlike the Palestinian suicide bombers who, in recent years, have terrified Israel, none of the Iraqis seems to receive a payment, such as an insurance premium, for their family. Those who die in Iraq are motivated by an ideology that has transformed death into a reward. Thus they are a free resource, costing al Zarqawi and his group nothing. Since the January 2005 election, a wave of suicide bombers has crashed into Iraq. In May 2005, there was on average one suicide attack every day in Baghdad alone. Sadly, people have learned to coexist with it.

In spring 2005, killing techniques were modified in Iraq to prevent the interception of suicide bombers. To guard against being shot before reaching their target, for example, suicide bombers are strapped to the steering wheel and have their foot taped to the accelerator. Soft targets, such as marketplaces, schools, and even hospital entrances, are chosen because they are not sufficiently guarded. The plague of suicide bombers resembles the sniper activity in Sarajevo during the 1990s war. They kill indiscriminately; their aim is to terrify the population, create chaos, and by so doing, destabilize and weaken the central authority of the state. Like the snipers in Sarajevo, suicide bombers do not see themselves as terrorists; they consider themselves members of an army that is seeking a better government for the Iraqi population. "Why, in the media, do you call them suicide operations and not martyrdom operations, and why do you use the word terrorists and not mujahedin?" an Iraqi jihadist asked the LBC television reporter he had kidnapped in al Qa'im in May 2005.[19]

A sophisticated, high-tech jihadist network hails suicide bombers as heroes. Using the Internet and CDs, it advertises suicide missions across the Muslim world as well as in the West. CDs showing the last moments of suicide bombers circulate among jihadists supporters. "Give away the martyr to his second home in heaven, give away the martyr with his wounds, blood, and clothes," sings one of these CDs obtained by the *Sunday Times*.[20] The ad campaign is relentless. Jihadist Web sites chart the martyrs' lives, list their family members, and present the details of the attacks carried out. A generation of Muslim Arabs seems to be fascinated with martyrdom via suicide missions, and because of this broad fascination, profiling future suicide bombers is a problem, as the sole common denominator among prospective bombers is their Muslim identity and origin. On one Web site 450 names are listed, including "Saudi university students, newlyweds, and an employee of the Kuwaiti defense department who resigned and headed across the border to Iraq."[21]

This new generation of jihadists aims to remove Americans from the Arab lands. They are totally focused on this task and cannot be dissuaded from it. Syrian officials in May 2005 arrested 137 Saudis as they were heading for the border. The commander who interviewed them said that their ideology was nonnegotiable. In mind and spirit they were already martyred; what they needed was someone to coordinate the attack, someone to tell them which target to hit, where to go, and how to complete their mission.[22] Al Zarqawi and his network of jihadists provide such information. Evoking the preparations performed by Christian warriors on the eve of their entry into knighthood to embrace a life in defense of Christianity, soon-to-be Iraqi suicide bombers spend the night before the attack alone, praying and getting ready for death.

SUICIDE MISSIONS: A COST-BENEFIT ANALYSIS

Suicide missions carried out by the second generation of suicide bombers in Europe are equally cost-effective. The July attacks in London may well be the cheapest to date carried out by a group in the West, costing no more than the price of the explosives and a rental car, the train and Tube tickets, and a trip to Pakistan for three of the bombers.

The unsuccessful suicide mission of Richard Reid, the so-called shoe-bomber, was equally inexpensive. Reid is part of a growing number of European-born suicide bombers operating in the West, including Zacarias Moussoui, a Frenchman of Moroccan origin, who pleaded guilty to playing a role in the 9/11 attacks. A Frenchman of Algerian origin unsuccessfully attempted to bomb the U.S. embassy in Paris in 2001. Ten Algerian and French-born jihadists also plotted to blow up a Christmas market in Strasbourg, France, in December 2001.

Members of the new generation of would-be suicide bombers have not gone through the camps in Afghanistan. They lack the requisite physical and psychological preparation to engage in direct combat in the jihad. In forging the new generation of jihadists, the recruiters are forced to skip combat training, because the camps have been destroyed, and they focus instead on psychological indoctrination. Although the invasion of Afghanistan pulverized al Qaeda's logistical apparatus and forced its leadership to run and hide, it did not destroy its radical message. In adapting to the new environment, the messianic call to arms has become a potent exhortation to martyrdom through suicide missions. It has evolved into a new anti-imperialist ideology: al Qaedism. This message has spread via the Internet, through thousands of jihadist Web sites and via an army of recruiters, some of them joining only after 9/11. These recruiters have been highly successful among the large numbers of often unemployed and disenfranchised young men in the Middle East as well as among middle-class European Muslims.

As proven by al Zarqawi's extensive use of suicide bombers in Iraq, these missions have become the core of the new ideology, and suicide bombers have replaced the concept of the mujahedin in the collective imagination of radical young Muslims. Followers of al Qaedism have gone underground, hiding their ideology. None of the perpetrators of the London bombings had shared his commitment to the jihad with family members. On the contrary, they hid their political ideas and their willingness to die for them.

The idea of death exercises a potent political appeal to the new generation of jihadists. Death by detonation seems to transcend reality, projecting those who choose to embrace it into a parallel dimension, populated exclusively by suicide bombers to be. Thus, mentally and emotionally, the departure from life takes place well before the loss of one's body. The mother of one of the London suicide bombers said that the night before the attack, her son fell asleep on the couch in the sitting room. One cannot help but wonder if he had been watching television and felt too exhausted to go to bed.

THE INTERNATIONAL FRONT FOR JIHAD AGAINST THE JEWS AND THE CRUSADER

Westerners find the idea of suicide missions profoundly shocking. For Londoners and others, perhaps the most disturbing and terrifying aspect of the 7 July bomb attacks was the realization that they had been masterminded by a suicide team.[23] Equally shocking in the Muslim world are images of Muslims dying at the hands of Western powers.

"I couldn't forget those moving scenes, blood and severed limbs, women and children sprawled everywhere," said Osama bin Laden in a statement after the 9/11 attacks, referring to the images of Beirut in 1982 during the Israeli occupation of the country. "Houses destroyed along with their occupants and high rises demolished over their residents, rockets raining down on our home without mercy. . . . And that day, it was confirmed to me that oppression and the intentional killing of innocent women and children is a deliberate American policy. Destruction is freedom and democracy, while resistance is terrorism and intolerance. . . . So with these images and their like as their background, the events of September 11th came as a reply to those great wrongs. Should a man be blamed for defending his sanctuary?"[24]

Towards the end of the 1990s, bin Laden used the images of the shelling of Beirut to justify a major strategic change: the return of the jihad to the international arena. By targeting America as the primary enemy, he broke away from the majority of jihadist terror groups. What caused such a drastic about-face? Undoubtedly, the prolonged presence of U.S. troops in Saudi Arabia played a big role; however, equally important was "the failure of the Islamist revolution in the Arab countries, [for example,] in Algeria and in Egypt."[25]

Throughout the 1990s, al Zawahiri's interpretation of the jihad had prevailed inside al Qaeda and among Salafi jihadist groups. Across the Muslim world, domestic terror groups such as the GIA, loosely linked to al Qaeda's leadership, had engaged unsuccessfully in domestic armed struggles. Only in Chechnya, where the mujahedin were fighting the Russians, had they succeeded.[26] Their leader, a young Saudi named Tamer Saleh Suwaylam, but better known as Khattab, was determined to keep the fight confined to Chechnya.[27]

Among all the jihadist leaders, Khattab offered the strongest opposition to Osama bin Laden's new approach. Backed by foreign Muslim parties, mostly in Saudi Arabia, which supplied him with funds and young recruits, Khattab quickly established himself among the jihadists, and his reputation took off. Unlike many other leaders, he had plenty of money because he had established a network of sponsors in the Gulf countries and controlled, to a large extent, the Arab fight in Chechnya. He even had his private media, which connected him to the outside world. He was clever, charismatic, and charming.[28] According to sources very close to bin Laden, Khattab's position in Chechnya until the start of the second Russian campaign in 1999 was stronger than that of Osama bin Laden's in Afghanistan.[29] Khattab's vision of the jihad and his commitment to keep it localized had tremendous weight inside the jihadist movement.

Although Osama bin Laden's attempts to win over Khattab were unsuccessful, he managed to convince Ayman al Zawahiri. In February 1998, the Egyptian shocked the Salafi jihadist world by forming the International Front for Jihad against the Jews and the Crusaders, a new organization under the leadership of Osama bin Laden. The fatwa attached to it stated that not only were Muslims permitted to kill Americans, both soldiers and civilians, but also that this action was compulsory for those capable of doing so. "What we see is the return to the international jihad," commented Nadine Picaudou.[30]

The fight thus returned to the global level. The enemy was once again the distant enemy, represented by an unjust world order firmly under U.S. domination, which subjugated and humiliated Muslims. "We have declared jihad against the government of the United States of America," said Osama bin Laden, "because it is an unjust government, aggressive and infidel. It has committed several criminal acts directly or indirectly through its support for the Israeli occupation of Palestine. . . . We believe that it is responsible for the killing of Palestinians, Lebanese, Iraqis."[31] With this statement, Saladin's jihad, the counter-Crusade, was back in the picture.

AL QAEDA'S INFIGHTING

In the fall of 2004, *al Sharq al Awsat*, the London-based Saudi newspaper, received a manuscript entitled, *The Story of the Arab-Afghans from the Time of Their Arrival in Afghanistan Until Their Departure with the Taliban*. The author is believed to be Abu Whalid al Masri, an Egyptian journalist very close to Mullah Omar, who lived in Kandahar where he ran a Taliban magazine. The work provides unique insight into the real al Qaeda. It argues that during the second half of the 1990s, far from being ideologically homogenous, the group was plagued by vicious infighting. It also reveals that at the core of the new battle to control al Qaeda was bin Laden's decision to relaunch the counter-Crusade, to target America, and to plan the 9/11 attacks.[32]

Since al Qaeda's relocation to Afghanistan in 1996, the moderate wing had resented bin Laden for having trusted a group of Saudis close to him, people who had bankrolled al Qaeda for more than a decade. These Saudis traveled freely to the United States and had the habit of reporting their impressions to bin Laden. They confirmed his idea that America was weak and that it could not withstand more than three blows: the U.S. embassy bombing in Africa, the attack against the USS *Cole,* and 9/11, America is weak, Osama bin Laden "stated at several expanded meetings [of al Qaeda] and as evidence he referred to what happened to the United States when the bombing of the Marines' headquarters in Beirut led them to flee from Lebanon. He then cited another incident, that of the clashes in Somalia, that made the U.S. troops flee in a hasty and disgraceful retreat; and another incident in Yemen, less known than the previous two, when the UN secretary general (Boutros Ghali) telephoned Yemeni President Ali Abdallah Salih to tell him that the U.S. troops were on their way to Aden to make it a rear supply base for the military operation in Somalia, codenamed "Restoration of Hope." But an explosion occurred in the Aden hotel, where the Americans were due to stay. [After the attack] the United States canceled its program in Aden."[33]

These were some of the key considerations that prompted the relaunching of the counter-Crusade and the plotting of the 9/11 attacks. Secretly, the moderates disapproved of Osama's support for the Saudis' naive analysis. They feared America's military retaliation. The Taliban, most of whom despised bin Laden and the Arabs for their lavishness and their arrogance, shared these fears.

Since his return to Afghanistan, bin Laden had been very unpopular among the Taliban leadership, who saw him as a liability to the newly established regime, to the emirate. His obsession with using Western media to publicize his hatred for America had more than once irritated the Taliban, including Mullah Omar, who judged such behavior immature and dangerous. Among those who opposed bin Laden's media frenzy was Mullah Muhammad Hasan. "[Hasan] was the leader and the most prominent symbol of the opposition wing within the Taliban ranks. He was a strong member of the Taliban's *Shura* Council and was foreign minister for a period of time. He believed that bin Laden had become the decider of foreign policy in the Emirate [Taliban regime]. [Bin Laden's] media activities had also aroused U.S., Pakistani, and Arab reaction. Under U.S. influence, Europe and the United Nations moved against the Taliban. The opinion of this wing of hawks was that bin Laden should be punished 'or expelled,' because he repeatedly refused to obey the instructions of 'the Prince of the Faithful' [Mullah Omar] to refrain from giving media interviews."[34] More than once the Pakistanis had advised Mullah Omar to make Osama keep quiet or give him up to the Americans, but the Taliban spiritual leader had refused. "I will not hand over a Muslim to an infidel," he repeatedly stated.[35]

Bin Laden was equally unpopular among al Qaeda's hardliners. Back in 1998, under the guidance of Abu Hafas al Masri, also known as Muhammad Atef, one of the founders of al Qaeda who died during the U.S. bombing attacks on Kandahar, the hardliners had put pressure on bin Laden to acquire weapons of mass destruction so that they might be stored inside the United States and deployed should the Americans invade Afghanistan after 9/11. Although Osama bin Laden never formally rejected the idea, he prevented al Masri from pursuing it to the point that al Masri even tried to resign from his position as al Qaeda's defense minister to voice his frustration.

The truth is that Osama bin Laden was uninterested in weapons of mass destruction. He did not see any point in using them against an enemy which, he firmly believed, was on the verge of collapse. Saudi arrogance may have been at the root of this analysis. Both bin Laden and his rich Saudi sponsors failed to understand the complexity of the West and of America in particular, nor did they foresee the strength of Western democracies. They simply superimposed their own stereotype of America onto U.S. society, seeing only a corrupt, deeply immoral country that has no backbone and is motivated by greed. Ironically, both Osama and his sponsors—wealthy elites who had interacted only with their own American peers—were victims of their own privileged background. Saudi arrogance may also explain why, in the aftermath of 9/11, al Qaeda did not plan any additional attacks inside the United States.

The Saudi sense of superiority also eroded bin Laden's status. A growing number of Islamist warriors were dissatisfied with Osama bin Laden's leadership; they did not dare express their opinion in public, but secretly, they judged his behavior as similar to that of Arab leaders, who made promises only to ignore them. Equally, increasing numbers of alienated young people began to see bin Laden as an extension of the Saudi elite. In 1999, many of these people saw Khattab, who had carefully kept the famous Saudi at arm's length, as a symbol of the spirit of the mujahedin and of independence from bin Laden; among them was al Gharib. Disillusionment drove young people towards new leaders.[36] The Stranger would soon become one of them.

CHAPTER FIVE

Return to Afghanistan

Oh, God, damn these tyrants, Arabs and non-Arabs,
condemn all religious renegade leaders, one by one, cut
them to pieces and do not spare anyone, Amen.
—al Zarqawi

In May 1999, the young, newly crowned king of Jordan, Abdallah II, granted a general amnesty to celebrate his ascension to the throne. Al Gharib and al Maqdisi, along with thousands of other political prisoners, were released from prison. "Although he [al Gharib] returned to his comrades and to the mosque of Zarqa, preaching and educating, instigating and mobilizing people, he was planning to leave Jordan," reveals Abu Hilalah, an al Jazeera journalist. "He realized that Jordan was inappropriate as a base for a jihadist organization."[1]

Members of the Stranger's family admit that he did attempt to fit into the everyday life of his hometown. He even considered buying a pick-up truck to start a business selling fruit at local markets.[2] He soon, however, found himself out of place. Saleh al Hami, his brother-in-law, confirms that al Gharib "was not very happy when he left jail. Somehow the conditions in prison were better than those of the easy, nothing-to-do, routine life. I felt that he was bored. I felt that he was bitter. I felt the spirit of jihad inside him. He was dying to get out of this country."[3] One day, the Stranger confided to his sister his dream of leaving Jordan, of going back to Pakistan and from there to Chechnya.

At the end of 1999, a few months after his release from al Suwaqah prison, al Gharib left Jordan for Pakistan. Al Maqdisi stayed behind and would soon after be imprisoned again. Their adventure together came to an end.

Al Gharib departed with his beloved mother, Um Sayel, who was suffering from leukemia. People close to the family claim that he hoped that the climate in Pakistan would improve her condition. However, his primary aim was to reconnect with his past experience in Peshawar and to find a way to get to Chechnya. He wanted to join the legendary Khattab, to participate in the second Chechnyan war against the Russians.[4] The Jordanian authorities, eager to get rid of troublemakers like him, once again facilitated his departure.[5]

Mother and son remained in Peshawar for six months until al Gharib was arrested because his visa had expired. "In those days many were imprisoned in Pakistan for the same reason. When I arrived he was already in jail," explains Saleh al Hami. "He remained for eight days. When he was released the Pakistani authorities kept his passport because they wanted him to leave." The authorities would not return al Gharib's passport unless he agreed to go back to Jordan, but he had no intention of doing so. Without a passport, he could only cross over the border into Afghanistan. "He told me he didn't want to enter Afghanistan," reveals al Hami. "The situation there was too dangerous, the Taliban were fighting Masoud Rajawi's forces." He was reluctant to participate in the fight between the Taliban and the Northern Alliance.[6] However, having no choice and "want[ing] a secure venue, in the end, he resolved to cross over to Afghanistan."[7]

Once again al Gharib missed the opportunity to become a warrior and prove his courage in battle. Once again he was forced to abandon his dream to fight and had to adapt to hostile circumstances. Once again, in Afghanistan, he was confronted with swarms of disorientated mujahedin—Muslim warriors who had returned to Afghanistan after the victory of the Taliban—and were desperately trying to recreate the unique atmosphere of the anti-Soviet jihad.

As al Gharib had envisaged, fighting fellow Muslims was not like battling with the Soviets. The Taliban struggle against the Northern Alliance lacked the "soul" of the anti-Soviet jihad, which was why the mujahedin were lost. "Some of them wanted to fight a new jihad. Others had no specific plans but they were used to living in the camps and Afghanistan offered such an opportunity. There were many Arabs without a specific task. They moved in groups of different sizes, some were twenty, others were only seven people. . . . Abu Mos'ab [al Zarqawi] gathered around him about 80–100 people, they were all from Palestine and Jordan. They did not have their own shelter, but they had a place in Lougar, far from the front. . . . They settled there and Abu Mos'ab was the leader of this group, who did not have a name or an agenda. What kept them together was the fact that they shared the ideal of the jihad."[8]

What was the jihad envisioned by al Gharib and his group? The revolutionary jihad of Khattab or the anti-American counter-Crusade of Osama bin Laden? The answer to this question comes from a key meeting between Osama bin Laden and al Gharib.

The encounter took place at the beginning of 2000 in Kandahar. Who organized it, nobody knows. Was it the Jordanian Jaafar al Hijar, from Salt? Upon his arrival in Afghanistan, al Gharib had encountered this legendary mujahedin captain who had participated in the battle of Khost. Or was the meeting arranged by al Qaeda, simply because al Gharib was the leader of a group of Arabs in Lougar? Whatever the circumstances, the meeting was not between equals: al Gharib was seeking protection and funding for himself and his group; Osama bin Laden was the emir of al Qaeda. However, when the latter offered him a chance to join his group, al Gharib refused for ideological reasons. He could not embrace the jihad against the United States.

Crucially and symbolically, the meeting took place between two men who come from opposite corners of the Arab world; one rich and powerful, the other a social misfit. Yet both men shared a common aim: the deliverance of Muslims. Both were passionately committed to such a goal, and yet, because of their different upbringing, they could not agree on the strategy for achieving it. Osama bin Laden, coming from a very wealthy family, having been in contact all of his life with the political elite, the international elite, had essentially a global vision of the conflict. Al Gharib, on the other hand, a working-class lad forged inside Arab prisons, was essentially an "outlaw." He had discovered the jihad through the melding of petty crime with Islamic insurgency; modern Salafi religious indoctrination was the vehicle of this transformation. Culturally, he could not cross the borders of the Arab state and grasp the international dimension of the jihad. In Kandahar, he was still much closer to old-style terrorism, the localized armed groups of the Irish Republican Amy (IRA) or the Basque separatist group Euskadi Ta Askatasuna (ETA), than to transnational al Qaeda.

Is it feasible that in 2000 a "small fish" like al Gharib, without financial backing or even a track record as a mujahed, refused Osama bin Laden's offer? According to those who have met al Gharib, this kind of behavior was perfectly in line with his personality. "He never followed the orders of others," admits a member of his group, "I never heard him praise anyone apart from the Prophet, this was Abu Mos'ab's character, he never followed anyone, he only ever went out to get what he felt was just to do."[9] In his relationship with al Maqdisi it is clear that he never saw his companion as a leader but only as a tutor, a mentor.

THE HERAT CAMP

The alliance that Osama bin Laden and al Gharib are said to have made in 1999 is one of the many legends which have been constructed around the life of al Zarqawi. No evidence of such an alliance has ever been provided. On the contrary, as early as 2000, one can see the emergence of major strategic differences between the two men.

Al Gharib was not alone in disagreeing with Osama bin Laden, as discussed in the previous chapter. People inside al Qaeda, as well as members of the Taliban regime, shared his views. Is this what prompted them to help him carve a small space for himself in Afghanistan? One event seems to confirm this interpretation. Soon after the meeting in Kandahar, Muhammad Makawi, also known as Seyf al Adl,[10] the man in charge of al Qaeda's military operations, encouraged al Zarqawi to set up a camp to train his group.[11]

Following his advice, al Gharib moved to northwestern Afghanistan, to the city of Herat, which lies close to the Iranian border. In the surrounding hills, he set up a training camp. At this point he changed his name again, becoming Abu Mos'ab al Zarqawi. Once again, he sensed a transition and assumed a new identity to fit his future life. The choice of the name is symbolic: one of his children is called Mos'ab; Mos'ab was also the name of a famous warrior of the Prophet; and al Zarqawi means "from the city of Zarqa." The name marked a new chapter in his life, the beginning of a new phase which would lead him, a few years later, to become al Qaeda's representative in Iraq.

It is unclear who sponsored the Herat camp. Some believe it was backed by the ISI, the Pakistani secret service. "Al Zarqawi's dependence for many years was entirely on Pakistan and its supportive jihadist parties, which in turn were getting their funds from the ISI. Al Zarqawi's most useful contacts were with the Pakistani militant wing of Jamiat Ulama al Islam (JUI), Maulana Samiul Haq's group, which had been training various groups of Islamic militants through its network of over 500 madrasas (religious schools) as a sort of cover job for ISI." The rationale behind this theory is that Pakistan, facing pressure from the Clinton administration to convince the Taliban government to expel Osama bin Laden, wanted to weaken the power of the famous Saudi. Backing al Zarqawi was part of this strategy.[12]

This theory has many faults. In 2000, al Zarqawi was too inconsequential to appeal to the ISI. At the time, there were several people like him, emirs of small groups of Arabs who gravitated around the Taliban and al Qaeda. Some of them had fought heroically in the anti-Soviet jihad and were well known to ISI. Osama bin Laden had many enemies inside Afghanistan, some more powerful than al Zarqawi. If the ISI wanted to undermine his authority, it could have chosen far more suitable candidates.

The presumed ISI link also clashes with al Zarqawi's past experiences in Afghanistan. He played an insignificant role in the anti-Soviet jihad. Many sources confirm that in the early 1990s he was just one of thousands of young Arabs who moved to Pakistan with the idea of becoming great warriors and melted into the masses of confused and lost mujahedin. "Due to his late arrival in Afghanistan, it is highly unlikely that [he] established any contact with the ISI," admits Abdallah Anas. "At that time he was an unknown young man." Even less plausible is the theory that al Maqdisi, his mentor, had such contacts, and that through him al Zarqawi had access to ISI leadership. It is equally unlikely that, on his return to Peshawar at the end of 1999, al Gharib met high-ranking officials of the Pakistani secret service; if he did, why was he arrested for having an expired passport? Why did he not use those contacts to get the passport back when he was released from prison?

It is more likely that in 2000 al Zarqawi succeeded in convincing the faction of the Taliban regime that most opposed bin Laden to allow him to establish a camp in Herat, possibly with the mediation of Muhammad Makawi and the help of the Palestinian and Jordanian factions inside al Qaeda.

The camp was near the Iranian border, in the mountainous frontier. This region was also Afghanistan's gateway to the north of Iraq and to Turkey. It was across those mountains that, in the 1980s, Iraqi Kurds had flocked to Afghanistan to participate in the anti-Soviet jihad. Herat also bordered the region that, in 2000, was still under the control of the Northern Alliance. Therefore, the Taliban must have thought that the presence of the training camp could act as a buffer against its enemies.[13] Indeed, after 9/11, the Northern Alliance attacked the camp, put it under siege, and eventually destroyed it.

Saleh al Hami, al Zarqawi's brother-in-law, confirms that the camp was funded by the Taliban. "I don't think Afghanistan in those days was only about bin Laden and al Zawahiri. What I know is that the Taliban were in charge, and all the Arabs who were in Afghanistan were sheltered by the Taliban. It was a safe haven for all those Muslims who felt persecuted."[14] The cost of setting up the camp was very small. According to key witnesses it was tiny and run on a shoestring. "Our lives were simple, no comfort, no luxury. Abu Mos'ab wanted us to live a very simple life," states Iyad Tobaissi, who trained in the camp.[15]

From a few dozen fighters at first, the camp quickly grew. New recruits arrived and the group came to be known as Jund al Sham, the Levant Warriors. Abd al Hadi Daglas and Khaled Arouri, former cell mates and long-term friends of al Zarqawi, were his right-hand men. While al Qaeda members came predominantly from Saudi Arabia and Egypt, the Levant Warriors originated from Palestine, Jordan, Syria, Lebanon, and Iraq. The camp was advertised by word of mouth, and the new recruits reached Herat through personal connections. Iyad Tobaissi, for example, heard of al Zarqawi back in Jordan; he had met people who had known him, who could describe his character and commitment. On the strength of these recommendations, Tobaissi decided to join him.

Some of the recruits were just children, like Anas Sheikh Amin, today a timid eighteen-year-old Syrian boy. In the documentary by Patrice Barrat, Najat Rizk, and Ranwa Stephan, *Zarkaoui: la Question Terroriste,*[16] he appears for what he is, an adolescent victim of a society which had denied him even the right to childhood. In the footage, he describes how he traveled to Afghanistan with his father, Abu Anas al Shami, author of "The Diary of Falluja" (see the appendix) and considered one of the main spiritual guides behind al Zarqawi. At the time Anas Sheikh Amin was no more than twelve years old. In the documentary he comes across as someone without a proper education, who expresses himself in simple language, using the local dialect. In Afghanistan, the adolescent Anas Sheikh Amin received military training, most likely in more than one camp, before starting his journey back to the Middle East. "I . . . went to Saudi Arabia," he said, "and from there to Turkey where I got my residency. I was assigned . . . to go to Amman in order to perform a military operation."[17] The young Syrian was supposed to die in the foiled bombing of the U.S. embassy in Amman in April 2004; at the time he was seventeen years old.

What was the purpose of the Herat camp? The answer to this question is key to understanding the role that al Zarqawi wanted to play in the Islamist jihadist movement. According to several sources, he concentrated his efforts on training fighters who would go back to Jordan, and possibly to neighboring Arab countries, to overturn existing regimes. The tale of Anas Sheikh Amin seems to confirm that the purpose of the Herat camp was to prepare recruits for suicide missions.

ANSAR AL ISLAM

In January 2002, an unusual funeral took place in Iraqi Kurdistan. A large contingent of Jordanian jihadists gathered together to pay their last respects to Raid Khuraysat, also known as Abu Abd al Rahman al Shami, and a group of his followers. They had died at the end of December 2001 in battles against the Kurdish Patriotic Union, led by Jalal Talabani, America's strong ally, and the president of Iraq from April 2005. Prior to 9/11, Kurdish forces had already clashed with the Jordanian jihadists, their presence being well known to the Kurdish secret services.

Al Rahman al Shami was from Salt, a Jordanian town similar to Zarqa. Flooded with Palestinian refugees, it had in the last two decades of the twentieth century turned into a stronghold of the Salafi jihadist movement. The tale of al Rahman al Shami differs little from the life story of many Jordanian jihadists who settled in Afghanistan and northern Iraq. He left secondary school before completing his studies and for a while he worked as a taxi driver. After a car accident in which two cousins died, he began to visit the local mosque and became more and more religious. Family and friends describe him as a quiet young man. One day he told his father he was going for a pilgrimage to Mecca. "I said all right. But deep inside me, I felt something different," said his father. "I heard then that many youths from Salt went abroad for jihad. I heard about that. I knew then that his intention was not to go for minor pilgrimage."[18]

Al Rahman al Shami was part of a group of about fifty people from Salt who reached Afghanistan after the Taliban victory. They stayed for only a short time before moving to northern Iraq, into the Kurdish area, where they sought to create a Taliban-style regime. Among these Jordanians were friends and acquaintances of al Zarqawi. Al Rahman al Shami was one of them.

Footage of his funeral shows, among the mourners, Nidal Arabiyyat. Also from Salt, he was a close aide to al Zarqawi, and a specialist at making booby-trapped cars. Arabiyyat had left Jordan in 1999, shortly after becoming religious and embracing Salafi jihadist thought; he had traveled to Afghanistan where he joined the Herat camp. On 17 February 2004, Arabiyyat died in al Khalidiyya, a section of Baghdad, in a clash with Coalition forces. In his "Falluja Diary," Abu Anas al Shami reports Arabiyyat's death and lists him among the martyrs of the jihad in Iraq. The presence of Arabiyyat at the funeral proves that, prior to 9/11, there were ties between al Rahman al Shami's group and al Zarqawi, who at the time was running the Herat camp. According to al Maqdisi's letter written in September 2004, al Zarqawi knew Rahman al Shami in Jordan.[19] Possibly, their relationship was cemented by the fact that Herat was the gateway from Afghanistan to Iraqi Kurdistan and that after 1995 "Kurdistan became a favored passage [to Afghanistan] and a less dangerous route than Pakistan, which [at that time] tightened its controls on passage to and from its territory."[20]

On arriving in northern Iraq, the Jordanian jihadists found fertile terrain. As in most of the Arab world, the proliferation of Islamist groups in Iraqi Kurdistan followed the Muslim Brotherhood's active proselytism. As early as 1952, the Brotherhood became politically active in northern Iraq. In 1971 the Iraqi Ba'ath party evicted it from the political arena by declaring the group illegal. Around the same time, modern Salafism began to penetrate the area thanks to the financial backing of Saudi charitable organizations.

The progressive marginalization of the region, the victory of the Iranian revolution, and the Soviet invasion of Afghanistan contributed to the growth of the Salafi jihadist movement in the region. In early 1980, the first armed groups began to appear. However, in the next two decades internal fights paralyzed the activity of these organizations. Moderate and reformist ideas constantly clashed with various jihadist tendencies. Thus, the impact of the radical groups upon local society was very limited. Hunted by Saddam and ideologically divided, they remained boxed inside the underworld of Iraqi Kurdistan "outlaws."

In 2000, this scenario began to change. Salafi jihadist groups grew in number and power. When al Rahman al Shami and his companions arrived in Iraqi Kurdistan, the jihadist movement was booming. On 1 September 2001, they became part of a new group, Jund al Islam, the Army of Islam. Headed by Abu Unaydallah al Shafii, the organization primarily consisted of former mujahedin who had reached northern Kurdistan from Afghanistan. By force, the group gained control of a frontier area of about 500 square kilometers (extending from Halabia to the border with Iran) with a population of about 200,000 people. Mimicking the Taliban regime, they imposed Sharia law on the ten villages under their control. They prohibited the sale of alcohol; music was banned, as were satellite dishes; shops had to be closed during prayers; and schools were forced to teach the Koran to students.

In December 2001, Jund al Islam merged with several other small jihadist groups to become Ansar al Islam. Its spiritual guide was Abd al Moneem Mustafa Halima, better known as Abu Baseer, another of al Zarqawi's countrymen. He had the task of producing fatwas to legitimize the activities of the new armed organizations.[21] Najm al-Din Faraj, better known as Mullah Fateh Krekar, was the emir. Ansar al Islam, whose logistical bases were in al Bajra, coexisted with several other jihadist armed groups.[22]

Thus in 2000, a conglomerate of shell-states[23] blossomed in Iraqi Kurdistan. These were small areas, near the border with Iran that had fallen into the grip of jihadist organizations.[24] These groups had taken over the socioeconomic structure of the society, forcing the local population to obey their rule in order to survive. Based upon the enforcement of Sharia law, relations between the Islamist armed organization and the local populations were tense. "They had with them Arabs from Baghdad, Saudi Arabia, Jordan and Syria. We did not mix or speak with them, but if they bothered us, we used to have discussions with them," explains a resident of Iraqi Kurdistan. It was, however, a period of relative stability. "During their time, there was security and stability. No one violated anyone else's rights. If one of them had a case at the courts and was in the right and had witnesses, they delivered a fair ruling." The resentment of the population was based upon the imposition of customs, predominantly Arab customs, which were mostly foreign to the locals. "There was no theft, but what was wrong about them was that they forced women to wear the head cover and the *aba* [long gown] when going to the fields to work. Such acts aggravated us because the Kurdish dress is a *hijab* in itself, so there was no need to force women to wear the aba on top of it."[25]

According to the Egyptian scholar Hani al Sibaii, Ansar al Islam was essentially a Salafi jihadist group that followed the teachings of Ayman al Zawahiri.[26] Ansar al Islam had a revolutionary vision of the jihad and was focused on fighting the near enemy: Saddam Hussein's regime and the Kurdish nationalist forces of Jalal Talabani. Because it lacked great military strength, it used guerrilla tactics.

After 9/11, the Kurdish secular parties began to link Ansar al Islam to al Qaeda and to Osama bin Laden; they claimed that al Qaeda had training camps in Iraqi Kurdistan and that it was running chemical laboratories to produce biological weapons.[27] Mullah Krekar strongly denied that such links with al Qaeda ever existed.[28] After the war in Iraq ended and Ansar al Islam was disbanded, no traces of al Qaeda training camps or chemical laboratories were found in the region.

Contrary to what the U.S. administration claimed, the relationship between Ansar al Islam, al Qaeda, and al Zarqawi was not structured; it was based exclusively on personal relationships, often cemented in the countries of origin. Al Zarqawi, for example, being from Jordan, had contacts with Jordanians from Salt such as al Rahman al Shami and Nidal Arabiyyat.

It was thanks to old ties, not to new ones created while running the camp in Herat, that, after the invasion of Afghanistan, al Zarqawi was able to cross over to Iran and from there, reach Iraqi Kurdistan.

FLEEING AFGHANISTAN

As anticipated by many in Afghanistan, the American response to the attacks of 9/11 was swift. Hitting back at al Qaeda was the paramount objective. On 7 October 2001, Coalition forces began bombing Afghanistan in an attempt to destroy the Taliban regime, which had refused to hand over Osama bin Laden and al Qaeda's leadership. The "war on terror" had begun.

The bombing campaign destroyed all mujahedin training camps and dispersed the jihadists, some of whom regrouped in Kandahar. In Herat the Northern Alliance surrounded al Zarqawi's training camp. He and his followers risked imminent capture. The tale of their escape is another of al Zarqawi's legendary adventures. Iyad Tobaissi, an eyewitness to the siege, recounts the event: "The dissidents (Northern Alliance) had by now encircled us. Al Zarqawi started to pray, seeking help from God, he was praying and crying; after his prayers he came out with a new strategy. He gathered some of the men and promised to fight his way through the siege in order to liberate us. That's what he did."[29]

According to Tobaissi, al Zarqawi and his followers (women and children included) arranged themselves in a convoy of up to four hundred cars. They headed from Herat southward to Kandahar. To their general surprise, the caravan was never stopped or shelled. "God was watching over this convoy as planes were circling over us," explains Tobaissi. "For some reason there were a lot of shooting stars in the sky, many of them, as if God was sending his angels to protect us."[30] One of the drivers was Yassin Jarrad, the father of al Zarqawi's second wife, who in August 2003 would drive a car bomb against the Imam Ali Mosque in Najaf.

It took the convoy four days to reach Kandahar, mostly because they were traveling with women and children. Upon their arrival, they were shocked to find the city a ghost town, the residents having fled the relentless bombing and shelling. Only a few buildings had survived; entire sections of the town were in ruins. At this point al Zarqawi decided to send the women and children to safety in Pakistan, and from there to Turkey. Tobaissi was given the task of escorting them to the Pakistani border. The rest of the group remained behind. The decision to evacuate them proved wise; soon after their departure the city was again attacked by the Northern Alliance.

When Tobaissi and the other escorts returned, Kandahar was still under siege. They managed to sneak inside and reach the safe house in which al Zarqawi's forces were barricaded. "Abu Mos'ab was there to greet us; he thought I was hurt in a car crash. I was taken into a side room, he followed me . . . he smiled and said, 'So you're back.' I replied, 'With God's will, yes.' To my surprise, the others told me that Abu Mos'ab was injured. Apparently he was in a house when a rocket hit it, his ribs were broken."[31]

Fouad Hussein's investigation for LBC television[32] reveals that from Kandahar, al Zarqawi and his warriors went to Tora Bora, where they took part in the famous battle against Coalition forces. Again, the legend says that al Zarqawi escaped safely with his group. "His withdrawal from Tora Bora with his followers, without suffering any serious casualties, shows his tactical qualities. Some believe he is a bad political leader—well, they are wrong. He's not a ghost, he's very much alive, he's God-sent, he knows how to deal with our problems, let the West label him as it pleases."[33]

Was al Zarqawi really at Tora Bora? It is difficult to establish this for certain, as many of his followers construct myths and legends around his person. However, if he participated in the battle, he fought out of loyalty to the Taliban regime, not to protect Osama bin Laden. After the defeat, in fact, those loyal to al Qaeda fled with bin Laden and al Zawahiri, while al Zarqawi headed for Pakistan and from there, on foot, to Zahdan in Iran.[34] "We were received by a grouping of Iranian Sunnis," recounts Tobaissi. "They gave us shelter and food, they looked after us very well. We then were taken from the border into the city of Zahdan in groups, into several rest houses. We stayed in Zahdan for about a week, then we were escorted to Teheran."[35]

According to Fouad Hussein's investigations, while in Iran, al Zarqawi and his followers were looked after by the Afghan warlord Hikmatyar, a former opponent of the Taliban and of the Northern Alliance. Those who were not in possession of legal travel documents went to northern Iraq; the others headed for Turkey. But the new base being established in Iraq was a deeply held secret; not even al Zarqawi's closest allies knew about it. "When we met with Abu Mos'ab," revealed Tobaissi, "I told him that I didn't know where to go next. He answered, 'We are going to Iraq, of course.'"[36]

One member of the group admitted that "Abu Mos'ab saw in Iraq a new arena for his jihad, a wide space; he was expecting to confront the Americans there once the war in Afghanistan was over, and God Almighty gave him the strength to become the new jihadist leader in Iraq. . . . It's naive to think that while the U.S. was preparing for its war against Iraq, someone like Abu Mos'ab was not getting ready to fight them there. He had been planning for this for a long time. Iraq was to be the new ground for jihad."[37] For al Zarqawi, Iraq would be a final test of courage, the opportunity he had dreamed of for a lifetime.

Fouad Hussein's investigations also reveal that al Zarqawi's movements in Iran were controlled; his presence was tolerated, but not favored. In early 2002, bending to U.S. pressure, the Iranian authorities shut down his bases and imprisoned more than twenty of his followers. Al Zarqawi responded by hastening his plans to move to Iraq; his troops went to northern Iraq ahead of time. Thanks to his connections with the Jordanian jihadists in Iraqi Kurdistan, al Zarqawi's men settled in the area and established two military camps. Al Zarqawi put his childhood friend Abd al Hadi Daglas in charge and secretly went to Baghdad to prepare for battle.

Clearly, returning to Jordan was not an option. "After Afghanistan many mujahedin couldn't come back to their homelands," explains Hussein. "They were forced to look for a new terrain for jihad. But just as the United States was looking for a new enemy after the collapse of the Soviet Union, the Islamists were also looking for a new enemy after they had defeated the Soviet forces in Afghanistan. The West, represented by the United States, was the new enemy."[38]

In Kurdistan, al Zarqawi's presence did not go unnoticed, nor did the fact that he came from Afghanistan. Soon after 9/11, the Kurdish secret services contacted the United States, claiming al Zarqawi was al Qaeda's man in northern Iraq. It was at that point that Abu Mos'ab al Zarqawi caught the attention of the American neoconservatives.

CHAPTER SIX

The Myth of Abu Mos'ab al Zarqawi

My dream is that the nearest to my heart of all my children will be martyred.
—al Zarqawi's mother, declaring her last wish

The first time the American authorities heard about al Zarqawi was a few days after 11 September 2001, from the Kurdish secret service. "I believe that Ansar al Islam is an inseparable part of al Qaeda," stated Dana Ahmad Majid, a Kurdish intelligence official, in a report about al Zarqawi broadcast on al Jazeera on 1 July 2004.

Before 9/11, al Qaeda planned to found another base to fall back on after the 9/11 operations. They knew very well that they would be attacked in Afghanistan after 9/11 and that they would have to turn to other areas. They got in touch with the leadership of Ansar al Islam, who were previously in Afghanistan, and studied the issue. They chose Bajara to be their second base should they have to leave Afghanistan. Their choice was based on several factors. The first was the presence of a base for their network in that area. The second issue was that the area has rough terrain and is similar to the areas in Afghanistan where they trained. The third issue was their relations with the Iraqi regime. The fourth issue was that they sensed that the government of the Kurdistan region is weak and incapable of resisting and they would be able to spread and take control. The other issue is that it was close to Afghanistan, and so they would be able to cross into Iran by various means to reach that area.[1]

Following this interpretation, al Zarqawi, in charge of the camp in Herat and with personal links to the Jordanians who had settled in Iraqi Kurdistan, was singled out as the intermediary between al Qaeda and Ansar al Islam.

Americans had nothing on al Zarqawi—they did not even know who he was. Nor did they have any idea about al Qaeda's infighting and the existence in Afghanistan of camps independent of al Qaeda. They believed the Kurds and began their own investigation.

It is likely that soon after the Kurdish secret service contacted the American authorities, Washington got in touch with Jordan to find out more about al Zarqawi. It is at this point that his name began to be linked to the Millennium Plot (not to be confused with the U.S.-foiled Millennium Plot to blow up Los Angeles International Airport).[2] The plot included the simultaneous bombing, during the millennium celebration, of the Hotel Radisson SAS in Amman; one of the border crossings between Jordan and Israel; Mount Nebo in Jordan; and the site on the river Jordan where John the Baptist is believed to have baptized Jesus.

Fortuitous circumstances prevented the attack. At the end of 1999, while al Zarqawi was preparing to move to Pakistan, Jordanian intelligence intercepted a call between Khadr Abu Hoshar, a Palestinian militant in Jordan, and Abu Zubaydah, who in the late 1980s had gone to Afghanistan to participate in the anti-Soviet jihad. During the conversation, Abu Zubaydah, who at the time was in Afghanistan, stated that the time for training was over. On alert for a year following a tip that an attack in the region was in the pipeline, the Jordanian authorities acted immediately. Because the attacks aimed to kill American and Israeli tourists, Jordanian and American authorities agreed to jointly conduct the investigation. U.S. and Jordanian authorities portrayed Abu Zubaydah as the man in charge of al Qaeda recruiting and training camps, though he was not even a member of al Qaeda.[3] On the basis of this false intelligence, the Millennium Plot became known as an al Qaeda operation.

In September 2000, eight of the twenty-eight men charged in the plot were sentenced to death, four in absentia. During the trial, nobody mentioned the involvement of Ahmed Fadel al Khalaylah, alias Abu Mos'ab al Zarqawi. The first time his name appeared in connection with the plot was on 21 November 2001, that is, after 9/11 and after the Kurdish secret service had alerted Washington to al Zarqawi's presence in northern Iraq.[4] It is unclear what role, if any, al Zarqawi played in the plot or how he got involved in it. It is possible that the U.S. and Jordanian authorities used Abu Zubaydah, whom al Zarqawi had met in the 1990s in Peshawar, to link him to the Millennium Plot. According to Abdallah Anas, they had both worked for the Arab-Afghan Bureau when they were younger.

After a second trial on 11 February 2002, al Zarqawi was sentenced in absentia, along with several other people, for his part in the plot. He received a sentence of fifteen years in prison. The Arab press covering the trial did not even include mention of his name, as he was unknown. This was the first time al Zarqawi was implicated in a terrorist act. Back in 1995, together with al Maqdisi, he had been found guilty of creating an illegal cell, not of committing a specific terrorist act.

In early 2002, the Jordanian authorities were also still investigating the killing of an Israeli citizen, Yitzhak Snir, a fifty-one-year-old diamond dealer living in Amman, that had taken place on 6 August 2001.[5] In a written message to the press, an unknown armed organization, the Honourables of Jordan (Shurafa al Urdun), had claimed responsibility for the murder and accused the victim of being an agent of Mossad. Then, on 28 October 2002, another brutal assassination took place as an American diplomat, Lawrence Foley, was gunned down in front of his house in Amman. Again the same organization claimed responsibility for the murder. But this time the authorities in Jordan were quick to link al Zarqawi to both crimes.

Soon after Foley's assassination, a Federal Bureau of Investigation (FBI) team flew to Amman. Although Muhammad Adwane, the Jordanian minister of information, had publicly declared the killing an attack against the national security of Jordan, the FBI took over the investigation, in a move that generated widespread criticism among Jordanian citizens. "What was so embarrassing was the involvement of the American security service. The FBI was operating directly on this case in Jordan," said Hussein Majaalli, a Jordanian lawyer and former president of the Jordanian lawyers' union. "All the findings were logged and studied and presented to the judiciary after they had been approved by the FBI, . . . which proved that they were de facto in charge, not the Jordanian authorities."[6]

The Americans focused their investigation on al Zarqawi. Linking him to the two assassinations and the Millennium Plot seemed to reinforce the Kurdish secret service's claim that he was part of al Qaeda. Several sources claim that FBI agents conducted the interrogations in which alleged members of the Honourables of Jordan admitted to being part of Abu Mos'ab al Zarqawi's web of terror, suggesting that American coercion may have been a factor in the confession.[7] "Three men were arrested, a Libyan, a Palestinian, and a Jordanian. They were accused of collaborating with al Zarqawi, they were said to have been armed and financed by him; they [the Americans] accused the Libyan citizen of having provided a space where al Zarqawi would meet his wife. However, all the clues were supplied by the FBI, in spite of the crime occurring on Jordanian territory, where normally only the Jordanian authorities are allowed to investigate."[8] However, it is more plausible that the Jordanians worked together with the Americans and that the Jordanians conducted some of the interrogations.

Al Zarqawi was charged with the murder of Lawrence Foley and the assassination of Yitzhak Snir, in addition to planning military actions against government targets in Jordan. This was the first time he was accused of masterminding a terrorist act. According to Hussein Majaalli, "There is no proof that links al Zarqawi to the organization [Honourables of Jordan] and there is no proof which links this organization to any local or international terrorist network."[9]

Was al Zarqawi framed to fit his new status as international terror leader? Many people believe that this is what occurred. Or were the Americans fed the wrong information by the Kurdish secret service and the Jordanian authorities? Both had much to gain from the myth of al Zarqawi. The Kurds wanted to convince the United States to help them get rid of jihadist groups, and the Jordanians were desperate to find the ringleader of a series of terror attacks. There is another interpretation of why al Zarqawi was, from the outset, the prime and sole suspect. Privately, some terrorist analysts believe that the U.S. authorities had some undisclosed information about him that caused them to single him out. This information may have come from Abu Zubaydah, who was arrested in March 2002 and handed over to the Americans. Abu Zubaydah may have mentioned his name as someone with strong leadership skills, someone likely to rise through the ranks of the jihadists. Unfortunately, this hypothesis cannot be confirmed as no one knows where Abu Zubaydah is being held captive.

MADE IN AMERICA

From 9/11 in 2001 to 20 March 2003, the United States built its case for attacking Iraq. Saddam's regime was accused of two things: possessing weapons of mass destruction and supporting terrorism. Although UN weapons inspectors spent a long time in Iraq searching for evidence of hidden arsenals, they had been unable to come up with any proof of their existence. Saddam's support for terrorism was, therefore, the only trump card the U.S. administration held with which to convince the world that the Iraqi dictator had to be removed. To play it, the administration had to demonstrate that Saddam and al Qaeda were connected. The link was Abu Mos'ab al Zarqawi. "When Colin Powell spoke about a link between al Zarqawi and terrorism we started to wonder why the Foley murder [had been] pinned on Abu Mos'ab. There was a need to create a connection between the Saddam regime and terrorism," said Fouad Hussein.[10]

On 5 February 2003, Colin Powell went to the United Nations and presented plenty of evidence to justify the forthcoming war in Iraq. Today, the world knows that much of this evidence was faulty, including al Zarqawi's alleged role as intermediary between Saddam and al Qaeda. Possessing no evidence of weapons of mass destruction, the U.S. administration focused on Abu Mos'ab al Zarqawi's alleged role in the build-up of Iraqi chemical weapons. "When our coalition ousted the Taliban, the al Zarqawi network helped establish another poison and explosive training center camp, and this camp is located in northeastern Iraq," stated Powell. He even showed pictures of the camp. "The network is teaching its operatives how to produce ricin and other poisons. Let me remind you how ricin works." Powell carefully displayed a small container of white powder to the Security Council and to an already terrified world:

> Less than a pinch—imagine a pinch of salt—less than a pinch of ricin, eating just this amount in your food would cause shock, followed by circulatory failure. Death comes within 72 hours and there is no antidote. There is no cure. It is fatal. . . .
>
> Those helping to run this camp are al Zarqawi's lieutenants operating in northern Kurdish areas outside Saddam Hussein's controlled Iraq, but Baghdad has an agent in the most senior levels of the radical organization Ansar al Islam, that controls this corner of Iraq. In 2000, this agent offered al Qaeda safe haven in the region. After we swept al Qaeda from Afghanistan, some of its members accepted this safe haven. They remain there today.[11]

On 23 March 2003, just over a month after Colin Powell's speech, U.S. forces fired thirty Cruise missiles into the area controlled by Ansar al Islam, killing fifty-seven members of the organization.[12] The United States justified the strike by saying that al Zarqawi was running the camps.

"The ricin that is bouncing around Europe now originated in Iraq," stated Powell, referring to the arrest of dozens of North Africans (mainly Algerians) in January 2003 in Britain, France, and Spain on charges of preparing ricin and other chemical weapons. Both the U.S. and U.K. governments used these arrests as proof that the threat posed by al Zarqawi's ricin network was real. However, in Spain, all the suspects were eventually released when the poisons turned out to be bleach and detergent; in France charges were dropped when ricin samples were revealed to be barley and wheat germ.[13]

Only in Britain was the alleged ricin-manufacturing cell put on trial. However, in April 2005, a London jury cleared all the defendants of being part of the ricin ring when it emerged that the laboratory report on the found substance had been altered. Instead of saying that no ricin had been found, the report stated that it had. Subsequently, the U.K. government issued an apology, citing a clerical error as the cause of the faulty report.

The investigative journalist Duncan Campbell tracked down for the British court the Web site that was believed to be the original source of the ricin formula. In an editorial in the *Guardian* on 14 April 2005 he wrote: "Yesterday's verdicts on five defendants and the dropping of charges against four others make clear there was no ricin ring. Nor did the 'ricin ring' make or have ricin. Not that the government shared that news with us. Until today, the public record for the past three fear-inducing years has been that ricin was found in the Wood Green flat occupied by some of yesterday's acquitted defendants. It was not."[14]

Several people now believe that the link between the "ricin ring" and al Zarqawi was a fabrication of the Americans. "The name of al

Zarqawi neither appeared in the confession of Meguerba [the Algerian who first mentioned the existence of a ricin cell in the United Kingdom] nor in any documentation produced by the U.K. investigators. The Americans used such investigations to prove that there was a link between Saddam Hussein and al Qaeda and for this purpose they came up with al Zarqawi," says Campbell.[15] Did the British encourage the Americans to use the ricin ring as proof of al Zarqawi's connections with al Qaeda? In the final analysis the information about the European ricin network came from London, not Washington.

On 5 February 2003, having sought to establish the role that al Zarqawi played in the build-up of chemical weapons in Iraq, Powell's speech moved on to show the link between Saddam Hussein and al Qaeda that would prove Iraq's involvement in global terror.

> We are not surprised that Iraq is harboring al Zarqawi and his subordinates. This understanding builds on decades-long experience with respect to ties between Iraq and al Qaeda. . . . As I said at the outset, none of this should come as a surprise to any of us. Terrorism has been a tool used by Saddam for decades. Saddam was a supporter of terrorism long before these terrorist networks had a name, and this support continues. The nexus of poisons and terror is new; the nexus of Iraq and terror is old. The combination is lethal. With this track record, Iraqi denials of supporting terrorism take their place alongside the other Iraqi denials of weapons of mass destruction. It is all a web of lies. When we confront a regime that harbors ambitions for regional domination, hides weapons of mass destruction, and provides haven and active support for terrorists, we are not confronting the past, we are confronting the present. And unless we act, we are confronting an even more frightening future.

A simple sentence then gave birth to the myth of al Zarqawi. "Iraq today harbors a deadly terrorist network, headed by Abu Mos'ab al Zarqawi, an associate and collaborator of Osama bin Laden and his al Qaeda lieutenants."[16]

According to Fouad Hussein, in the Arab world even children laugh at the thought of a relationship between Saddam Hussein and al Qaeda. Ideologically they are opposites. Saddam Hussein's regime was secular, firmly rooted in the separation between religion and state, though in the 1990s it had became more Islamized as a reaction to UN economic sanctions. Al Qaeda is an Islamist movement that believes in the political role of religion. When Saddam invaded Kuwait, Osama bin Laden wanted to create an army of mujahedin in Saudi Arabia to fight against Iraqi troops. When the House of Saud rejected the idea and allowed U.S. troops into the country, bin Laden denounced the decision. On the night before the 2004 U.S. presidential election, Osama bin Laden issued a video in which he stated that the United States had substituted an old servant, Saddam Hussein, with a new one, Iyad Allawi.

Was Washington unaware of these important factors? Or did it simply ignore them as superfluous to its search for a reasonable justification for the war in Iraq? In his speech at the United Nations, Colin Powell offered a weak dismissal of the antagonism between Saddam's regime and al Qaeda: "Some believe, some claim, these contacts do not amount to too much. They say Saddam Hussein's secular tyranny and al Qaeda's religious tyranny do not mix. I am not comforted by this thought. Ambition and hatred are enough to bring Iraq and al Qaeda together, enough so al Qaeda could learn how to build more sophisticated bombs and learn how to forge documents, and enough so that al Qaeda could turn to Iraq for help in acquiring expertise on weapons of mass destruction."

Ignorance of the complexity of the Muslim world and its internal battles facilitated the spread of the myth of al Zarqawi. Politicians and the media are equally responsible for the widespread campaign of misinformation. Sufficient evidence of the true relationship between the Salafi jihadist movement, al Qaeda, and Saddam Hussein was readily available, yet it was ignored. People who might have possessed key intelligence, like the former Jordanian parliamentarian Layth Shubaylat, a member of the opposition movement who not only knew al Zarqawi from the time they spent together in al Suwaqah prison, but who also was personally acquainted with Saddam Hussein, were never interviewed. Layth Shubaylat could have offered a more realistic reading of events. "First of all, I don't think the two ideologies go together, I'm sure the former Iraqi leadership saw no interest in contacting al Zarqawi or al Qaeda operatives. The mentality of al Qaeda simply doesn't go with the Ba'athist one." When he was in prison, "Abu Mos'ab wouldn't accept me," said Shubaylat, "because I'm opposition, even if I'm a Muslim."[17] How could he accept Saddam Hussein, a secular dictator?

Layth Shubaylat's analysis is backed by al Zarqawi's accusation that the Iraqi Ba'ath party is guilty of apostasy. "They [the Americans] tried before to hide the truth of the battle and to distort the image of the pure banner of jihad. They deluded the world into believing that it is the remnants of the defunct regime and the elements of the infidel Ba'ath that are waging the resistance operations so that the nation would not back the battle and hail the epic. But these are only lies and fabrications. The heroism, sacrifice, and resolution that you heard in dealing with the enemies was, praised be God, the work of your sons, the knights of the nation."[18]

Shubaylat brings forward a further argument against the purported link between al Qaeda and Saddam Hussein: the refusal of the former Iraqi dictator to allow any form of opposition inside his regime. "I met with President Saddam twice to discuss a major issue; namely that opposition should be allowed. The opposition is dealing with the Americans and the Jews [I told him]. None of us accept this. But the opposition is a legitimate right. A state cannot exist without opposition. Two years later, when I saw him again, I told him: 'Mr President, your people have not contacted a group [from the opposition] that is asking to cooperate with the regime to protect Iraq. They are Iraqis and are speaking on this basis.' So, I do not believe that the issue reached the extent of coordinating with al Qaeda because [Baghdad has] even failed to coordinate anything with the opposition."[19]

Why did the world believe Colin Powell? How could he link two enemies, using an unknown Jordanian as a go-between, without any evidence? In February 2003, the planet was still shell shocked; the images of 9/11 were constantly flashing on television; people were scared. Without knowing it, the world had already plunged into the politics of fear and the apocalyptic, nightmare scenario that led to the war in Iraq.

CHAPTER SEVEN

Facts and Fiction about al Zarqawi's International Network

Destruction is freedom and democracy, while resistance is terrorism and intolerance.
—Osama bin Laden

After Colin Powell's speech, the world found a new enemy and the jihadists a new leader. His name is Abu Mos'ab al Zarqawi.

The birth of this myth coincided with a media frenzy over al Zarqawi's terrorist activity. However, unlike Osama bin Laden, who actively pursued and manipulated Western journalists, Abu Mos'ab had no contact with the media; on the contrary, he kept himself well away from it. The United States boosted his media profile in its desperation to find a link between al Qaeda and Saddam Hussein. "There are hundreds of men like al Zarqawi among the jihadists, committed fighters with leadership qualities," explained a former mujahed who resides in London. "Abu Mos'ab became famous because Colin Powell went to the United Nations and presented him as the new global terror leader."[1]

How was he presciently singled out by the Americans as a key terror player in Iraq? After Colin Powell's speech, media, intelligence, politicians, and a growing number of "terrorist experts" rushed to find an answer.

In his address to the United Nations, the U.S. secretary of state had warned that al Zarqawi had planned operations in France, Italy, Russia, Britain, and Spain, so European investigators searched for his connections with local jihadist groups. According to Abu Hilalah, a journalist at al Jazeera, suddenly every bombing attempt anywhere in the world was attributed to him.[2] He was linked to all major operations that took place in the aftermath of 9/11, including masterminding the creation of cells in Spain, Germany, and Istanbul. He was charged with the Casablanca attack and accused of having participated in the Madrid bombing. Confidentially, some investigators admit that after Powell's speech his name became well known, and therefore easier to recognize and single out among the endless lists of Arab names produced during interrogations.

The myth of al Zarqawi also boosted jihadist ideology. Though he was not a member of al Qaeda, the fact that he was portrayed as a key player in that organization helped keep al Qaeda in the limelight. At the same time, the fact that America presented him as the operational leader and new icon of al Qaeda facilitated the transition of his organization from a small, highly integrated terror group into the architects of the global anti-imperialist ideology of al Qaedism. Thus the decision to use al Zarqawi to justify military intervention in Iraq provided radical young Muslims with a focus for their desire to confront America. The Americans themselves transformed a minor jihadist leader into a figure of global importance. Throughout the official and unofficial war in Iraq, al Qaedism became the ideological umbrella under which groups of sympathizers and supporters could gather in the Middle East and Europe. Al Zarqawi came to embody this ideology for Western, and especially American, audiences in the years after the invasion.

Al Zarqawi's status as international terror leader was reinforced on 6 April 2004 when a Jordanian court sentenced him and ten of his followers to life imprisonment in absentia (later modified to the death penalty) for the murder of Lawrence Foley and Yitzhak Snir. According to Hussein Majaalli, "this whole affair demonstrates how American and Israeli interests in Jordan are untouchable. This is a murder case just like any other. One doesn't know who the murderer is. The investigation was conducted in a manner that a murderer had to be found. In the end this was nothing but an organized scenario."[3] Did the sentence reflect the interests of the United States and Israel, or those of the Jordanian authorities who were desperate to find the ring-leader of several terror attacks?

On 14 April 2004, the Jordanian authorities foiled another attack against the U.S. embassy and the Jordanian secret service building in Amman, masterminded (and subsequently claimed) by al Zarqawi. In a televised interview, the would-be perpetrators declared that the bombing was going to kill between 80,000 and 160,000 people with a chemical bomb of twenty tons.[4] Al Zarqawi responded in a statement posted on his Web site a few weeks later. "The tons that were manu-factured were raw materials that are sold in markets as brother Azmi al Jayyusi said, may God set him free," he began.[5] "As for the chemi-cal bomb and poisons, they were fabrications by the evil Jordanian agencies. This has been very clear, as the signs of torture were evident on the brother's face and hands. Yes, the plan was to completely destroy the building of the General Intelligence. The operation was planned against the source of black evil in our country."[6] "If I had had chemical weapons," he concluded, "I would have used them before against Tel Aviv."[7]

At the end of April 2004, the Honourables of Jordan released another statement, claiming responsibility for killing both Lawrence Foley and Yitzhak Snir. The message was accompanied by the shells of the bullets that had been fired at Foley and Snir; the statement denied any involvement by al Zarqawi.[8]

Accusing al Zarqawi of having planned the Millennium Plot and of the assassinations of Foley and Snir without solid evidence was part of the strategy to present him as a top-ranking al Qaeda member. It paid off in December 2004 when, as we shall see, Osama bin Laden made him the head of al Qaeda in Iraq—the Islamists often seem to follow a script provided by their enemies. The claim that the attack against the

U.S. embassy in Amman was going to be carried out with a chemical bomb, made without any evidence that such a bomb had ever existed, apart from the confessions of those involved in the attack, was also part of the construction of the terrorist myth of al Zarqawi. This strategy, masterminded by the Kurdish secret service, the Jordanian authorities, and the Americans, had tragic consequences. It diverted the investigation from pursuing the real perpetrators of the Millennium Plot and of the two assassinations, so that to date very little is known about the Honourables of Jordan. At the same time, sympathy for al Zarqawi grew in the Arab world with many seeing him as the victim of an American-Jordanian conspiracy. This phenomenon contributed to the maintenance of his image as a respectable mujahed while in reality, al Zarqawi was already a terror leader plotting deadly attacks in Jordan.

AL ZARQAWI'S NETWORK

From February 2002 onwards, it becomes increasingly difficult to distinguish fact from fiction in the life of al Zarqawi. As the myth took shape, the life of the man faded into its own legend. He was a chemical engineer, an expert on explosives, a legendary mujahed, a close associate of Osama bin Laden. He lost a leg in battle defending al Qaeda from U.S. raids, he had been operating in Iraq under the protection of Saddam, and at the same time he had been seen in the Pankisi Gorge, in Europe, and in the Middle East. Abu Mos'ab al Zarqawi had been transformed into the globetrotter of terrorism, soon to surpass Osama bin Laden in notoriety.

It is unreasonable to believe that al Zarqawi had the time or means to build such a global network, or to travel to so many places, whether with one leg or two. Until May 1999, he was in jail in Jordan; soon after he spent six months in Peshawar until he was arrested by the Pakistani authorities; at the beginning of 2000 he crossed over to Afghanistan where, towards the end of spring, he succeeded in setting up his own camp in Herat. In October 2001, the United States invaded

Afghanistan and al Zarqawi was once again on the run. Thus, in barely a year and a half, between late spring 2000 and October 2001, he is supposed to have managed to create an international network of cells to rival that of al Qaeda.[9] During the same time, members of his camp claim that he shuttled between Herat, where his second wife lived, and Kabul, where his first wife resided, and that he dealt with the recurrent incursions of the Northern Alliance and kept in touch with the Taliban leadership, which was bankrolling his camp.

The U.S. media and several terrorist analysts are adamant that, while in Herat, Abu Mos'ab al Zarqawi had the time and means to put in the pipeline the series of terror attacks against Europe that took place after 9/11. However, no hard evidence has been produced to back this claim, apart from transcripts of interrogations held (often under duress) in Jordan and other countries in which former terrorists confess to being part of al Zarqawi's network. Yet the trail of these individuals does not lead to him or to the Herat camp. By contrast, the trail of the hijackers who took part in 9/11 led to al Qaeda's camps in Afghanistan and to Osama bin Laden. Investigators could also retrace the links between al Zarqawi and those arrested in all the attacks for which he claimed responsibility, including the foiled bombing of the U.S. embassy in Amman; most of those perpetrators had been trained in the Herat camp.

When talking about the al Zarqawi network, it is unclear whether one is referring to the al Qaeda network or the Salafi jihadist network. Islamist armed organizations tend to be formed via social bonds, and al Zarqawi's movement is very different from the al Qaeda network, which masterminded the destruction of the Twin Towers. It is not cohesive and highly integrated like the IRA, the Red Brigades, or the al Qaeda that existed before 9/11.

Undoubtedly, al Zarqawi's notoriety in this context is enormous. "After Colin Powell's speech, any jihadist wanted to be related to al Zarqawi, any group wanted to have contacts with him," admits a former mujahed. "He is the symbol of the fight, he is much more important than Osama bin Laden."[10] His importance stems from the fact that he is operational in Iraq. Thus, the association with Abu Mos'ab al Zarqawi seems a spontaneous phenomenon, mediated through many loose social links and thanks also to virtual links, as his presence on the Internet is overwhelming.

Analysts who support the claim that al Zarqawi is at the heart of a web of terror in Europe[11] also maintain that his terror campaign in Europe targets Jews and Jewish interests.[12] If true, it would suggest that al Zarqawi has shifted the focus of his jihad from the near to the distant enemy. Can we believe that the man who in 2000 refused to join Osama bin Laden because he did not share the infamous Saudi's idea of targeting the United States, would soon after target Europe, a second fiddle to America and Israel in the Islamist counter-Crusade? The analysis conducted by the Arab media[13] is more sophisticated. It stresses that, while in Herat, al Zarqawi had not one, but two main objectives: to prepare the Jordanian cells and at the same time shape the European ones.[14] But this is surely wrong. He may have had some links with Islamists in Europe, but he had no means or time to play much of a role in organizing them. The Arab media sought to show him fighting both the near and the distant enemy: the Jordanian regime and the European democracies.

THE EUROPEAN NETWORK

Both analyzes seem implausible in light of the fact that in 2000 and 2001 Abu Mos'ab al Zarqawi did not have sufficient backing to set up a network of cells anywhere. He could not even afford to pay for the transportation of his recruits; those who traveled to Herat admit to having funded the journey themselves. More likely, when al Zarqawi arrived in Afghanistan, he was already part of a loose network of Salafi jihadists who were on the move. As we have seen, people from Salt went via Afghanistan to Iraqi Kurdistan; others remained in their countries, in Jordan, Syria, or Lebanon; some others traveled to Herat. The connection between Arab countries and Europe already existed; it dates back to the 1980s and 1990s when people who were persecuted in their own countries moved to Europe, seeking refuge. At the time, al Zarqawi was the bully of Zarqa; later, he was in jail. Today, there is no evidence that he controls the European network. Indeed, one of the founders of Ansar al Islam, Mullah Krekar, based in Norway, was cleared of the charge of supplying suicide bombers to Iraq for the al Zarqawi network in November 2004.

The myth of al Zarqawi would have us believe that his network is a sort of Islamist Comintern, a well-structured organization, highly pyramidal and integrated. The truth is very different. "The Islamist international does not exist," argues Nadine Picaudou. "Neither al Qaeda's nor al Zarqawi's networks are structured as such. What we have is a nebula of groups that forge alliances whenever it suits them, alliances which can be broken at any time. We cannot regard them as a homogeneous entity."[15] This, in a nutshell, is al Qaedism—a global anti-imperialist doctrine that rose from the ashes of al Qaeda. Al Qaedism is a creed embraced by a highly unstructured web of people and groups, whose most powerful weapons are suicide missions.

Members of the jihadist nebula keep in touch through a web of personal contacts, including family and ethnic ties, which constitute the milieu of the jihadist movement, not only in Europe, but all over the world. Osama bin Laden and al Zawahiri, who originate from the Arab elite, have strong links with the Gulf countries and the United States. They are tapped into this network, while al Zarqawi, partly because of his modest Jordanian origins, has links with the European network.

The heart of the European network is the grid of radical mosques and informal places of worship scattered across the continent. Following the bomb attacks in London in July 2005, investigations revealed the existence of informal mosques, and underground prayer rooms in private houses and universities. These are places where the recruiters of the second generation of suicide bombers have been able to move freely. European counterterrorism is adamant that the presence of large Saudi investments in Europe facilitated the funding of such a network across the continent. This network is perceived today as the most powerful instrument for recruiting, funding, and coordinating the activity of cells and armed groups linked to Islamist terror in Europe and abroad. Until the Madrid attack of 11 March 2004, its strength was not fully recognized. Al Qaeda is also tapped into it. Spanish counterterrorism officers have defined European mosques as "havens for al Qaeda planning and fund-raising."[16] Before the Madrid bombing, counterterrorism intelligence may have underestimated the role played by such a network in bankrolling Islamist terror during the preparatory stages for 9/11.

With Colin Powell's speech at the UN and the beginning of the war in Iraq, it became increasingly easy for al Zarqawi and his followers to tap into the European network. A European undercover agent admits that many jihadists and radical preachers had never before heard of al Zarqawi; the fact that his name was mentioned by the U.S. secretary of state gave him the necessary status to be regarded as a leader. "In the Arab world, as everywhere, when people see something on TV they immediately believe it," says Abdallah Anas. European investigations confirm that after the beginning of the war in Iraq, the jihadist network in Europe began supplying Muslims to carry out suicide missions for several groups, including al Zarqawi's.

One of the men in charge of the export of European suicide bombers to Iraq is known as Mullah Fouad. Described as the "gatekeeper" of Iraq, he was arrested in Syria in June 2005.[17] Mullah Fouad was born Mohammed Majid; he is an Iraqi Kurd believed to be a member of Ansar al Islam. Before fleeing to Syria in 2003, he lived in Parma, Italy, for several years. The Italian authorities are convinced that he is in charge of smuggling European suicide bombers through Syria into Iraq.[18] According to Jean-Louis Bruguiere, the French antiterrorism investigative magistrate, dozens of European recruits have entered Iraq since the summer of 2003.[19] In a conversation intercepted by the Italian authorities, Mullah Fouad asked a member of the Italian cell to send more people "like those that were in Japan,"[20] referring to the kamikaze. Mullah Fouad is believed to have been one of several Syrians working with al Zarqawi.

THE SYRIAN CONNECTION

Al Zarqawi's strongest weapon in Iraq has been an endless supply of suicide bombers, some of whom come from his native Jordan. On 28 February 2005, a suicide bomber blew himself up outside a health clinic in the city of Hilla, Iraq, killing about 125 people. This was the single biggest massacre since the beginning of the Iraq war. Among the scattered corpses were the remnants of the young Jordanian, Raed al Banna, who had carried out the attack. According to family members and friends, al Banna had spent time in the United States and was mesmerized by American culture. It was only in 2003, after he was refused entry into America, that his radicalization began to take place. He became more religious and started gravitating towards jihadist groups in Jordan. He made a pilgrimage to Mecca and as soon as he returned he vanished. His family was told that he had found a job in Saudi Arabia; al Banna even called several times pretending to be living and working on the Arab Peninsula. In reality, he had crossed over to Iraq through the Syrian border and blended into the throng of Abu Mos'ab al Zarqawi's army of suicide bombers.[21]

After his death, the Arab media reported that relatives held celebrations to commemorate his martyrdom.[22] The family even ran an obituary in the *ad Dastour* paper announcing that he had "won martyrdom in the land of Iraq." Yet, when interviewed by *Time* magazine, all the family members uniformly denied that they were backing the Iraqi insurgency or that they had any knowledge of al Banna's involvement with al Zarqawi. His father even confessed that he hoped that the entire affair was a mistake and that one day his son would knock at his door.

The tale of al Banna is emblematic of the mystery that envelopes the insurgency in Iraq, the involvement of neighboring countries, and the role that al Zarqawi's recruitment network plays among young Middle Eastern jihadists, many of whom end up as suicide bombers. Several are Iraqis, or from neighboring countries—Saudis, Kuwaitis, Jordanians—while others, coming from different Arab and European countries, reach Iraq via the Syrian connection, a network predominately composed of Syrians, including expatriates. In the Middle East, these soon-to-be suicide bombers come from Palestine, Jordan, and Syria. The investigation conducted by Fouad Hussein for LBC television in Beirut reveals that these are the countries where al Zarqawi's recruitment network is particularly strong.

Khaled Darwish, better known as Abu al Ghadia, has been identified as one of the key players in the enrollment of Syrians and Palestinians on behalf of al Zarqawi. A Syrian orthodontist, Abu al Ghadia is an expert in explosives and document falsification. He acquired these skills while training in various countries: Afghanistan, Iran, Turkey, and Lebanon. According to Jordanian television, several jihadists convicted in the foiled attack against the U.S. embassy in Amman admitted that Abu al Ghadia had supplied them with money and false identities.[23]

It is unclear when al Zarqawi recruited Abu al Ghadia. It could have happened at any time since 1999, after he left the al Suwaqah prison, to October 2001, when the United States attacked Afghanistan and he fled that country. Abu al Ghadia spent some time in Herat, training recruits in the use of explosives, as confirmed by members of the camp.[24] "I was trained in Herat, I trained in explosives on a very high level," explains Azmi al Jayyusi, who was supposed to die as a martyr in the foiled attack against the U.S. embassy in Amman.[25] Abu al Ghadia was part of the same operation. Possibly he even masterminded it with the help of the Syrian connection. Azmi al Jayyusi had in fact come to Amman from Syria. Indeed, the plot was discovered when some of al Zarqawi's followers were arrested in Syria; from them the Syrian authorities learned of the plot to bomb the buildings in Amman and alerted the Jordanian secret service.

Porous borders between Iraq and neighboring countries facilitate the movement of al Zarqawi's supply of recruits; one of the most permeable is the Syrian border with Iraq. However, this fact alone does not prove the involvement of Syria in such trade. Yet, both the Coalition forces and the Iraqi government accuse Syria of supporting al Zarqawi. In February 2005, al Iraqiya, the government-controlled Iraqi television station, set up by the Coalition, broadcast several confessions of Arab jihadists, members of the Liberation Army (a mixed group of Iraqis and Arabs, who had crossed into Iraq from Syria). They claimed that the Syrian secret service had supplied them with explosives, detonators, and instructions on how to behead hostages, as well as other information about acts of sabotage against the police and members of the national guard. According to these confessions, the Syrian secret services funded their activities in Iraq. A Sudanese even remarked that he received fifty dollars per beheading.[26] Nevertheless, no evidence of the involvement of the Syrian secret service has been provided.

The Iraqi government also accused neighboring countries of supporting former members of the Ba'ath party. In February 2005, during the Riyadh conference on terrorism, the Iraqi delegation admitted that terrorist activity in Iraq was masterminded by members of the old Ba'ath regime, and then denounced Egyptian, Syrian, and Jordanian nationalist groups' support of the insurgency. According to the delegation, the common belief is that what is taking place in Iraq is not terrorism but national resistance to defend the Arab identity of the country. The delegation accused Syria, Jordan, and Yemen of harboring former members of the Ba'ath party, renamed in Iraq "the backward party" (Hizb al Awda), through their national Ba'ath parties.[27]

Although, after the fall of Saddam's regime, several members of the Iraqi Ba'ath party took refuge in Syria and now use this country as a base from which to fund and equip armed groups, these activities do not take place under the protection of the Syrian government. So far, Damascus has fully cooperated with the Americans. Though porous at crucial segments, the border between Syria and Iraq is jointly patrolled by Syrian and U.S. troops.[28] By accusing neighboring countries of supporting the insurgency, the Iraqi government is attempting to hide the strong anti-American sentiment that is widespread among its own and neighboring populations.

The blind commitment of young Arabs who join the Iraqi insurgency, including al Zarqawi's group, seems to confirm the Iraqi government's fear that what in the West is commonly defined as terrorist activity is regarded in the Arab world, including in Iraq, as national resistance against an occupying foreign power. Young people are particularly drawn to the insurgency. "I followed Abu Mos'ab al Zarqawi everywhere he went, I never even discussed it, I just followed all his orders," explains al Jayyusi. "After the fall of Afghanistan I met with Abu Mos'ab again in Iraq. He was accompanied by the Jordanian Muafaq Adwan, whom I knew from Afghanistan. We were assigned to go to Jordan, Muafaq Adwan and I, in order to build a military operation in Jordan [that was supposed to carry out the bombing of the U.S. embassy in Jordan]."[29]

According to the U.S. authorities, Abu al Ghadia, who is a member of al Zarqawi's *shura*, or high council, is also in charge of contacts with Palestinian recruiters who select future suicide bombers. On behalf of al Zarqawi, for example, he is accused of having transferred $10,000 to Abu Muhyin, head of Asbat al Ansar, a group based in the Ayn Helwa refugee camp in Lebanon.[30]

Several investigations have identified Abu al Ghadia as one of the main financial channels through which al Zarqawi's activity in Iraq is bankrolled. Again, the Syrian connection plays an important role in such funding. Abu al Ghadia is tapped into the network of Syrians in Europe who left the country in 1982, when the regime clashed with the Muslim Brotherhood. Over the last two decades, these groupings, persecuted inside and outside of their homeland, have become more fundamentalist. According to Fouad Hussein, they are today among the most important sponsors of al Zarqawi via Abu al Ghadia.[31] In 2005, the United States nominated Abu al Ghadia to the UN list of terror financiers in the hope of stopping his activity. According to John Snow, U.S. treasury secretary, Abu al Ghadia supplies al Zarqawi's network in Iraq with $10,000–$12,000 every month; the money is delivered by a fleet of couriers who regularly cross the border between Syria and Iraq.[32]

There is mounting evidence that al Zarqawi is also receiving money from individual sponsors in the Gulf. Ironically, the surge in oil prices has increased liquidity in the region. "Sponsors have more spare cash at their disposal," admitted a Saudi source. Although al Zarqawi does not have the same status as Osama bin Laden in Saudi Arabia and other Gulf states, he is fighting on the frontlines, while bin Laden is trapped in the region between Pakistan and Afghanistan.

CHAPTER EIGHT

Insurgent Iraq

Mission accomplished.
—George Bush on the war in Iraq

At 19.30 on a Friday evening, Ayatollah Muhammad Sadeq al Sadr, the popular leader of the Shi'ite Muslims in Iraq, left his office on the outskirts of the holy city of Najaf, near the Euphrates River, southwest of Baghdad. He had just finished delivering his sermon inside the crowded Masjid al Kufa Mosque, where thousands upon thousands of people flocked every Friday to listen to him. Sadeq al Sadr was a superstar cleric, regarded by Shi'ites across the world as a holy man. As usual, that Friday he had addressed the faithful wearing his funeral shroud, a symbol of his readiness to be martyred.

Two of his sons, Mustapha and Mu'ammal, who acted as his chief assistants, escorted the old man to the car along with their driver. In the golden evening light of this ancient city of Mesopotamia, the four of them, dressed in traditional Shi'ite clothes, seemed inhabitants of a timeless age. Suddenly, without warning, bullets were flying from all directions and the four men were hit. A few minutes later, their bodies rested motionless inside their vehicle, parked on the dusty square adjacent to the historic mosque. Iraqi security forces immediately sealed off the area and did not allow even an ambulance to drive through.[1]

This is not another terror tale from "liberated" Iraq; the assassination of Sadeq al Sadr and two of his sons took place on 18 February 1999. The killers were sent by Saddam Hussein, who was determined to silence the leader of the Shi'ite opposition to his regime.

The murders triggered a violent revolt, which was crushed by an equally violent repression. The British newspaper the *Independent* reported that "inside the mosque weapons were handed out and a pitched battle soon raged. Several security vehicles were set on fire. But Saddam's forces eventually shot their way into the mosque, killing some 200 people."[2] Hundreds more died in street fighting; others were imprisoned, tortured, and executed.

Repression was particularly brutal in "Saddam City," the infamous Baghdad ghetto where more than two million Shi'ites lived in appalling conditions. "People were massacred by Saddam's police forces," recalls a resident. "They were butchered in the streets like animals." In this large, miserable section of Baghdad, the assassinations only bolstered popular allegiance to Ayatollah Muhammad Sadeq al Sadr. In martyrdom, as in life, he came to represent the voice of the victims of Saddam. On 9 April 2003, when Saddam Hussein's regime fell, residents of the area covered a plaque at the entrance of the neighborhood that read "Welcome to Saddam City" with a hand-painted sign reading "Welcome to Sadr City."

Ironically, the Iraq insurgency was born here, in Sadr City (Medina as Sadr), in the Shi'ite slums of Baghdad, among the very people who were happiest to see the arrival of the Americans. While Ba'ath loyalists were regrouping inside the Sunni Triangle and al Zarqawi was waiting to launch his terror offensive, the voice of the unemployed, dispossessed, persecuted Shi'ites of Sadr City rose against the breakdown in law and order, the shameful looting, appalling living conditions, and political corruption that followed the victory of the Coalition forces. Their spokesman was the youngest surviving son of Ayatollah Mohammad Sadeq al Sadr, the preacher Moqtada al Sadr.[3]

THE SHI'ITE INSURGENCY

"We had hoped that some of the problems might have vanished by now," said a pro-Sadr cleric at a prayer meeting in Sadr City in

November 2003. What were these problems? The lack of law and order, rampant unemployment, lack of basic services in Shi'ite urban areas—and Coalition disregard for the cultural and societal norms of the population. The Shi'ite political leader best able to undertake that challenge was none other than [Moqtada] al Sadr."4 As chaos gripped post-war Baghdad, pro–al Sadr preachers organized vigilante committees to guard neighborhoods and to prevent the looting of public institutions. Others distributed food and water. In the midst of this remarkable outpouring of solidarity, Moqtada al Sadr launched his inflammatory populist sermons. He denounced Coalition forces as occupying forces and the interim government as American puppets; he condemned the governing council as composed largely of Iraqi exiles, people who had lived outside the country during Saddam's regime; he also lashed out at the traditional Shi'ite religious authorities for remaining silent about these abuses.

Moqtada al Sadr's rhetoric was drenched in the Shi'ite masses' disillusionment with a transitional regime that was planning to exclude them from power. He was and still is regarded as a political leader, not as a religious authority.5 The young preacher warned against the creation of a new ruling elite that would once again marginalize poor Shi'ites. His voice became a rallying cry for the Shi'ite majority (about 60 percent of the Iraqi population) to fight for its rights. During the first months, he stopped just short of a direct and unambiguous call for violence, yet he skillfully distanced himself from the three other main, moderate, Shi'ite political groups: al Daawa, the Supreme Council of the Islamic Revolution in Iraq (SCIRI), and Ayatollah Ali al Sistani's al Nayaf. Today all of these groups are represented in the new Iraqi parliament. So, too, is Moqtada al Sadr.

Traditionally and ideologically, Iraqi Shi'ites have been divided into three main streams. Al Daawa, the oldest party, was created in the 1950s. It is in favor of a reformist Islam, a parliamentary regime, and a decentralized State. Al Daawa has declared itself against the presence of American forces in the Middle East and, at the same time, has kept its distance from Iran. Today, it is the weakest among the Shi'ite parties. "[It is] led by Ibrahim Jaafari, who returned to Iraq from exile in London after the fall of the Ba'athists. Jaafari holds a seat on the Governing Council, and acted as its first president. Though influential, Jaafari's views do not necessarily reflect the full spectrum of ideologies and allegiances within the Daawa Party. According to some observers, the party is still too fractured and secretive to play a decisive role in Iraqi politics."[6]

The Supreme Council of the Islamic Revolution in Iraq was created in 1982 as a spin-off of al Daawa under the leadership of Muhammad Baqer al Hakim. In 2003, after his assassination, his brother took over the leadership. Although it took part in the National Iraqi Council under the supervision of the United States, it has gradually distanced itself from it. SCIRI is in favor of a decentralized and democratic parliamentary model. Its military branch, the Badr Brigade, consists of about 10,000–15,000 men, mainly people who went into exile in Iran and returned after the fall of Saddam. Under the Coalition process, SCIRI joined the Iraqi government.

The strongest party is led by Iranian-born Ayatollah Ali al Sistani who settled in Iraq in 1952 and assumed leadership of al Nayaf after the murder of Muhammad Sadeq al Sadr. The party is based around the Hawza al-Ilmiya, a network of religious schools in Najaf that are run by Iraq's highest-ranking clerics (*marjayya*), who tend traditionally to be quietists, rather than followers of the Iranian ideology of rule by clerics. The marjayya have supported the Coalition occupation of Iraq to only a limited degree and stress that civil rule should be returned to the Iraqi people in a controlled fashion as soon as possible. "Al Sistani is the Shi'ite leader most criticized by the Sunni and the mujahedin because he called on the civilian population to stop holding up the advance of the allied forces. . . . His influence is based on the traditional principle of obedience to the spiritual authority. His followers consist of clans, students of religious schools, men of religion, traders, artisans and government employees."[7]

In the summer of 2003, al Sadr created his own militia, Jeish al Mahdi (Army of al Mahdi). He claimed that it was not armed and that it carried out social tasks in poor Shi'ite neighborhoods. However, members of the militia simply hid their arms, acquired from looted Iraqi military arsenals; the central offices of Moqtada al Sadr's movement, scattered around the country, supplied ammunition. Recruitment took place predominantly in urban ghettos, where people had no experience in guerrilla fighting.

> Few of the "rank and file" within the lower levels of the militia—often young illiterate kids who had migrated from rural areas into urban centers—had any training in arms or small-unit tactics whatsoever. Recruits to the Moqtada insurgency indicate the clear class and social basis of the movement. Moqtada catered to the most dispossessed elements within the long-suffering Shi'ite community. Disgruntled and unemployed young men, who would stand at street corners for hours on end every day, would eventually be enticed into attending Friday sermons, after which their entry into the movement began. His constituency was derived from towns such as [Sadr City]—a large, sprawling, squalid and fetid suburb of Baghdad where the unemployment rate hovers around seventy percent—and al-Kut [about one hundred miles southeast of Baghdad], which faces a similar unemployment problem.[8]

The size of the Jeish al Mahdi has been estimated at between three thousand and ten thousand members.[9]

With a strong following also from Najaf and Karbala, both Shi'ite pilgrimage destinations, in the late spring of 2003 Moqtada al Sadr launched his opposition to Ayatollah Ali al Sistani on the basis that al Sistani could not preach to the Iraqis about how to deal with the occupying forces because he was Iranian. At the same time, al Sadr demanded the immediate departure of all foreign troops.

Intra-Shi'ite rivalries between al Sadr and al Sistani are not a new phenomenon. They had erupted in 1999, when al Sadr's father, Muhammad Sadeq al Sadr, began his campaign against Saddam Hussein. "He had previously avoided friction with the Ba'ath regime, and so his sermons against Saddam immediately won him huge support with younger Shi'ite. Attendance at his sermons ballooned. Grand Ayatollah Sistani objected to Sadr's preaching because he feared the regime would retaliate in devastating fashion against the entire Shi'ite community."[10] After the assassination of Muhammad al Sadr, his family, and in particular Moqtada, did not forgive al Sistani.

As early as April 2003, Jeish al Mahdi began its violent activity inside Iraq against both moderate Shi'ites and Coalition forces. On 10 April, the armed group assassinated the moderate Ayatollah Abd al Majid al Khoi. Moqtada al Sadr's agenda was clear: create a parallel state and government under his leadership, with the militia as its military arm and the special religious tribunals, such as those in Najaf and Karbala, as its judicial one.[11]

Fueled by the sermons of Moqtada al Sadr, the Shi'ite insurgency soon spread across the country. It was forceful, violent, and rooted in the poverty of its supporters. From spring 2003, clashes and rioting began to plague "liberated" Iraq, with many areas resembling full-fledged civil war zones. In late spring 2004, Jeish al Mahdi, which by now had become a terrorist group, kidnapped two South Korean human rights activists. Coalition troops had to battle daily even against the preacher's supporters in Najaf, Karbala, and Sadr City, strongholds of his militia.

Despite the violence, Moqtada al Sadr's popularity grew. An opinion poll conducted by the Provisional Authority in six Iraqi cities[12] between 14 and 23 May 2004 showed that 81 percent of those interviewed had a better opinion of al Sadr than three months earlier and that 64 percent regarded his actions as part of a national resistance that had served to unify the country.[13]

THE SUNNI INSURGENCY

While al Sadr's followers were gaining new momentum, the Sunnis launched their own offensive. Their insurgency started in May 2003 with the first outbreaks of violence in Baghdad, Ramadi, and Falluja. The core of the social unrest was in the Sunni Triangle, an area predominantly populated by Sunnis with strong tribal traditions. Contrary to what many believe, the insurgency was not conducted exclusively by a minority of people who had enjoyed special privileges under Saddam; the Sunni commercial and middle classes also joined in.

Ironically, these social groups had welcomed the arrival of American troops, convinced that they would protect them from the widespread criminality and economic harshness which had plagued the country for over a decade. In 2000 Saddam had released 200,000 convicts, some of whom formed criminal gangs that terrified the population. The war boosted their ranks. The breakdown in law and order, which followed the fall of Saddam's regime, the release of thousands of common criminals from prisons, and the massive looting convinced the Sunni middle class that the Americans were unable to keep the country under control.

By early summer 2003, Coalition soldiers became the target of both Shi'ite and Sunni violence. The insurgencies violently expressed grievances with the occupying power shared by Shi'ites and Sunnis alike: both groups felt betrayed by their "liberators." What Iraqis had expected from the United States was a better life; what they got was a nightmare worse than the one they had endured under Saddam's regime. "If the Americans had come and developed our general services, brought work for our people, and transferred their technology to us, then we would not have been so disappointed," explained an Iraqi to a *Guardian* newspaper correspondent in spring 2004. "But it is not acceptable to us as human beings that after one year America is still not able to bring us electricity."[14]

In retrospect, the failure to address the grievances of the Sunni commercial and middle classes was a tragic mistake. America could have benefited from their support—a vital backing needed to smooth the process of transition. But the United States was unprepared or unwilling to take control of the country. It had relied entirely upon its advisers, a group of exiled Iraqis, to provide all their information, most of it incorrect, regarding the logistic and economic conditions of the country. These informants had painted a far-too-optimistic picture. In reality the country's socioeconomic infrastructure had been eroded by more than a decade of economic sanctions, and the war had brought them to a total collapse. Due to the effects of sanctions, Coalition forces inherited a nation with no running water, no electricity, and no proper sewage system, where over 60 percent of the population survived on food rations linked to the UN oil-for-food program. Faced with this scenario, the Bush administration had no plans for the transition period following the defeat of the dictator. America had ill-advisedly focused all its efforts first on justifying the war and then on fighting it, as though removing Saddam were the sole objective.

As the country slid into chaos, Americans barricaded themselves inside the Green Zone, oblivious to what was happening outside. A Norwegian journalist who entered the Green Zone during the first assault against Falluja in spring 2004 was astonished to discover four American diplomats, who had not left the compound in several months, engaged in a heated discussion about how to structure Iraq's stock exchange. "I had just arrived from Falluja," said the journalist, "and the city was on fire. It was surreal to watch these men planning a stock exchange while the country was in the grip of civil war."[15] Life inside and outside the Green Zone is shockingly different. Those sheltered inside have decision-making powers, but no sense of the state into which the country has been plunged. "Young and inexperienced soldiers were sent to patrol Iraqi streets while officers stayed behind," as the wife of an American reserve officer explained to me, "to prevent losses of 'important' lives."

Americans also failed to understand the complexity of the insurgency. The Sunni resistance, for example, was multifaceted and included a strong Islamic nationalist faction. Former Iraqi army officers and security personnel belonged to this group. Islamic nationalism was a by-product of the economic sanctions. To counteract the UN embargo, which was crippling the country's economy, Saddam had made strategic concessions to appease the clergy and the tribal leaders who ruled according to Sharia law. Women were the first victims of this new regime. Overnight, Saddam halved unemployment by banning women from working outside their homes, a decree that was subsequently revised to prohibit women from working altogether. Saddam also allowed honor killing to go unpunished. Under Sharia law, any male member of the family has the right to kill a female who has dishonored the family merely by having a boyfriend or even by talking to a man without the permission of her family. Tribal leaders, with whom Saddam had always had problems, supported these changes. But it was towards the end of the 1990s that the Islamization of Iraqi society accelerated. In 1999 the regime launched *al hamla al-imaniyah* (enhancement of Islamic faith), a de facto Islamist campaign. Opening hours for drinking and gambling establishments were restricted and secular practices were greatly reduced, while the government actively promoted religious education. Secular schools were closed down and girls were kept at home.

During the 1990s, the regime also tolerated the spread of modern Salafism, which became a powerful religious movement among Iraqi Sunnis, especially in the Sunni Triangle. After the fall of Saddam, "The [radical] Salafi . . . contributed to the increasing violence of the insurgency by targeting leaders of other communities, promoters of 'moral laxity,' and non-Muslims. They . . . derided the Shi'ites and their rituals and . . . even attacked and defaced posters of Shi'ite religious figures. In the fall of 2003 Islamists [Salafi] were particularly active in Mosul, where they attacked a nunnery, killed a well-known writer, bombed a popular cinema, and torched four liquor stores."[16]

Support for the Sunni insurgency also included secular groups. The spectrum ranged from students, intellectuals, and middle-class professionals to former soldiers and farmers. In the summer of 2003, due to the actions of its secular and nationalist elements, the Sunni insurgency came to be known as a resistance movement, the social upheaval of a proud nation against an occupying power. This phenomenon won the admiration of Iraqi Sunnis everywhere, including moderates and those far from the frontlines.

The capture of Saddam Hussein in December 2003 delivered a serious blow to the Ba'ath loyalist faction of the resistance, those who were fighting for the dictator's return to power. In sharp contrast, the Islamo-nationalist insurgency, a front composed of religious and secular groups, formed in the summer, and was greeted with a new popularity. They blamed Saddam's foolish policy for the invasion and fought to regain control of Sunni territory. Their political platform was simple: get rid of the occupation and bring law and order to those regions under their leadership.

During the fall and winter of 2004, the Islamo-nationalists gained new momentum, carrying out several successful attacks against Coalition forces. This was due to strategic factors, in particular, their ability to recruit professional military personnel. Many of these people became part of the resistance after the United States had dismantled the army; in the process, they had lost both their salary and their social status. Former army officers trained new recruits in guerrilla tactics. Thus the Islamo-nationalists achieved considerable tactical successes against American forces and, at the same time, reduced their losses considerably.

At any given time the Sunni resistance was never short of men or weapons; however, the biggest intake came from Sunni tribes, which supplied a die-hard breed of fighters. Towards the end of 2003, for example, 50,000 men from the Albuseissa tribe joined the resistance in the area surrounding Falluja alone. "Its members have claimed that it was their fighters who shot down the U.S. Army Chinook that resulted in the deaths of 17 U.S. troops in early November 2003."[17]

At the root of the Sunni tribes' opposition to the Americans lie traditional, economic, and behavioral factors, realities that the Bush administration never took into consideration. Traditionally, tribal leaders have always been reluctant to submit to an outside authority; even Saddam had problems with them and was forced to grant them special autonomy. Americans are regarded as infidels because they are not Muslim, which largely contributed to the lack of trust in them. U.S. soldiers' ignorance and disregard for tribal tradition—evidenced by their practices of searching homes in the absence of the male head of the family and having male soldiers perform body searches on women—fueled a resentment which easily erupted into violence. Finally, economic grievances, similar to those of the Shi'ites, convinced tribal leaders of the Americans' inability to bring economic stability to the country.

Another key factor in the growing popularity of the Sunni insurgency is its financial wealth. Neither Shi'ite nor Sunni insurgents are short of money. While the Shi'ite insurgency can count on financial sponsors from Iran and from sympathizers abroad, the Sunni resistance has financiers and arms suppliers inside the country. Saddam Hussein had taken into account the high cost of resistance if the country were invaded. Loyalists had hidden large quantities of money in various locations. The U.S. army discovered some of these hideouts and captured insurgents with large amounts of cash; however, this has not stopped the flow of funds, as much more is still hidden. At the same time, private citizens donate money to the resistance, generally people from rich families from the Sunni Triangle.

Thus both the Shi'ite and Sunni insurgencies have plenty of men, weapons, and money to stage a long and bloody resistance against the occupying power.

CHAPTER NINE

The New Mongols

Americans are the new Mongols.
—*Bashaer* magazine

Before the official war, there existed no link between al Qaeda and Saddam Hussein; as soon as the invasion began, however, enraged Salafists from all over the Middle East flocked to the country to fight the Coalition forces. Ironically, the fall of Saddam hastened the influx of foreign fighters and jihadists, some of whom were linked to local Iraqi Salafi groups based inside the Sunni Triangle, in places such as Ramadi, Falluja, and Mosul. Al Zarqawi was one of them. He entered the country before the official war started and began organizing his support network ahead of all the others. This factor alone gave him a tremendous advantage over other jihadist leaders.

Throughout the 1990s, modern Salafism swept Iraq thanks to the process of Islamization launched by Saddam. Sunni Triangle residents' shared radical Salafi religious beliefs, a factor that alone played an important role in the acceptance of foreign fighters in Iraq. A member of Falluja's administrative council, for example, referred to foreign insurgents as mujahedin, or holy warriors. "Al Anbar [the province where Falluja is located] has a bigger nationalist consciousness than the rest of Iraq," he added. "We are also more religious. We consider this resistance a religious duty and a nationalist one as well."[1] This sentiment is widespread among the middle class. During the UN economic sanctions, religion became a source of comfort for the impoverished

Sunni middle class. Islam was a way to cope with harsh economic conditions. In occupied Iraq, Islam became a means to regain independence from the Americans and to grow economically once again.

To be effective, the foreign jihadists required the support of all the local resistance groups, including secular nationalists and tribal members. This was readily forthcoming. The entire spectrum of the Sunni resistance, from modern Salafi to Saddam loyalists, willingly supported the "freelance" foreign fighters. All groups offered protection, concealment, and the necessary resources to carry out attacks. This readiness to offer foreigners a support network is related to the importance that this relatively small group of people has inside the Sunni resistance. This minority is willing to carry out operations that Iraqis are not—such as suicide missions.

The presence of foreign fighters and of suicide bombers is one of the key elements that differentiates the Sunni resistance from the Shi'ite insurgency. Another is the background and motivations of the two groups. While the latter is essentially a class struggle, the former is a counter-Crusade and a civil war. From the outset, Moqtada al Sadr's Shi'ite revolt sought political recognition for his followers and a share of the political pie for himself; Sunni insurgents, instead, are engaged in a full-fledged war against an occupying power.

As early as spring 2003, the timeless, apocalyptic rhetoric of the Iraqi Salafi jihadist movement justified the call to arms with a powerful historical comparison: the thirteenth-century invasion of the Mongols. Coalition forces are viewed as the new Mongols who have invaded Iraq. Images of Mongols and Tartars during the sack of the splendid city of Baghdad in 1258 are, for Sunni Iraqis, evocative of shameful memories. "In the Sunni Triangle, the sense of history is very strong," explains Saad al Fagih. "People are proud of their origins, of their strength, and remember past humiliations for generations and generations. This tribal area has given birth to Saladin, the winner of the Second Crusade. While in power, Saddam often compared himself to the legendary Muslim leader, who, like him, was born in Tikrit [in Saladin's time, a Kurdish town]. We are talking about ancient Mesopotamia, the cradle of our civilization."[2]

Soon after the fall of Saddam's regime, a vast literature became available on the Internet about the new Mongol invasion. In the virtual magazine *Bashaer*, the reader is told that before reaching Baghdad, the Mongols invaded the kingdom of Huwarzim (today Uzbekistan and Turkmenistan), just as Coalition forces attacked Afghanistan before invading Iraq.[3] Mongols and Tartars forged an alliance to wage war against Baghdad, as did the United States and the United Kingdom before bombing Iraq. In both circumstances, Baghdad was attacked from the east and west, the siege lasted twenty-one days, the military superiority of the invaders was enormous, and people were so afraid that they did not pray on the first Friday after the attack had begun. In the thirteenth century, as in modern Iraq, the rivalry between Shi'ite and Sunni weakened the central power. Mongols and Tartars came with armies of mercenaries who participated in the invasion and sacked the city; Coalition forces stood by as their Iraqi supporters looted libraries and cultural institutions and killed women and children. The Mongols and the Tartars left with most of the wealth of the caliphate; Americans took control of the oil fields and other natural resources of Iraq. After sacking Baghdad, the Mongols conquered al Sham (the great Syria); today America is warning and threatening Syria.

The *Bashaer* magazine analogy ends with a prediction drawn from the historical close of the Mongol invasion: two years after the sacking of Baghdad, the Syrian and Egyptian armies, together with groups of Arab volunteers, defeated the Mongols and the Tartars at Ayn Jalut. "We are sure that God will punish America for good," concludes *Bashaer*. "When will the new Ayn Jalut take place?"[4]

SHI'ITES AS THE ALLIES OF THE MONGOLS

In the summer of 2003, al Zarqawi used the analogy of the Mongol invasion to launch his offensive against the Shi'ites. Ibn al Alqami, the vizier of Baghdad, explained al Zarqawi, helped the Mongols in their conquest of Baghdad.[5] His followers conspired with the Mongols and the Tartars, encouraging them to invade Baghdad. In a similar fashion the Shi'ites conspired with the Americans and welcomed them into Iraq. This was the first time that the issue of sectarian infighting between Sunnis and Shi'ites surfaced within the Iraqi insurgency.

Jihadists were immediately drawn to this analogy because they operate with a timeless frame of reference. For them, historical forces are essentially static. "History repeats itself," declared al Zarqawi, "the logic of what happens through time does not change; what changes are the people, one player replaces another, machines improve, but what does not change is the theatre where the operations take place and the history of fighting is only one: truth battles with falsehood."[6] The appeal of al Zarqawi's historical analogy among jihadists is apparent once put in the context of their overall fight. "The jihadists are convinced that they are reliving the time of the life of the Prophet," explains Nick Fielding, senior correspondent of the *Sunday Times*, "that they are part of the fight between Mecca and Medina."[7] Thus, what to us looks merely like an historical comparison is, to al Zarqawi and his followers, their daily reality. They exist outside the metaphysical boundaries of the Western world.

Initially, no other Sunni group involved in the resistance supported al Zarqawi's condemnation of the Shi'ites. The Sunni insurgency, far from being sectarian, had all the characteristics of a counter-Crusade, an insurgency against a foreign occupying power. Nobody was interested or willing to fight another enemy. Opening a new front against the Shi'ites also shocked al Qaeda's leadership. Osama bin Laden was very much in favor of a united front of all Muslims against the Americans, not only in Iraq but everywhere. Even al Maqdisi, al Zarqawi's former mentor, had abhorred the idea of Muslims fighting Muslims. To the majority of Sunnis, al Zarqawi's vitriolic rhetoric against the Shi'ites was not only incomprehensible, it was unjustified and unfair.

Even before the official war in Iraq started, Shi'ite groups had maintained an ambiguous relationship with the Americans. None of them had "embraced" the occupation. On the contrary, they had all, in various ways, voiced their dissent. Al Sadr's followers had gone so far as to take up arms against Coalition forces. It is hard to deny that Sunnis and Shi'ites had a common enemy, and so, in the summer of 2003, it was possible that, under the umbrella of Iraqi nationalism, Shi'ite insurgents would unite with their Sunni counterparts against the occupying power. Iraq had already experienced a similar phenomenon. In 1920 both groups had cooperated and staged a nationalist uprising against the British. As in the past, the united front would have strong secular and nationalist connotations. It was precisely to avoid this outcome that al Zarqawi decided to target the Shi'ites.

The idea was to drive a wedge between the two insurgencies to prevent any cooperation and alliance between Shi'ites and Sunnis that might leave the jihadists on the fringes of a strong nationalist, secular movement. But the Mongol analogy was not enough to ignite a sectarian war. Thus al Zarqawi used the concept of takfir to accuse the Shi'ites of apostasy. "Community of Islam, you must know that the schism does not belong to Islam," he said. "They [Shi'ites] have always been a thorn in the heart of Islam."[8] To reinforce this statement, he presented them as enemies, people who had forged a political alliance with Coalition forces. "The Shi'ites have done terrible things. They work with the United States against a purely Sunni state."[9] Al Zarqawi went so far as to rename them *al Rafidin* (rejectionists), explains Gilles Kepel, a French professor of Islamic studies, and to speak of the Shi'ites as though they are non-Muslim, worse than the Americans, Europeans, and Israelis.[10] In reality the only Iraqis who had "embraced" the Americans were the exiles who had advised the Bush administration, people who were as unpopular with Iraqi Shi'ites as with Sunnis.

Al Zarqawi's propaganda campaign was relentless and included special fatwas against the Shi'ites. The fight against the Iraqi Shi'ites became part of a much bigger battle between good and evil, between his vision of the world and the one projected by the enemies of Islam.

From spring 2003 to summer 2004 this rhetoric was reinforced by the different treatment given to the Shi'ite insurgency vis-à-vis the Sunni resistance. Thus the contraposition between Shi'ites and Sunnis assumed clear political connotations. Although both Coalition forces and Shi'ite moderate groups condemned Jeish al Mahdi as a terrorist group,[11] there were continuous efforts to bring al Sadr's militia back into the "legitimate" political arena of the new Iraq. Shi'ite political forces close to the transitional government protected Moqtada al Sadr because they were conscious of the power he exercised over the masses. The popularity of the young preacher, coupled with the widespread dissatisfaction of the Iraqi population with the transitional government prevented the criminalization of the Shi'ite insurgency and set it completely apart from the Sunni insurrection. Coalition forces as well as the international media not only accepted this situation, but also promoted a policy that predominantly criminalized Sunni insurgent groups.

Scholar Nadine Picaudou warns of the danger of viewing the context in which the armed confrontation between Sunnis and Shi'ites took place in Iraq as a problem solely of religious dogma. "It must be analyzed within the relationship of power between these two groups. There is a struggle to control the future of Iraq, the new state, among groups who use their Sunni and Shi'ite origins as a political tool."[12] In this context, Professor Kepel poses an interesting question: is Abu Mos'ab al Zarqawi a jihadist or a seditionist?[13] Most likely he is a seditionist, someone who wants to tear apart Iraqi national identity to create a new state, a racially pure Sunni regime. This explains how, in the context of a political, and not religious, conflict between Shi'ites and Sunnis, al Zarqawi the seditionist eventually was able to win over Ba'ath loyalists as well as Islamo-nationalists.

Against this scenario, al Zarqawi's attempts to group the Shi'ites together with the Americans should be regarded as a tactic to drag the Sunni community into a sectarian war, a revolutionary jihad, while maintaining the fight against the Americans. Strategically, suicide missions, the most spectacular and effective terror weapons, were used to drive this wedge between the Shi'ite and Sunni resistance deeper and deeper, and to provoke Shi'ite retaliation.

Thus in insurgent Iraq, for the first time, the two interpretations of the modern jihad—the revolutionary jihad and the counter-Crusade—merge. Al Zarqawi resolved the dilemma of the jihadist movement. From spring 2003 to fall 2004, the nature of the Iraqi jihad and the role of the Shi'ites was the main topic of discussion between al Zarqawi and Osama bin Laden, thanks, among other things, to the ruthless campaign of kidnappings and beheadings carried out against Western hostages that boosted the Jordanian's profile as a terror leader in Iraq.

THE CRIMINAL INDUSTRY

On 4 March 2005, Nicola Calipari, an Italian special agent, secured the release of journalist Giuliana Sgrena from a group of Iraqis who had been holding her captive. While driving her to freedom, their car came under fire. Calipari died protecting Sgrena with his own body. The world stood in shock when it became clear that the bullets had been fired by American soldiers guarding a road block near Baghdad's airport. Amidst mounting criticism, George W. Bush launched a partial investigation into the shooting.[14]

The tragic incident added to the general confusion about the kidnapping industry, a booming business in Iraq since the fall of Saddam Hussein. Common criminals—most of them freed from prison after the victory of the Coalition forces—as well as terror groups are part of this industry. According to Ali Faysal, the head of the Iraqi kidnapping unit, the groups include families of criminals and gangs of students.[15] Criminals are another main player in the Iraqi nightmare; they are motivated by money and will work with or for anybody.

Tragically, kidnapping is a daily occurrence in Iraq. Contrary to what many believe, the majority of kidnappings are carried out by criminals, and over 70 percent of the victims are Iraqis or people from neighboring countries. They include doctors, engineers, and business-men.[16] More recently the children of rich families have been targeted. Official data from the Iraqi government show that over the eighteen-month period ending in January 2005, one in five thousand Iraqis was kidnapped; only a few of them worked for Western companies. Police forces are simply overwhelmed by the number of people who disap-pear. Often they do not even start an investigation.

According to Colonel Yabbar Anwar, head of the anticrime unit in Baghdad, the main objective of the kidnappings is financial; accusing the victim of a connection with Western companies is merely a strat-egy to force relatives to pay the ransom. Ransoms range from just a few hundred to half a million dollars. The authorities are convinced that these kidnappings have nothing to do with funding insurgent groups.[17]

Terror groups use hostages primarily to inflame Western public opinion, not to raise money. Hostages are released only if the politi-cal demands attached to their freedom are met. Thus a fundamental difference exists between criminal and terrorist motivation. In "Wisaya li-l-mujahedin" ('Recommendations for the Mujahedin'), al Zarqawi explains this disparity. "We have decided not to free these infidels [hostages] even if they pay a ransom equivalent to their weight in gold. We do not compromise in front of God to free prisoners in exchange for money. . . . The enemies of God must be told that in our heart there is not mercy for them: either if they are set free or if they are beheaded." Referring specifically to the kidnapping of Nico-las Berg, he adds, "Some mediators attempted to convince us to let him free in exchange of a large sum of money. Even if we needed the cash, we decided not to take it and revenge our sisters[18] and our commu-nity."[19] To justify the beheading of hostages, al Zarqawi then made reference to the Prophet who, according to some interpretations, gave the order to kill prisoners after the battle of Badr.[20]

Terror groups are part of the kidnapping industry only when they get involved in the commercialization of hostages, that is, when groups exchange prisoners amongst themselves for cash, arms, and ammunition. This is not a new phenomenon. During the civil war in Lebanon, Western hostages were frequently bought and sold. Hussein Kemal, in charge of intelligence for the Iraqi Ministry of the Interior, believes that there are commercial relationships between Iraqi criminal and terror groups. "Sometimes terrorists pay criminal gangs to kidnap hostages, other times criminal groups sell the hostages to terror organizations; this happens when they play a political role or when relatives are unable to pay the ransom."[21]

In Iraq, as in Lebanon, the kidnapping industry flourishes in highly destabilized areas such as war zones where there is no strong central authority to administer law and order. What is relatively new is the recourse to kidnapping by jihadist groups. This practice was unknown during the anti-Soviet jihad. Political blackmail through hostage-taking springs from the introduction of terror techniques to the jihad. One of the first examples took place in Chechnya under Khattab, when three British hostages and one New Zealander were beheaded. The most dramatic case happened in the summer of 2004 in Beslan, where an entire school was held hostage.

Radical religious scholars have legitimized the kidnapping of Western hostages with several fatwas[22] that include reference to the beheading of hostages.[23] All armed groups active in insurgent Iraq have been involved in kidnapping. They use their own interpretation of these fatwas to justify targeting their victims. The Movement of National Islamic Resistance,[24] for example, took eight Chinese citizens hostage even though China was against the war in Iraq. They justified the kidnapping on the basis that China was helping the U.S. army, but eventually released them. Ansar al Sunna, an organization formed in September 2003 from the groups that had merged into Ansar al Islam, took twelve Nepalese hostages and killed them, showing the executions on the Internet. On 19 March 2005 the Patriotic Movement for the Liberation of Mesopotamia, a new group, claimed responsibility for the kidnapping of two Egyptian engineers in Baghdad. The group stated that the hostages "were working and cooperating with the illegitimate government of Iraq, which does not represent the Iraqi people but the occupying American troops." The statement ended with a chilling warning to the world: "We will show no mercy to anybody who enters Iraq, Arab or non-Arab, and works for the occupying power or for the new government."[25]

Widespread criminality contributes to the sense of despair of both Shi'ite and Sunni. It outlines the failure of the Coalition forces to bring peace and stability to the country.

CHAPTER TEN

The Iraqi Jihad

They are the enemies. Beware of them. Fight them.
By God, they lie.
—Abu Mos'ab al Zarqawi on the Shi'ites

On Friday, 29 August 2003, in Najaf, Yassin Jarrad, the father of Abu Mos'ab al Zarqawi's second wife, crashed a car laden with explosives into the Imam Ali Mosque. The explosion killed 125 Shi'ites who were leaving the mosque after prayers, among them Ayatollah Muhammad Baqer al Hakim, the spiritual leader of the Supreme Council of the Islamic Revolution in Iraq, head of the Shi'ite political party. Al Hakim had resided in Iran for more than twenty years before returning to Iraq in May 2003, after the fall of Saddam's regime. Many Iraqi politicians considered him a relatively moderate voice, who had called for unity among Shi'ite groups.

Symbolically, this attack marked the beginning of al Zarqawi's active fight against the Shi'ites, though its significance was not immediately understood. As mentioned in the previous chapter, the motive for the bombing seemed incomprehensible and those who carried it out were unknown. In the summer of 2003, Coalition forces were battling al Sadr's militia, considered the primary armed opposition, and the Sunni insurgency, primarily remnants of the Ba'ath party and Islamo-nationalists. This explains why al Zarqawi's name took so long to surface in the Western media.

The attack came a few days after a truck bomb exploded at the UN headquarters in Baghdad, killing the head of the UN delegation and several of its members. This bombing also carried the signature of al Zarqawi. Yet the connection between the two attacks escaped Western analysts. In August 2003, it was a common belief that the conflict in Iraq was a bilateral fight between Coalition forces and their supporters on one side and Moqtada al Sadr's Shi'ite militia and Saddam's loyalists on the other.

The fact that the two attacks came a few days apart is highly symbolic. From the outset, al Zarqawi launched his jihad on two fronts: one against the Coalition forces and the other against the Shi'ites. Thus, he made clear that the anti-Crusade and the revolutionary jihad were equally important aspects of the Iraqi jihad. For strategic reasons, he waited until August 2003 to broadcast his message to the world. According to one of his fighters, he did not want to get involved, nor did he want to kill Americans during the war. He could not compete with the B52s, missiles, and other high-technology weapons in America's arsenal. He waited until the situation in Iraq had calmed down and the occupation was in place. "To think that a man like al Zarqawi would not fight the Americans in Iraq is naïve," explained another fighter. "He prepared himself during a long period of time; he waited until Iraq was ready for the jihad."[1] Al Zarqawi also waited until his support network among the Sunni resistance was fully in place. As a foreigner, he was highly dependent upon it.

If the Coalition forces failed to understand the importance of the Imam Ali Mosque massacre, the Shi'ites sensed what was about to happen. Hours after the news of the bombing reached them, three hundred members of the Badr Corps, the armed wing of the Supreme Council of the Islamic Revolution in Iraq (SCIRI), departed Baghdad heading for Najaf. They wore militia-style uniforms and carried guns and rocket-propelled grenades.[2] The conflict between Sunnis and Shi'ites in Iraq had come into the open.

From the end of August 2003 until December 2004, when Osama bin Laden officially recognized al Zarqawi as the head of al Qaeda in

Iraq, al Tawhid wa al Yihad,[3] the armed group formed by al Zarqawi in Iraq, battled against the distant enemy, the Coalition forces, as well as against the near enemy, the Shi'ites. Al Zarqawi made a point of using the same terrorist techniques, ranging from car bombings to the beheading of hostages, against both enemies. During the same period, he continued to correspond with Osama bin Laden, the core of their dialogue centering upon the revolutionary jihad against the Shi'ites.

In a document sent in February 2004 to Osama bin Laden and Ayman al Zawahiri, al Zarqawi described the situation in Iraq. Beyond the heavy rhetoric and flowery style is a detailed political analysis of the Shi'ite forces and of their final objective. "The most important components of a state are 'security and economics,' which in Iraq have both fallen in the hands of the Shi'ites," al Zarqawi wrote. "Shi'ites control the institutions of the state, the security services, the army, and they have infiltrated the economic infrastructures of the country."[4]

Al Zarqawi's analysis of Moqtada al Sadr's political plan showed a great understanding of the true nature of the infighting within Shi'ite forces. The Sadr Brigade, he wrote, is a political and military force; its aim is to get even with the Sunnis. The violence unleashed by Sadr after the end of the war against the Coalition forces had now been extended to the Sunni population. The multifaceted scenario of the Iraqi conflict included the Shi'ites, and this was precisely the problem. While fighting the Americans was easy because they are visibly identifiable as they patrol the streets and man road blocks, confronting the Shi'ites was not easy. They look like us, al Zarqawi pointed out; they know who we are and where we live. Fighting them presented a real challenge. He had no doubt that their ultimate goal was to create a Shi'ite state in Iraq and subjugate the Sunni population.

Al Zarqawi expressed his concern to bin Laden that the insurgency might develop into a national resistance, with Shi'ites and Sunnis fighting together in a resistance that would necessarily be secular. These fears were confirmed in spring 2004, when al Sadr's revolt attracted admiration among Sunni insurgents. Pictures of the preachers were plastered on the walls of the neighborhoods where Sunnis lived. During the first attack against Falluja, rumors circulated that members of the Mahdi militia had tried to enter the city and fight next to Sunni insurgents. Thus, in his correspondence with bin Laden, al Zarqawi relentlessly stressed the need to prevent Iraqi Shi'ites and Sunnis from uniting around a genuine nationalism. If this were to happen, he concluded, the jihadists would be cut out because they were foreigners and the insurgency would become secular.[5]

How to avoid this outcome? For al Zarqawi the answer was simple. "If we can drag them [the Shi'ites] into a sectarian war, then we can wake up the Sunnis because they will understand the danger posed by the Shi'ites."

Al Zarqawi's analysis also suggested that the Americans were drawn towards the Shi'ites. They were convinced that they would defeat the insurgency only if they accepted that the Shi'ites would control the state. The trouble is that in the long run a Shi'ite state would inevitably be pro-Iran and presumably unfriendly to the United States. The Americans were, therefore, caught in a quagmire. This was partly due to the fact that in launching the war, they had relied on poor information from secular Shi'ite exiles abroad, whom they had proposed as their candidates to replace Saddam's regime. The Americans soon realized that these people were not welcomed by the population, and that they had to engage in a dialogue with Iraqi religious leaders, several of whom had spent years in exile in Iran. Unable to fight on two fronts, against the Shi'ites and the Sunni insurgency, and looking for an exit strategy, concluded al Zarqawi, the Americans would have no choice but to back the Shi'ite religious leaders.

It is hard to believe that a simple man from Zarqa could produce such a detailed and thoughtful political summary of the new Iraq. Many believe that among his followers there are well-educated people who have joined him since the growth of his myth and who are able to produce political analyzes and communicate his strategy with a high degree of sophistication. Al Zarqawi is still a man guided by his instincts; he may have great intuition, but ideologically and politically, he lacks the necessary strategic tools. Ironically, the myth constructed around him is at the root of his transformation into a political leader. With Osama bin Laden trapped in the tribal belt along the border between Afghanistan and Pakistan, Abu Mos'ab al Zarqawi became the new symbol of the fight against America, a magnet for whomever was looking to be part of the struggle.

As the dialogue with bin Laden progressed, al Zarqawi began to reveal his long-term plan. His strategy was to stop the Shi'ites by triggering a civil war on the grounds that they had pledged loyalty to the Americans, and by so doing, declared war on the Sunni population. Tactically, the revolutionary jihad had to take priority over the counter-Crusade because fighting the Shi'ites was the only way to get the umma, the community of Sunnis, to rally around the fight. Al Zarqawi's reference to the umma is very important. It shows that he lacks the authority to mobilize it: he is neither a preacher nor a scholar.

In addition, his relationships with the Iraqi ulemas, the religious authorities, before and after the battles of Falluja had been rocky. The religious leaders resented the fact that, after the first attack, his group had taken control of part of the city and had refused to avert the United States' second attack with his departure, as the Coalition forces had required. The ulemas wanted to save the city by accepting the U.S. ultimatum. This seems to confirm al Zarqawi's analysis as presented to bin Laden: the ulemas did not want to, or were unsure whether or not to confront the Americans.[6]

Relations between nationalist insurgents and the jihadists were also tense.

In early summer 2004, nationalist insurgents in Fallujah were about to assault a group of foreign jihadists based in the Jolan suburb and who were led by a Saudi with the nom de guerre Abu Abdullah. Later in the summer the insurgent "authorities" in Fallujah—largely made up of former military personnel and Iraqi police and led by clerics—succeeded in kicking out a number of non-Iraqi terrorists. But this did not resolve the tensions between them and native-born extremists who have the solid backing of a number of Salafi clerics within the city.[7]

The challenge, al Zarqawi argued in his letters to bin Laden, was how to get the ulemas to back the counter-Crusade against the Americans. Al Zarqawi offered a solution: to mobilize the umma, the Sunni population, by presenting the Shi'ites as enemies, as allies of the United States. He argued that the Shi'ites had already begun to criminalize the Sunnis by claiming their insurgency was being waged by Saddam loyalists. Under the pretext of hunting members of the old regime, he explained, both the Iraqi sectarian police and the army, composed of Kurds and Shi'ites from the south, had penetrated the Sunni Triangle where his bases were. There were only two possible alternatives: to fight them, which would cause tension among the local population because the Iraqi army and police are locals; or to leave and search for another country, as they had done before. Time was running out, he concluded. They must come to a decision soon, because each day their Shi'ite enemy was getting closer.

Why was al Zarqawi, the man who in early 2000 rejected al Qaeda, so keen from February 2004 onwards to get Osama bin Laden's approval? The answer rests on the fact that al Zarqawi lacked the religious authority to rally the Iraqi Sunni population around him against the ulemas. He desperately needed legitimacy and Osama bin Laden was the only one who could help him obtain it.

In February 2004 Osama bin Laden was conscious of al Zarqawi's motivations but failed to grasp the complexity of the situation in Iraq as described by the Jordanian. Most likely he relied upon other sources. According to Saad al Fagih, al Qaeda sent two hundred men to Iraq just before the war started to observe the situation.[8] These people established good relationships with members of the army who had strong

Islamic tendencies, possibly even with members of the Iraqi ulemas. As such, it is reasonable to believe that at the beginning of 2004, bin Laden could count on alternative sources of information, some of which may have disagreed with al Zarqawi's analysis. His reluctance to accept the Jordanian's views might also be related to arrogance. At the beginning of 2004 al Zarqawi was still a small fish in the jihadist pond.

THE TRIUMPH OF THE SHI'ITES

By the spring of 2004, the death toll in Iraq was beginning to hurt George W. Bush's political standing. Several members of the Coalition forces were looking for a way out of the conflict. Americans troops were overstretched and the White House asked the British army to help them fight the Sunni insurgency, which then posed the most serious threat to peace and stability in Iraq. Falluja, in particular, represented a problem, as the city was believed to be a stronghold of al Zarqawi's group, al Tawhid wa al Yihad. Against this background, Shi'ite moderates attempted once more to bring Moqtada al Sadr's forces back into the legitimate political arena. Washington welcomed this move. Now Shi'ites and Americans had a common goal: to clamp down on the insurgency before the November presidential elections in the United States and the Iraqi election in January 2005. With Moqtada al Sadr in the fold, Coalition troops could focus exclusively on the Sunni insurgency.

Shi'ite leaders, such as Ayatollah Ali al Sistani, who had pledged their support to the new regime and had backed the call for Iraqi elections, became instrumental in the dialogue with al Sadr. Negotiations lasted until early summer when a truce was reached. Then, on 5 August, tensions began to rise again. Moqtada al Sadr called on his followers to rise up again and fight U.S. troops. Clashes broke out in Najaf, Karbala, and Sadr City between the Shi'ite militia and U.S. and Iraqi security forces. The truce was clearly over.

By 6 August, the U.S. military estimated that it had killed three hundred militants in the city of Najaf alone; nineteen died in the streets of Sadr City. Moqtada al Sadr's spokesmen sent mixed messages: one saying that the preacher wanted to reinstate the truce and another urging his followers to fight on.

On 7 August 2004, Iyad Allawi, the Iraqi interim prime minister, issued a limited amnesty that pardoned insurgents who had committed minor crimes but had not killed anyone. To qualify for the amnesty, insurgents had thirty days to turn themselves in to Iraqi security forces. Thus Allawi offered an olive branch to Moqtada al Sadr, allowing him a chance to distance himself from the violence of his militia and to take part in the political process. "I have been having positive messages from Moqtada al Sadr," said Allawi in early August. "That is why we don't think that the people who are committing the crimes in Najaf and elsewhere are his people. We think they are people using his name. We invite, and I invite from this platform, Moqtada al Sadr to join the elections next year." Previously, Moqtada al Sadr had rejected invitations to participate in the national conference and national council and had shown no willingness to take part in the upcoming elections. His attitude at the beginning of August 2004 had not changed. On 9 August, in response to Allawi's offer, al Sadr vowed to fight the "occupation of Najaf" until the "last drop of blood" was spilled.

In the summer of 2004, al Sadr's rhetoric became distinctively anti-imperialist and nationalist. Under the religious banner, he used his sermons to meld economic, nationalist, and Islamic issues together. He packaged them as indictments of the Americans' intention to exploit the economy of Iraq and to oppress Arabs in defense of Israel. Using the wave of Shi'ite and Sunni insurgencies against Coalition forces that had shaken the country since the spring, he called for unity between the two groups. To win over the Sunnis, he declared that his final aim was to oust foreign powers and transform Iraq into an independent and free country.

Al Sadr's rhetoric was motivated by two main factors: his failure to attract the support of Shi'ite merchants and middle classes, and the military weakness of the armed wing of his insurgency. Although the cleric's popularity had grown, it had done so within his original constituency, the poorest segment of the Shi'ite population, a group that accounted for only 10 to 20 percent of a total population of twenty-five million. Moderate Shi'ites did not welcome the political vision of al Sadr. They rejected the idea of having politicized clerics, and they abhorred the use of violence. Economic considerations also played an important role among the commercial classes. In Najaf and Karbala, for example, money changers, hotel and restaurant owners, tourist guides, and anybody who stood to gain from the influx of pilgrims to the holy cities after the fall of Saddam's regime, strongly opposed the fighting in these cities. The insurgency was keeping away pilgrims, especially those who came from Iran.

Failure to gain support from these classes had greatly reduced the funding for al Sadr's insurgents, which explains the lack of military training of Sadr's militia. Though well armed—the country was awash with sophisticated weapons—the militia was unable to carry out guerrilla warfare, the house-to-house fighting at which the Sunnis excelled; they did not know how to maximize the advantages of urban guerrillas and lacked snipers, a vital element in urban warfare.[9]

In August 2004, al Sadr was able to overcome the above impediments by using the holiest places, such as the cemetery of Najaf and the Imam Ali Mosque, as strongholds for his militia. Americans were very wary of assaulting such sacred sites. By strategically outplaying the enemy, al Sadr thus checkmated the U.S. troops and the interim government despite having a weak militia and the support of only a fraction of the Shi'ite population.

Summer 2004 was the closest the Shi'ite and Sunni insurgencies came to forming a united front. However, the creation of a genuine, nationalist Iraqi resistance was not obstructed by al Zarqawi's terror techniques against the Shi'ites, but by one of America's key allies in Iraq, Ayatollah Ali al Sistani.

The August stalemate between al Sadr and U.S. troops prompted al

Sistani, who was still in London for health problems, to announce his return to Najaf with a proposal for a peaceful solution. On 26 August, an agreement was reached with Moqtada al Sadr.[10] Al Sadr's militia was allowed to leave the holy city of Najaf and all the sacred places in safety. The fighters were not asked to lay down their weapons, which were instead hidden, ready to be taken up again a few months later when, as we shall see, the militia began to engage in the counterinsurgency against the Sunnis. Members of the militia did not acquire a criminal record, nor were their names listed; they simply disappeared into the Shi'ite population. The U.S. troops withdrew and handed over responsibility for security to the Iraqi police force, which was composed of Shi'ites. The keys to the sanctuary were given to Ali al Sistani.

A few days later the Shi'ite religious authorities issued a fatwa to voice their opposition to any armed action against the forces of occupation. The fatwa was reinforced by al Sadr's call to his followers to cease the armed struggle and to participate in the political process in preparation for the elections of 30 January 2005. This action marked the end of the Shi'ite insurgency; American troops were now ready to concentrate on the Sunni resistance in Falluja.

Both the Bush administration and the Iraqi interim government considered al Sadr's entry into the "legitimate" political arena a great success. It was, however, a Pyrrhic victory. The removal of al Sadr's fighters from the insurgency would prevent the union of Shi'ite and Sunni insurgents under the nationalist banner, a scenario that terrified both the U.S. and the interim government; however, it confirmed al Zarqawi's claims that the Shi'ites were traitors. The Sunnis responded with sectarian violence. As the Shi'ite militiamen had not laid down their arms, they began to engage in ethnic violence that soon degenerated into ethnic cleansing. Thus the end of the "official" Shi'ite insurgency marked the beginning of a civil war inside Iraq, albeit one obscured by continuing conflict with the Americans.

In the spring of 2004, al Zarqawi had foreseen this scenario. In a letter sent to Osama bin Laden on 5 April he had put as a condition of their future alliance bin Laden's support for his strategy in Iraq to give priority to the fight against the Shi'ites.[11] Osama bin Laden waited until December 2004 to accept this condition. By then, events in Iraq had proved the correctness of al Zarqawi's analysis over and over again.

CHAPTER ELEVEN

Slipping into Civil War

*They [Shi'ites] have always been a thorn in the heart
of Islam.*
—Abu Mos'ab al Zarqawi

On 24 March 2004, American troops entered Falluja, encountering unexpected resistance. A week later, four employees of Blackwater Security Consulting were lynched by a mob, their bodies paraded through the streets of Falluja amidst cheering crowds in an episode eerily reminiscent of the killing of American soldiers in Somalia. For the United States and the world, Falluja came to symbolize the ultimate nightmare in Iraq.

By the time the first assault against Falluja took place, it had become clear that the Sunni resistance was engaged primarily in urban guerrilla warfare. Cities provided safe havens for the various groups involved in the resistance: loyalists of the Ba'ath party, Islamo-nationalist groups, and jihadists. Falluja, for example, was "a haven for the remnants of the regime of Saddam Hussein, which included mostly secular elements (members of the Ba'ath party, special forces, and former military and police). At the same time, it . . . attracted members of fundamentalist Islamic Iraqi organizations, such as Jaish Mohammad, Ansar al Sunna, Ansar al Islam, al Jaish al Islami, as well as elements of al Qaeda that have filtered across the borders."[1]

Guerrillas are unable to defeat conventional armies in open battle and therefore need safe havens from where to plot and launch their attacks. "From these locations guerrillas can treat the wounded, train and arm new recruits, and plan future campaigns without harassment. The Vietnamese used North Vietnam, Laos, and Cambodia as political safe-havens from American forces. Guerrilla armies from China to Cuba used inaccessible terrain such as mountains or dense jungles to hide from road-bound government forces."[2]

Logistical considerations are at the root of Iraqi insurgents' decision to use cities as their strongholds and battlefields. The north of the country, where the terrain is similar to Afghanistan and ideal for concealment, is controlled by the Kurds; the rest of the country is flat, crisscrossed by rocky desert areas. Cities, therefore, offer the best hideouts. Within them, guerrillas are able to find the support network they need. When the Americans wanted to arrest Moqtada al Sadr, he took refuge in Najaf, among the Shi'ites he represented. In Falluja, insurgents were widely supported by the majority of the residents and by the clerics.

The vast arsenal of weapons at the disposal of the resistance is also hidden inside the cities. According to Ibrahim al Jaafari, Iraq's prime minister, the Iraqi police have even discovered car-bomb factories in Baghdad.[3] Saddam Hussein is responsible for the quantity of arms, ammunitions, and explosives available in Iraqi cities. He had anticipated the possibility that a full-fledged resistance against Coalition forces would take place in Iraq and made sure that the country was awash with weapons before the official war began. He lifted the gun control law that was in place and distributed small arms to the population and to various militias. He hoped Iraqis would mount a Somali-like resistance against Coalition forces, along the lines of the lynching in Falluja. According to Scott Ritter, former UN weapons inspector in Iraq, "The Mukhabarat [the secret service], under instructions from Saddam Hussein, had been preparing for some time before the invasion of Iraq on how to survive, resist and defeat any U.S.-led occupation of Iraq. A critical element of this resistance was to generate chaos and anarchy that would destabilize any U.S.-appointed Iraqi government."[4]

Yet Coalition forces are also responsible for the large quantity of arms in the possession of the insurgents. After the official war was over, the occupation authority disbanded the Iraqi army without disarming it. "Many soldiers went home with their weapons, and explosives from unguarded ammunition dumps are being found among the equipment of captured insurgents."[5] The widespread looting that took place after the arrival of Coalition forces included Saddam's vast arsenal of small arms.

AL ZARQAWI'S BIG GAMBLE

Following the lynching, acts of resistance multiplied. The brutal killings galvanized the various groups involved in the urban guerrilla war until, on 5 April 2004, the American offensive against Falluja began. Ironically, its aim was to "pacify" and control the city. The attack lasted until the end of the month, when U.S. troops were forced to withdraw to the city's outskirts. The long siege—a preamble to the second major offensive of November 2004—had a tremendous impact on the collective consciousness of the Sunni population; it bolstered the Salafi jihadists' ideal of resistance and heroism. Thus, Falluja came to represent the Sunni bastion against the new Mongols.

In this atmosphere of heightened tension, al Zarqawi kidnapped and beheaded Nicholas Berg. This was the first of several kidnappings and brutal executions broadcast on the Internet. These acts became part of a counter-Crusade against Coalition forces, a clear response to the American military push inside the Sunni Triangle and, in particular, against Falluja.

The event immediately relaunched al Zarqawi's myth. While intelligence was busy involving him in all the major terror attacks in Europe, the Middle East, and North Africa, the chilling images of Berg's execution seemed to confirm his international status as a ruthless terror leader. Borrowing from Colin Powell's speech at the United Nations, several in the Western media described the beheading of Berg as the ultimate confirmation of al Zarqawi's links to al Qaeda. In reality, his entry into the business of kidnapping and beheading hostages was one of many strategies designed to build his status in Iraq and win the approval of Osama bin Laden for his plan to fight against the Shi'ites.

In beheading Nicholas Berg before receiving recognition or backing from al Qaeda, al Zarqawi took a big gamble. He undoubtedly evaluated the advantages and disadvantages of such a radical decision carefully. As stated in his message of 5 April 2004 to Osama bin Laden, he had two options: stay in Iraq and confront the opposition of some Iraqis to his methods, or leave and search for another country in which to wage the jihad. The kidnapping of Berg on 9 April was a clear signal that he had decided to stay and face the consequences with or without the approval of Osama bin Laden.

As anticipated, the reaction of the Iraqi religious scholars was negative. The already rocky relationship between al Zarqawi and Iraq's Sunni authorities reached a breaking point. In November 2004, the Association of Muslim Ulemas in Iraq (AMUI) publicly condemned the kidnapping and beheading of hostages as actions prohibited by the Sharia.[6] The spokesperson of the AMUI, Omar Galib, stated that al Zarqawi did not represent the Iraqi resistance because he was not an Iraqi and because he was part of al Qaeda, whose sole aim was to persecute Americans wherever they are. "The objective of the beheading," he added, "is to diminish the Iraqi resistance whose actions are limited to fighting against the occupying forces."[7]

In the following six months, al Zarqawi claimed responsibility for ten kidnappings—of American, British, Italian, Somali, South Korean, and Turkish citizens. He also took hostage several members of the Iraqi security services. Other groups followed suit. The gruesome beheading of hostages coincided with the unveiling of the brutal face of the Coalition forces: the abuses and humiliations at Abu Ghraib prison, the assaults on mosques, the assassination of civilians, including the cold-blooded murder of the wounded, and the home searches that violated the honor of Iraqi families.

Against this background, in spring 2004 the AMUI attempted to mediate among the Sunni resistance and the interim Iraqi government, and the American forces, a decision which contributed to the ulemas' loss of credibility. Al Zarqawi publicly denounced the ulemas, saying "the only thing they want is to appease the resistance, end the jihad and serve as a bridge so that the enemy can finish off the umma."[8]

The interim government attempted to reach an agreement to neutralize the Sunni insurgency, as it had done a few months before with Moqtada al Sadr in Najaf. Initial negotiations took place with the Falluja resistance. The interest of the Iraqi interim government in peacefully resolving the Falluja crisis rested on the fear that a prolonged armed conflict would jeopardize Sunni participation in the election, delegitimizing the final outcome. However, all attempts to repeat the successful resolution of al Sadr's revolt failed.

Various factors prevented a positive outcome. The interim government refused to accept the negotiating committee of Falluja as an authentic representative of the armed resistance, whereas the committee claimed that the government did not agree to accept merely a cease-fire to begin negotiations, but demanded a handover of arms, the entry of the U.S. army into the city, and the departure of foreign combatants.[9] When an agreement was finally reached on these points, the interim government of Iyad Allawi added a new demand—the handing over of Abu Mos'ab al Zarqawi—something beyond the power of the representatives of the city. As we shall see in the appendix, al Zarqawi was not in Falluja, nor had he been there during the first U.S. offensive. The request was interpreted by the negotiating committee as a way of sabotaging the talks.

As the negotiations were underway, the media latched on to the story of al Zarqawi's latest atrocities in Falluja. With the tacit backing of the Coalition forces and the interim Iraqi government (who wanted to play down the Iraqi nature of the resistance), they portrayed him as the ruler of Falluja and as the leader of the Sunni insurgency. Only at this point did terror sponsors in the Arab world begin taking him seriously, reports a Saudi source. Money from Saudi Arabia started to flow north to Iraq to fund his activities. According to Saad al Fagih, Saudis see Iraq as the new terrain of the jihad and are willing to fund it. There is mounting evidence that *zakat* (religious almsgiving) money and individual donations from Arab sponsors are reaching Islamist armed groups in Iraq via Islamic banks. Cash is withdrawn from bank accounts and delivered across the border by a fleet of couriers. One of the favored smuggling routes is via Syria. According to al Fagih, in February 2005 the son of a high-ranking Saudi politician was stopped near the border between Syria and Iraq with a suitcase containing $50,000 in cash. He was waiting to deliver the money to people linked to Abu Mos'ab al Zarqawi. According to bin Laden, the weekly operating cost of al Zarqawi's group in Iraq is 200,000 Euros.[10]

During the siege of Falluja, which lasted from April to November 2004, al Zarqawi's kidnapping and beheading of Western hostages, an activity that, according to the U.S. intelligence, took place in his Falluja stronghold, served to reinforce his myth. He came to be regarded as the supervillain of insurgent Iraq. At the same time, his myth assumed a new dimension in the Arab and Muslim world, where the Western media are met with deep suspicion. Segments of society came to regard him as the new hero of the anti-American cause. Jihadist Web sites all carried tales of his heroism. His life story captured people's imaginations: a child of Arab slums, a former petty criminal, a bully who through the study of the Koran was able to quote the great scholars and wise men of Islam, a man who had become the symbol of the jihadists' fight against the hegemonic power of the West.

By the summer of 2004, al Zarqawi's big gamble was beginning to pay dividends. His myth was growing fast and Osama bin Laden could not ignore it.

THE BATTLE OF FALLUJA

The second and final battle of Falluja officially began on 8 November 2004. Twenty thousand American soldiers were mobilized together with two thousand members of Iraq's national guard, whose presence was thought necessary to lend legitimacy to the assault. Sectarian groups were engaged in the battle, the Peshmerga as well as Shi'ites from the south. Some of the Shi'ites went into battle holding pictures of Ali, Hussein, and Hassan, their saints. Inside the city, whose civilian population had largely evacuated, five thousand fighters waited for the attack. The battle had been planned for months; relentless air strikes, which began in the summer, had cleared the road for the invasion.

Gradually, the United States and Iraqi forces pushed the main insurgent force into the southwest of the city, using a "hammer-and-anvil" strategy, carefully conducting house-to-house searches and securing areas of the city, block by block. The idea was to force the insurgents into the open desert where they would be without cover. By late November most of the insurgents had been killed or captured. However, pockets of guerrilla resistance lasted until January 2005, with insurgents hiding in tunnels dug before the battle began.

By the time the battle was over, Falluja resembled Stalingrad in 1943, a city in ruins. Over fifty U.S. soldiers had been killed and several hundred wounded. According to U.S. military estimates, as many as two thousand insurgents may have died. Reports suggested a heavy toll as well among the remaining civilians in the city.

The final victory was celebrated as a great success for both the United States and the interim government, which hurried to announce that Falluja's inhabitants could return to their homes. At the end of December 2004 the Organization of Muslim Ulemas in Iraq declared the city uninhabitable and denounced the government's statement as election propaganda. In April 2005, Falluja was still a ghost town.

Located at the heart of the Sunni Triangle, Falluja is about fifty-six kilometers west of Baghdad and held some 350,000 inhabitants. Situated on the highway linking the Iraqi capital with Amman and Damascus, the city was a commercial center and a location of strategic importance. It was known as "the city of the minarets" because of its many mosques.

The town's population had strong tribal cohesion entrenched in its traditions. The fiercely held conservative values of its inhabitants were reinforced by the active role played by the ulemas in the daily life of the people, especially after 1991. Falluja, like other Sunni cities, had always been a strong supporter of Saddam Hussein's regime. A large number of its inhabitants belonged to Saddam's Republican Guard and the special guard, while others were employed by the national intelligence agency. Back in 1991 it was one of the cities that refrained from participating in the uprising against Saddam Hussein. It later received preferential treatment in return.

Saddam's regime, which until 1991 had strongly repressed the Islamist currents in the city, considered Falluja a strategic point for the defense of Baghdad. According to Saad al Fagih, before the war started Saddam distributed arms and munitions to the population and trained them in guerrilla warfare. Al Fagih is convinced that it was the Iraqi resistance and not al Zarqawi's Salafi jihadists who battled against the Americans in the summer and fall of 2004.

This interpretation is in sharp contrast with the analysis of the Bush administration and the Iraqi interim government. They blamed al Zarqawi for the chaos in the Sunni Triangle that preceded the first battle of Falluja. Falluja, they claimed, had become "a city without law, controlled by the foreign combatants" who, thanks to the power vacuum, were able to create the Consultative Council of the Mujahedin (Majlis shura al mujahedin), which managed the affairs of the city.[11] The media wrote about the Islamic Republic of Falluja and yet residents offered reporters conflicting views: "Nobody knows who governs here, we cannot distinguish between reality and rumor. Some days ago they applied the Sharia law and imposed lashings on vendors of alcoholic beverages and on those who consumed them, and in the presence of the police . . . have set fire to shops selling CDs because they sold 'libertine' films. . . . This is done by the mujahedin. . . . They are cleaning the city of bad people." Another resident declared that the Consultative Council of the Mujahedin had issued a fatwa prohibiting the work of all political parties, adding that they had forbidden barbers to shave beards.[12] In the summer of 2004, Falluja was also singled out as the "international market-place for kidnapping."

The propaganda of the Coalition forces and the Iraqi interim government portrayed Falluja as a city taken hostage by al Zarqawi's jihadists, claiming that the population was hostile to his forces and would welcome American soldiers as liberators. By doing so, the Coalition forces and the Iraqi interim government attempted to delegitimize the Sunni resistance. This strategy has been tested before. During the anti-Soviet jihad, explained al Fagih, the Soviets claimed that those who were fighting them were not the Afghans but the mujahedin, foreign brigades, who had taken the entire country hostage. The truth was very different: the Afghans themselves represented the strongest component of the resistance against the Soviets.[13]

In his "Diary of Falluja," Abu Anas al Shami, a member of al Zarqawi's group (see appendix), confirms that the presence of foreign jihadists in the city was very small, representing just a fraction of the overall resistance. The diary also suggests that al Zarqawi was not in control of Falluja, and that jihadists and residents willingly fought together. Thus, it is reasonable to believe that in spring 2004, at the outset of the Coalition forces' renewed military effort in the Sunni Triangle, al Zarqawi's fighters and elements of the Iraqi resistance had forged an alliance. Their refusal to accept the January 2005 elections, which foreshadowed a major change in the balance of power inside the country, cemented their partnership.

This interpretation is confirmed by a statement issued at the end of November 2004 by the Ba'ath party. The message was directed "to the great Iraqi people and to our glorious Arab community regarding the bat-

tle for the liberation of Iraq and the heroic battle of Falluja."[14] It highlighted the uniting of the heroes of the "patriotic and Islamic resistance"
to "liberate" the country. The battle, whose protagonists were the "sons
of Iraq," had been a lesson in "valour, jihad, and moral values," according to the statement. The result was a well-planned, well-studied operation waged against the United States and its allies, "the traitor
government." The Ba'ath party then thanked all the Iraqi mujahedin for
their high level of coordination. To counter American propaganda,
which identified the resistance with al Zarqawi's jihadists, the party
pointed out that the battle of Falluja, "the city of sacrifice and the gateway to liberation," was carried out by Iraqi patriots and believers belong-
ing to the different resistance groups and from different tendencies, all
of which participated in the "revolution of liberation." The communiqué repeatedly combined the concepts of resistance and jihad.

Contrary to what has been said by the Iraqi authorities, during the
battle of Falluja, the Americans confronted a strong armed opposition composed of both popular resistance against the occupier and an
international jihadist brigade, motivated by strong anti-American sentiment. Thus the city became symbolic of Iraq's Sunni resistance
against the new Mongols and, at the same time, of the epic struggle
of the Salafi jihadists led by al Zarqawi. The battle transformed these
men into heroes of the Sunni world. Although Hollywood is planning to cash in on the American interpretation of the battle of Falluja—
that the city was held hostage by al Zarqawi—by producing a
blockbuster film centered upon the heroism of a U.S. army captain,
in the Muslim world and in some corners of the Western world the city
will forever be associated with the resistance of those, residents and
jihadists, who confronted U.S. and Iraqi forces.

AL QAEDA IN IRAQ

Heroes and martyrs are often closely associated with the physical
site—a city, a village, a building—of their martyrdom or heroic act.

Often these become places of pilgrimage, locations where people can be reminded of their heroic gestures even after the acts themselves are long gone. Stalingrad, Masada, and now Falluja are associated with the traumatic experiences of those who died defending them.

Insurgent Iraq is inextricably linked to the violent gestures of Abu Mos'ab al Zarqawi. While the West associates him with the most gruesome aspects of the war in Iraq and its endless atrocities, in the Arab and Muslim world the symbiosis between man and country takes on a different meaning. The more the United States demonizes him, the more he is singled out as the supervillain of terror, the more the media broadcast that he has been arrested or cornered by Coalition forces, is injured or even dead, the greater his supernatural myth grows. He is capable of surviving in the midst of the chaos of a country at war, and, at the same time, he is able to plan attacks all over the world and escape from his pursuers at the last moment.[15] He is the Arab Zorro, who belittles the Americans and demands the liberation of Iraqi women prisoners; he is the Arab hero of the battle of Falluja.

In reality he has a limited following in Iraq. He was unable to sabotage the elections in January 2005. He has many enemies among the Sunni population, including the ulema who, some insist, have been trying to kidnap him in an effort to neutralize his violent attacks.

Abu Mos'ab al Zarqawi's association with the battle of Falluja was the long-awaited test of his courage. He had been preparing for it all his life. It secured his role as a leader of the jihadist insurrection and valuable ally of the Sunni resistance. Against this background, Osama bin Laden's attention was fixed on the event and on the man who distinguished himself in battle.

After the battle bin Laden sent a letter to the inhabitants of the city, describing Falluja as a "heroine" who has taught the Americans a lesson reaffirming the power of faith, a power that is greater than "that of the missiles and the planes."[16] In the letter, he compared the massacre carried out by Saddam Hussein's regime in the Kurdish city of Halabja with the massacre of Falluja imposed by "the Pharaoh of our age," U.S. president George W. Bush. Bush, bin Laden charged, is responsible for the assassination of several thousand people in Falluja in the name of the "bloodthirsty Zionist crusade." The notorious Saudi then goes on to describe American military operations in the region as a "total war against Islam" and Muslims.

For bin Laden, the siege of Falluja was of positive consequence because it spread the spirit of jihad across Iraq and beyond its borders. Falluja "has entered into history through the great door," it has been converted into "an example of resoluteness and resistance to the American barbarians," it "has written a new page of glory into the history of our community of believers." For bin Laden, the victims of Falluja are martyrs, "some of whom," he specified, "I have had the honor to know."[17]

On 27 December 2001, in a communiqué broadcast by al Jazeera, Osama bin Laden finally granted recognition to al Zarqawi and agreed to support him in his fight against the Shi'ites. "The Emir mujahed, the noble brother Abu Mos'ab al Zarqawi and the groups which have united with him are the best [of the community of believers]. We are pleased by the brave operations they have carried out against the Americans and the apostate government of Allawi, as we are pleased that they have followed the orders of God and his Envoy in regard to unity. . . . We in al Qaeda welcome your union with us, it is a great step on the road to the unification of efforts of the mujahedin to lift the State of Truth and suppress the State of Lies . . . and so that it be known, the brother mujahed Abu Mos'ab al Zarqawi is the Emir of the al Qaeda organization in Iraq and the brothers of the group in the country should swear to him an oath of obedience. The last call is for the unification of the jihadi groups under a single standard which recognizes al Zarqawi as the Emir of al Qaeda in Iraq." Al Zarqawi was free to lead the insurgency towards a Sunni Islamic state with the blessing of the Great Emir, Osama bin Laden.

At the end of October 2004, the anti-American counter-Crusade and the revolutionary jihad against the Shi'ite-majority Iraqi government finally and officially merged. From the slums of Zarqa to the battle of Falluja, the extraordinary life of Abu Mos'ab al Zarqawi was celebrated by his greatest achievement, not his entry into al Qaeda as its emir in Iraq but rather giving the modern jihad a new meaning.

By nominating al Zarqawi the emir of al Qaeda in Iraq, Osama bin Laden effectively franchised the al Qaeda trademark. This phenomenon illustrates a new trend discussed by bin Laden's former personal bodyguard, al Bahari, in an interview with the London-based newspaper *al Quds al Arabi* published at the end of March 2005:

AL HAMMADI: Does this [the role of al Zarqawi as al Qaeda Emir in Iraq] mean that the Iraqi events created or might create a new al Qaeda organization?

AL BAHARI: This is possible. Al Qaeda organization will then be the brain guiding others. Sheikh Osama bin Laden has recently called on all armed groups to merge under the leadership of Abu Mos'ab al Zarqawi. Merger is a very strong trend. I believe that many organizations will come under the leadership of Abu Mos'ab al Zarqawi. Al Zarqawi and his small group alone could do much against the U.S. forces in Iraq, so imagine how things will be when all unite under one leadership. Bin Laden's endorsement of al Zarqawi as an Emir in Iraq means that al Qaeda organization is reshuffling its cards in Iraq quite well.

AL HAMMADI: In view of the current events in Iraq, do you think al Qaeda has a large presence there?

AL BAHARI: Yes, al Qaeda members are present in Iraq, but I do not know the size of their presence. Their presence is now clearer, especially after Sheikh Osama's call on all fighting groups in Iraq to join al Zarqawi's group and declare allegiance to him. I think this will expand the circle of al Qaeda activities there and increase the number of the members present there. After the fall of Saddam Hussein's regime in Iraq, many of the former Iraqi members of al Qaeda began to contact each other and form a united front to fight the U.S. forces there. They formed a nucleus for the ones who followed them in raising weapons against the U.S. invaders.[18]

Since October 2004, many groups, both in the West and in the East, have attempted to come under the umbrella of the new al Qaeda. What unites them is the new anti-imperialist ideology, al Qaedism, of which Abu Mos'ab al Zarqawi is one of the leading voices.

CHAPTER TWELVE

The True Nature of the Iraqi Insurgency

Guerrillas move among people like fish move
through water.
—Mao Zedong

The myth of al Zarqawi has been beneficial to the main combatants in the "war on terror": the United States, one of the myth's main architects, and al Qaeda, the subject of the myth.

The Americans were able to present al Zarqawi to the world as the link between al Qaeda and Saddam Hussein. This connection never existed but was deliberately constructed to justify the invasion and the regime change in Iraq, an opportunity that the United States had sought unsuccessfully for more than a decade. When the official war ended and the situation in Iraq degenerated, the legends woven around the life of the Jordanian gave the United States the opportunity to personalize the enemy, putting him in the same league as Saddam Hussein and Osama bin Laden, and providing a face behind which to hide the true nature of the Iraqi insurgency. Thus the terrifying myth of al Zarqawi allowed the Bush administration to reinforce the false notion of America's popularity in the Muslim world, a popularity supposedly boosted by its commitment to bring freedom and democracy in Iraq. For the average American, the Iraqi resistance is not represented by citizens rebelling against the yoke of occupation, but by al Zarqawi, an evil man, and his bunch of religious fanatics.

Al Qaeda was equally able to manipulate the myth of al Zarqawi to its own advantage. It successfully franchised its trademark in Iraq, a country where it had never had any support or connections. By crowning al Zarqawi the leader of al Qaeda in Iraq, Osama bin Laden became, in the eyes of the world, a major player in the insurgency. Ironically, while its leader was trapped in the tribal belt between Afghanistan and Pakistan, al Qaeda was able to steal the leadership of the Iraqi resistance from all the other groups. In a script reminiscent of the anti-Soviet jihad, what the media defined as Arab fighters, new mujahedin, and al Qaeda's jihadists took center stage in a conflict that increasingly resembles a sectarian war. This is the picture projected to the outside world from war-torn Iraq; however, the daily reality that confronts Iraqis is very different.

Far from being liberators, Americans are regarded as an occupying power. Most Iraqis resent them and wish they would leave their country. As for the myth of al Zarqawi, Iraqis have no illusions; they know that it was created by the United States and that it is an instrument in the hands of the military. "The actions of al Zarqawi have been used by U.S. forces as an excuse for bombing Iraqi towns," said Liqa Makki, an Iraqi political analyst. "If he were to disappear, U.S. forces would lose their pretext for such assaults and many Iraqi towns would be spared further misfortune."[1] "Double standards" and "bullying" seem to be the expressions most used by Muslims to describe American policy in Iraq.

Muslims also have no doubts about the nature of the insurgency: it is fueled by Iraqi nationals. They are aware of the attempts of al Qaeda and of the jihadists to manipulate the resistance and are conscious of their claim that Sunni insurgency is under their control. However, most people believe that the majority of the resistance is composed of residents of the Sunni Triangle, among which are people who were prepared and armed for the invasion by Saddam Hussein. Falluja was defended by Iraqi brigades, made up mostly of residents who were protecting their city and their houses, by Islamo-nationalists, and by former Ba'ath party loyalists. The jihadists, some from al Zarqawi's group and some from Iraq, were fierce and die-hard but a minority.

The Kurdish secret service agrees that the core of the resistance is nationalist and that the Ba'ath party plays an important role. Mosul is the party's new stronghold. More than one third of Saddam's officers came from this city. In the summer of 2004, the party was reorganized. It expelled more than half the membership, including anyone who had had dealings with the United States, the Iraqi government, or even humanitarian aid groups. "The new Ba'ath leaders are Mohammad Younis al Ahmad and Ibrahim Sabawi, [Saddam] Hussein's half-brother and the former head of Iraq's general security directorate. . . . The insurgents are using the infrastructure of the old Iraqi army," said Sadi Ahmed Pire, in charge of the Patriotic Union of Kurdistan's security operations in Mosul.[2] As long as the United States focuses on al Zarqawi, former members of the Ba'ath party are able to move freely.

Both Islamic groups and Ba'ath loyalists use Mosul as a base from which to access a network of people willing to carry out terrorist attacks. "They pay from $50 to thousands of dollars, depending on the tasks," Pire said. "There's 75 percent unemployment in Mosul. Maybe some of these young people are not terrorists, but they have to make some money."[3] Unemployment in Mosul and all over Iraq is skyrocketing, which makes young people very willing to be employed by armed groups.

The nationalistic nature of the insurgency in the Sunni Triangle is America's major obstacle to bringing the region under control. The battle of Falluja, for example, far from ending the insurgency, fanned its flames. Insurgents fleeing the city filtered into northern Babilon province, Mosul and Baghdad itself. As a result, violence increased sharply and engulfed the area. In this region, Coalition forces were attacked with mortars and helicopters were shot down with missiles. These semimilitary operations were carried out by the Iraqi insurgency, not by the jihadists—possibly by former members of Saddam's army and those trained by it.

Thus far, al Zarqawi's jihadists have masterminded the campaign of suicide and car bombings that mainly affects Iraqi civilians, predominantly Shi'ites living in the Sunni Triangle. The ranks of suicide bombers are made up largely of foreigners; many Arabs who enter Iraq to join the fight ultimately meet their end as human explosives. Tactically this strategy is aimed at maximizing their usefulness. Many of these people have no military training or guerrilla experience, several have never even used a weapon. To be deployed as fighters, they would need to be trained and al Zarqawi's group lacks the time and infrastructure to prepare them. The best possible usage is to make them blow themselves up in a crowded area. Their handlers look at them not as people or jihadists, but as weapons.

Direct confrontation with Coalition forces, on the other hand, is waged largely by Iraqis, not foreigners. In May 2005, reports from the U.S. offensive in al Qa'im on the western Iraqi border corroborates this view. Al Qa'im, with a mostly Sunni and Bedouin population, is located along the main road linking Jordan and Iraq, which was an important commercial artery until UN sanctions crippled the Iraqi economy. Al Qa'im is also a former industrial town built around one of Iraq's biggest chemical plants. The city is the last Iraqi town before the Syrian border, which is nothing more than an endless stretch of rocky desert shared by the two countries. It is impossible to patrol the area; only those who were born and raised in this desert know how to navigate it. Bedouin tribes still cross it in caravans. Because of its geography, the Syrian border is one of the most popular entry routes to Iraq. Though Americans have accused the Syrians of deliberately allowing Arab volunteers across the border to join al Zarqawi's group, the truth is that the United States and the newly trained Iraqi army are unable to seal the border because they simply cannot patrol it effectively.

"Military experts say that without stationing thousands of troops along the border, the military has little chance of controlling it."[4] In effect, the Americans blame the Syrians for their own failure.

When, in May 2005, the United States launched its offensive against al Qa'im, local Iraqis, not foreigners, defended the city. The LBC television correspondent in Iraq, Ahmad al Askari, was kidnapped with his crew for a few hours by a group of insurgents near al Qa'im, right after a major American operation against them had ended. While in captivity, Ahmad al Askari asked his captors if Arab volunteers had been flocking from Syria to join them. One of them replied, "God be praised, you have been in this place and you have not seen any Arabs. But this is the excuse of the infidel enemy."[5] The reporter and the crew believe that they were prisoners of a group of Iraqi insurgents; the captors explained that they opposed the Iraqi government because it was apostate and that they wanted an Islamic state. The captors were loosely linked to, but were not members of, al Qaeda in Iraq.

Although blindfolded, the correspondent and the crew guessed where they were. "Our journalistic sense gave us the feeling that we were in a big base for armed men who opposed the United States."[6] Al Qaim is near one of the largest phosphate mines in the Middle East; the porous, phosphate-bearing rocks beneath the town are honeycombed with caves, some as high as a cathedral, and tunnels. This is an underground maze navigable only by locals. Most likely the insurgents use the mines as their headquarters, a location from which they have eluded capture.

Scott Ritter, former UN weapons inspector, believes that the myth of al Zarqawi has also been beneficial to the Ba'ath party. He claims that sources in Iraq have revealed that "the Bush administration's singling out of al Zarqawi prior to the war, highlighted by Colin Powell's presentation to the Security Council in February 2003, made the Jordanian an ideal candidate to head the Mukhabarat's disinformation effort. According to these sources, the selection of al Zarqawi as a front for these actions was almost too easy. The Mukhabarat was desperate for a way to divert attention from the fact that it was behind the attacks against Iraqi civilians. Iraqis killing Iraqis would turn the public against the resistance. It needed a foreign face, and al Zarqawi provided it. A few planted CDs later, and the al Zarqawi myth was born."[7]

Although this interpretation is extreme and fails to take into account growing Islamist feeling within Iraq, it is unquestionable that the U.S. counterinsurgency strategy has focused on al Zarqawi and his followers. This has resulted in much less attention being dedicated to other insurgent groups. Kurdish officials concur that the myth of al Zarqawi benefited the Iraqi Ba'ath party, which remains the driving force of the insurgency in Mosul and in the surrounding area. They confirm that the majority of people they have arrested are Iraqis, not foreigners.

Beyond the myth of al Zarqawi there is a much more frightening reality made up of complex forces: independent Iraqi jihadist groups that gravitate towards al Qaeda in Iraq; Islamo-nationalist and Ba'ath party resistance fighters opposing Coalition forces; ethnic conflict among the Sunni, Shi'ites, and Kurds; fully armed and active ethnic and religious militias; and an endless stream of foreign suicide bombers. This is the scenario that may well haunt Americans for decades; it is the true nature of the Iraqi insurgency.

THE PLAYERS IN "DEMOCRATIC" IRAQ

Despite the January 2005 elections, America's Iraqi allies are deeply ambiguous about the presence of foreign troops and the meaning of the new democracy; this reality is beginning to filter through to the Western media. In a *New York Times* editorial published on 15 May 2005, America's confusion about the fractured nature of the insurgency came through strongly. The author questioned the motivation of the insurgency and admitted to being puzzled by the fact that the various players are seeking different goals. "The insurgents in Iraq appear to be fighting for varying causes: Ba'ath party members are battling for some sort of restoration of the old regime; Sunni Muslims are presumably fighting to prevent domination by the Shi'ite majority; nationalists are fighting to drive out the Americans; and foreign fighters want to turn Iraq into a battlefield of a global religious struggle. Some men are said to fight for money; organized crime may play a role."[8] To this list one may add sectarian militias pursuing ethnic cleansing in strategic areas.

Faced with this scenario, American public opinion is at sea. The media have failed to explain the final aim of the insurgency, as, clearly, getting rid of Coalition forces is not the sole objective. Far from following the classic model of insurgency and counterinsurgency of the Cold War era, Iraq resembles more and more the outburst of violence that plagued the Balkans in the 1990s. As in Yugoslavia, in Iraq a cluster of ethnic groups, deeply suspicious of each other, had been kept inside the borders of the same country by a strong dictatorship which used secular, socialist values to homogenize the country. The removal of the dictator unleashed forces that had been simmering for decades. The infiltration of jihadists groups and their targeting of Shi'ites acted as a catalyst to set off the "Balkanization" of Iraq. This may well be al Zarqawi's terrifying legacy.

Although the media reports that the insurgency is powered by Sunnis, Shi'ites from Sadr City ignited it. Today all players are still engaged in violence. Because the jihadists control the suicide bombers' "spectacular" operations, as they are defined in the jargon of the Coalition forces, these foreign Sunni fighters receive disproportionate media coverage. On any given day in Iraq, hundreds of kidnappings, beatings, and killings take place; these actions, however, are carried out by ethnic militias, paid criminal gangs, and civilians, often in retaliation for kidnappings and murders.

This was the case with the Khudair family. In March 2005, rumors spread in central Baghdad that twenty-six-year-old Sab'ah Nisan Khudair had insulted the name of Imam Hussein, one of the most important imams of the Shi'ites. Soon after, the family received a note insulting them as Sunnis. A few days later Sab'ah was kidnapped.

"What came next has become typical for Iraq as sectarian tension and violence rise. Khudair's family formed an armed group of more than twenty relatives and neighbors who demanded Khudair's release and vowed to kill those responsible. 'If something happened to my brother, no Shiite would be safe,' Khudair's brother, Sameer, said at the time, convinced that Shiite militia members were behind the kidnapping."[9] Sab'ah's body was found a few days later, dumped in the street. The body showed signs of torture; death was due to a shot in the face. While the family mourned Khudair's death, on the rooftop of the house stood a group of relatives with AK-47s.

Behind the extraordinary outbreak in violence that has followed the January 2005 elections there are three main Iraqi forces: the Kurds, the Shi'ites, and the Sunnis. None of them is a homogeneous force and each group is deeply divided over how to deal with Coalition forces and neighboring powers, such as Iran and Saudi Arabia. They all share a common uncertainty about the future Iraqi state.

THE KURDS

Since the end of 2001, America's best allies in the effort to bring about regime change in Iraq have been the Kurds in northern Iraq, who account for anywhere between 15 and 20 percent of the population. Today, they continue to show pro-American sentiment and an almost unanimous distaste for anti-Coalition violence. However, Kurdistan is protected by its own militia, including the Peshmerga, an informal army that fought against Saddam's regime. Even after the January 2005 election, the Peshmerga were not dismantled or merged into the Iraqi army; they remain independent and fully armed. Thus far they have cooperated with the Coalition forces and the new government. In 2003, they were instrumental in the destruction of Ansar al Islam in Iraqi Kurdistan; they have been used by the Americans and by the newly elected government to fight the Sunni insurgency, and they were employed to guarantee security on election day. However, their loyalty is not to the new democratic Iraq, but to those who fund and arm them in Kurdistan. The use of ethnic militias is a clear sign of the weakness of the Iraqi army. Vice President Abd al Mahdi admitted that "it is essential to use all our people's forces, the Peshmerga and Badr forces, and the Iraqi army and Iraqi police. If these forces are plunged into the battle, we will correct the imbalance we have witnessed so far."[10] But what if ethnic tension explodes within the elected political parties? The sectarian militia will immediately engage in ethnic clashes.

Politically, Kurdistan is split between two parties, the Kurdistan Democratic Party (PDK), and the Patriotic Union of Kurdistan (PUK), which dominated the parliament elected in 1992 but has been inactive since 1995. According to a survey held by ABC News, the PDK has 11 percent of Iraqi support and the PUK 10 percent. The PDK stronghold is in the northwestern part of Iraqi Kurdistan, while the PUK has support in the southeastern part of the region, near the Iranian border. The Kurds of northern Iraq demand a unified and ethnically homogeneous region, an autonomous area that will administer its own natural resources. However, due to the richness of the region, Iraqi Arabs oppose this. If the Kurds decide to break away, the Sunni and Shi'ite militias will not hesitate to assert their right to exploit these resources.

Though twenty-five political parties have been formed in Iraqi Kurdistan since the invasion, two blocs have emerged: one consisting of Kurdish political parties, the other of Islamic political parties. Thus, inside the Kurdish ethnic enclave, religious forces are also at play.

THE SHI'ITES

America's other allies in Iraq are the Shi'ites, Iraq's largest ethnic group. The Shi'ite population lives mainly in the south and in parts of western Iraq. About 63 percent of Iraqi Shi'ites live in the western region, which is also populated by a Sunni minority. Persecuted during Saddam's regime, the Shi'ites welcomed the arrival of Coalition forces;

before March 2003, about 50 percent of them believed that "the U.S.-led invasion was right. This claim was supported particularly by Shi'ites in the Mid-Euphrates region (56 percent), compared to Shi'ites elsewhere (44 percent)."[11]

A report from the Israel-based International Institute of Counter Terrorism (IICT) research center, published at the end of December 2004, confirms that the Shi'ite political landscape, far from being homogeneous, is varied and patchy.

> Many of the Shi'ite parties and militias have had overt or covert help from Iran. Eastern cities like Baqubah and Sadra came under Shi'ite control soon after the fall of the Ba'athist regime, apparently with backing from Iran. The Iranian-backed Supreme Council for Islamic Revolution in Iraq (SCIRI) has amassed enough popular support in some cities, such as Kut, to be a force to be reckoned with. Nasiriyya appears to be virtually ruled by the. . . al Daawa Party. Iran is reportedly backing the return to Iraq of many Shi'ite Kurds, or Failis, who fled to Iran under Saddam Hussein's regime. A Faili militia from Iran is reported to have taken over the eastern city of Basra.
>
> Thus many Shi'ite-majority areas are now controlled by religiously-oriented factions [some loosely linked to Iran]. The secular Shi'ites have been increasingly marginalized in this process, due in part to the fact that, unlike the religious factions, they have not organized themselves into parties and militias. Among major Shi'ite population centers, only in Basra is the influence of the secular Shi'ite middle and working classes still felt.[12]

The increasingly religious character of the Shi'ite ruling factions hinders a smooth normalization in Iraq. Some Shi'ites seek the formation of an Islamic state, similar to Iran; this is a source of constant conflict with the Sunni and Kurdish populations who refuse to be ruled by ayatollahs or by a strict imposition of Sharia law. Clashes occur daily as all the factions have their own militia. The ethnic divide risks forcing moderate and secular Shi'ites to support religious parties because they have the majority and are the main political bodies to guarantee a regime dominated by the Shi'ites.

Each Shi'ite group has its own militia. The SCIRI has the Badr Brigade, its military wing; Allawi and his followers can count on the Muthana Brigade; and Shi'ites in Baghdad have the Defenders of Khadamiya (this unit was created in northern Baghdad, with the primary task of guarding the Shi'ite shrine there). "There is good reason for the unit. The shrine at Khadamiya draws some 800,000 Shi'ite pilgrims each year and poses an attractive target for Sunni terrorists like Abu Mos'ab al Zarqawi eager to set off a Sunni-Shi'ite civil war. But some U.S. military officials worry it could be used in internecine battles between rival Shi'ite clerics. Because the Defenders of Khadamiya force appears so closely aligned with the prominent Shi'ite cleric Hussein al Sadr, some U.S. officers worry that other Shi'ite clerics might use the unit to justify forming their own unauthorized militias. In particular, radical Shi'ite cleric Muqtada al Sadr might try to revive his Mahdi militia, which U.S. troops battled in Najaf and Sadr City in summer [2004]."[13]

Informal armies and militias are a necessary protection in a country where the central authority cannot guarantee law and order and, are at the same time, a sign of destabilization. According to a report filed by Tom Lasseter, a Knight Ridder correspondent in Iraq, Adil Abdel Mahdi, Iraq's finance minister, a Shi'ite candidate for vice president, and senior leader of the SCIRI, expressed concern about militias roaming Iraqi streets: "Imagine if you had a political crisis and each militia will go and support their party or political force, then you would have a very critical situation," he said. "Instead of having a political crisis, maybe you would have more than that."[14] However, Lasseter noticed that security outside Mahdi's home and office was provided by the Badr Brigade. Badr members patrolling the street wore camouflage pants and carried AK-47s. The bodyguard in charge of Mahdi's security admitted to Lassiter that he did not trust the Iraqi police and preferred to use the Badr Brigades because he knew who they were and because they came from his ethnic and religious group.

Another dangerous sign of sectarian division is the systematic use of ethnic policing in the Iraqi streets. Falluja, for example, is patrolled only by Shi'ite troops. "In Baghdad's notoriously violent Haifa Street area. . . many of the Iraqi troops who patrol the Sunni neighborhood are Shi'ite. 'The Shi'ite people believe that we are a Shi'ite militia, and so they welcome us,' said Sameh Walid, a Shi'ite soldier based near Haifa. Another soldier, Haider Jawad, said Shi'ite neighborhoods on the edges of Haifa have formed militias to enforce the sectarian boundary."[15]

According to military analyst William Lind, the proliferation of Shi'ite militias whose task is to fight Sunni insurgents puts pressure upon Iraq's Sunnis to support the insurgency. "Add to this the use of Kurdish Peshmerga militias also against Sunni Arabs and there is an increasing likelihood that civil war may result."[16]

THE SUNNIS

Sunnis are the third player in Iraqi politics. Although they make up the majority of Muslims worldwide (above 90 percent), in Iraq they are a minority (about 20 percent). Sunnis have opposed Coalition forces from the beginning. "Most Sunni Arabs believe that at this point, Iraq needs 'a single strong leader' (85 percent), and not an Iraqi democracy (76 percent), while in the long run, the same amount of Sunnis (35 percent) would like to see an Iraqi democracy as a dictator-ship. Only 15 percent of Sunnis crave a religious theocracy."[17] Sunni militias are part of the resistance.

In "democratic" Iraq, a cluster of ethnic and religious groups, not al Zarqawi or al Qaeda, are at the root of the Iraqi insurgency. "Al

Zarqawi does not represent the Iraqi resistance," explained Liqa Makki to al Jazeera, "for one reason, because he is not an Iraqi and for another, because his ideological agenda differs considerably from that of the Iraqi resistance."[18]

However, his legacy—the merging of Saladin's jihad with the revolutionary jihad and the creation of an army of suicide bombers ready to die—is likely to influence the fight, forcing the players to come out into the open and retaliate, abandoning their support for or opposition to Coalition forces. If this happens, Iraq will be plunged in an outright civil war with strong ethnic and religious divides, similar to what we saw in the Balkans in the 1990s. Thus the myth of al Zarqawi could mark the future of Iraq. Even if he is caught and killed, the insurgency will not stop. On the contrary, his capture or death would enlarge his myth and strengthen his legacy.

CHAPTER THIRTEEN

The Balkanization of Iraq

*When a government has come to power through some
form of popular vote, fraudulent or not, and main-
tains at least an appearance of constitutional legality,
the guerrilla outbreak cannot be promoted, since the
possibilities of peaceful struggle have not yet been
exhausted.*
—Che Guevara

In mid-May 2005, a group of Iraqi scavengers discovered the corpses
of a dozen men while sifting through garbage at the local dump in
northwestern Baghdad. Some of the victims had been blindfolded and
shot in the head; others had their hands tied behind their backs. Families identified the bodies as farmers who had mysteriously disappeared
on their way to a market in Baghdad to sell their produce. The Association of Muslim Scholars, an important and well-known group of
Sunni clerics, denounced the killing as the execution of Sunnis from the
Madain region, about twelve miles southeast of the capital. Madain is
considered a Sunni insurgent stronghold inside what is known as the
Triangle of Death. This is an area where retaliatory kidnappings and
killings between Shi'ite and Sunni groups take place frequently.

Many Iraqis linked the killing to the discovery, a few weeks earlier,
of scores of bodies in the Tigris River, in the vicinity of Madain. The
victims had been executed in a similar fashion. At the time, the Iraqi
president, Jalal Talabani, denounced the murders as evidence of the

mass kidnapping and killing of Shi'ites in the area. However, when Iraqi security forces raided the town, no hostages were found, nor did they find the killers.

In "democratic" Iraq, it is increasingly common to find corpses of soldiers and civilians—who appear to have been executed and sometimes tortured before being killed—in dumps, mass graves, or on river beds. This is the latest chapter in the Iraqi insurgency.

Too often, the Iraqi authorities are reluctant to release the identity of the victims or to provide information about the killings. Overall, they tend to blame the common criminals and local gangs which operate freely in the highly destabilized environment. But no signs of robbery were found on the corpses in Baghdad or Madain. The most profitable business for criminals remains kidnapping and smuggling, not mass execution. What the government is afraid to say is that Shi'ite, Sunni, and Kurdish militias are all involved in retaliatory actions, including kidnapping, torture, and gruesome executions. The mysterious killings could well be the prologue to ethnic cleansing, similar to what took place in the former Yugoslavia. The majority of Iraqis fear that these killings are the work of death squads.

POP-UP MILITIAS

The proliferation of mass executions is a clear sign that ethnic tensions are rising. In "liberated" and now "democratic" Iraq, sectarian divisions have been woven into the political tapestry by the politics promoted by the United States, the new Iraqi elites, and al Zarqawi. Instead of cementing the national unity, the new democracy pulverized it, which in turn further encouraged the growth of ethnic factions. Sectarian forces have been institutionalized in the new parliament and government as well as inside the structure of the police and armed forces.

The presence of ethnic factions prevents Iraqi militia, intelligence, and secret services from trusting each other or the newly formed Iraqi police force. Kurdish officials, for example, claim that the insurgency has infiltrated all branches of Iraqi government. It has supporters and sympathizers among the police, the National Guard, the ministries, and the local governments and municipalities. Some people are black-mailed into passing on information, others do it willingly. Resistance infiltration is the reason sectarian officers do not exchange informa-tion with each other. "If we or the Americans get ready to launch an operation, the terrorists will know about it within an hour," said a Kurdish officer.[1] On 9 November 2004, for example, insurgents in Mosul took control of two-thirds of its police stations, leaving the city without protection. This was possible because several members of the police force cooperated with the insurgents.

These events are emblematic of the failure of the United States and the interim and new Iraqi governments to create a national Iraqi army and police force. So far this effort has cost $5 billion, paid predomi-nantly by American taxpayers. Often, American soldiers end up fight-ing Iraqis they have trained a few months earlier. During "Operation River Blitz," U.S. troops raided several towns along the Euphrates River, west of Baghdad. Finding insurgents dressed in police clothes, they rounded up and arrested members of the police force.[2]

At present, the Coalition-recruited Iraqi police force has no national identity and is in shambles. In March 2005, the police in Tikrit went on strike in retaliation for U.S. and Iraqi soldiers having raided their headquarters and arrested two officers. In Hit, police officers who had been dismissed because they were suspected of sup-porting the insurgency, demonstrated in the streets armed with Kalashnikovs in an effort to get their jobs back. In January 2005, a few weeks before the elections, both U.S. and Iraqi officials were franti-cally searching for new police recruits after thousands had resigned in protest against the U.S. occupation. According to the Americans, people left their jobs because they had been intimidated by members of the resistance. In November 2004 the Mosul police force num-bered five thousand members; by mid-January 2005 it was down to one thousand. Similar mass resignations took place all over the Sunni Triangle.[3]

Against this background, both U.S. and Iraqi authorities are using irregular armies and militia, better known as pop-ups, instead of the regular Iraqi army. In February 2005, the *Wall Street Journal* reported that "the pop-ups started to emerge last fall [2004] out of nowhere, catching the American military by surprise. These dozen disconnected units totalling as many as 15,000 soldiers are fast becoming one of the most significant developments in the new Iraq security situation."[4] On election day, 30 January 2005, security was entirely in the hands of pop-up militia, including Peshmerga and the Badr Brigade. Shi'ites, mostly from the south, were deployed in Sunnis areas.

The most famous pop-up militia is the Special Police Commando (SPC) whose origins extend back to the beginning of the Iraqi insurgency. On 11 December 2003, the *Washington Post* reported that CIA officers had held a meeting with Allawi to discuss the creation of "an Iraqi intelligence service." This organization had the task of spying on groups and individuals who were targeting U.S. troops and Iraqi allies working towards the formation of a new government. Members of the Iraqi intelligence service were carefully selected from former government officials, that is, former members of the Ba'ath party. On 20 June 2004, before he assumed the post of interim prime minister, Allawi held a press conference in which he announced that a major reorganization of security forces was taking place. He also specified that "special police units would be created to be deployed 'in the frontlines' of the battle against terrorism and sabotage, and [that] a new directorate for national security [would be] established."[5] The next day Major General Adnan Thabet al-Samarra was appointed as the new security adviser, tasked with creating a security force modeled on the former General Security Directorate (GSD), one of Saddam's intelligence agencies, ironically dissolved by the Coalition Provisional Authority in May 2003. The main task of the new GSD is to hunt down terrorists, and its personnel was selected from former members of Saddam Hussein's Mukhabarat, the infamous security services. In a bizarre twist of fate, Saddam's henchmen were given the task of hunting down Saddam loyalists, former colleagues who were organizing the insurgency.

Author Milan Rai argues that among members of the new regime are other prominent former members of the Ba'ath party. The minister of defense is Hazem al-Shaalan, a former Ba'athist from al Hillah, and Brigadier General Muhammad Abdullah Shahwani, an old-time Ba'ath officer, is now head of the Iraqi secret police.[6]

The GSD prepared the ground for the formation of the Special Police Commando, a de facto militia, charged with many counterinsurgency tasks. The head of the Special Police Commando is General Adnan Thabit, who took part in the failed 1996 coup against Saddam Hussein masterminded by Allawi. Thabit was imprisoned and released shortly before the U.S. invasion in 2003. Ironically, his right-hand man is one of his former jailers in the infamous Abu Ghraib prison. Thabit is the uncle of Iraq's former interim interior minister, Falah al Naqib, who also happens to be the son of a former prominent Ba'ath official.

General Thabit single-handedly created the Special Police Commando, initially a force of only thousand soldiers, billeted in the ruins of the former Republican Guard base. The commandos lived in bombed-out quarters without electricity or running water. Yet their arms and ammunition were impressive and very sophisticated. The SPC attracted the attention of the United States when high-ranking army officers went on patrol with Thabit's group and were so impressed that they decided to fund them. Today the unit numbers over ten thousand men, making it the largest army contingent in Iraq second only to the Americans.

Undoubtedly, the United States considers the SPC an important weapon against the insurgency. On 16 February 2005, Secretary of Defense Donald Rumsfeld, addressing the Senate Appropriations Committee, praised the militia as one of the most efficient forces fighting the insurgency. Some U.S. military officers, however, worry that the group's allegiance is as much to their leader as to the Iraqi government. "If you tried to replace General [Thabit] he'd take his brigades with him. He is a very powerful figure. You wouldn't get that from other units," said Colonel Dean Franklin, a senior officer in General Petraeus's command, to *Wall Street Journal* reporter Greg Jaffe. "Pound for pound, though, they are the toughest force we've got."[7]

THE SALVADOR OPTION

Iraqis are convinced that the Special Police Commandos are being used to conduct death-squad operations in what is becoming known as the "Salvador Option."[8] This strategy was launched by the Reagan-Bush administration in the 1980s to support El Salvador's right-wing security forces, including clandestine death squads whose task was to "eliminate" Marxist guerrilla leaders and their supporters. "Many U.S. conservatives consider the policy to have been a success—despite the deaths of innocent civilians."[9] The use of death squads predates the war by proxy in Central America. According to Scott Ritter, "the Salvador Option. . . has its roots in the Phoenix assassination program undertaken during the Vietnam war, where American-led assassins killed thousands of known or suspected Vietcong collaborators."[10]

The decision to employ death squads in Iraq is linked to the failure to quell the insurgency. In a *Newsweek* article published in January 2005, a senior U.S. military officer stated that "what everyone agrees is that we can't just go on as we are. We have to find a way to take the offensive against the insurgents. Right now, we are playing defense. And we are losing."[11] The idea is to punish the Sunnis, as was the case with the population of El Salvador, for supporting the resistance. "The Sunni population is paying no price for the support it is giving the terrorists. . . . From their point of view, it is cost-free. We have to change that equation."[12]

It is unlikely that the United States will be able to replicate the success of the wars by proxy it funded in Central America. Iraq is not El Salvador. It is awash with weapons and the insurgents have plenty of money; its population is better trained in guerrilla warfare and it is geographically located in a region deeply hostile to America. "The war in Iraq has undermined U.S. standing elsewhere in the Middle East and around the world. Images of U.S. soldiers sexually abusing Iraqi prisoners, putting bags over the heads of captives and shooting a wounded insurgent have blackened America's image everywhere and made cooperation with the United States increasingly difficult, even in countries long considered American allies."[13]

Unlike El Salvador, Iraq is a country in which the ruling elite has been obliterated and replaced with a new one that is ambivalent towards the Americans. In El Salvador, U.S. allies defended existing privileges that would have been lost without U.S. backing; in Iraq the new rulers are fighting for future privileges. Many Iraqis are not convinced that the best way to gain them is by fully backing a prolonged U.S. occupation. The Bush administration has also disbanded the former Iraqi army and the police force. Officers, soldiers, and policemen, people who had the necessary training to join the death squads, have instead entered the resistance or become part of sectarian militias. Thus a different dynamic exists in Iraq. U.S. forces are left with few reliable local allies to carry out counterinsurgency operations. They will have to rely on sectarian militia, such as the Special Police Commando, whose loyalty is to their leaders and not to the Americans. This option is confirmed by *Newsweek*, which reported, "one Pentagon proposal would send Special Forces teams to advise, support and possibly train Iraqi squads, most likely hand-picked Kurdish Peshmerga fighters and Shi'ite militiamen, to target Sunni insurgents and their sympathizers, even across the border into Syria, according to military insiders familiar with discussions."[14]

Another major shortcoming in an American counterinsurgency plan is that Americans and Iraqi authorities do not know the identity of insurgency leaders, hence the excessive attention given to al

Zarqawi and to the jihadists—a small minority inside the Sunni resistance. Neither the Shi'ite nor the Sunni insurgency has been infiltrated. Above all, the fight is not between two groups, but rather it involves an increasing number of factions, all of which are pursuing different goals using identical terror techniques, including death squads. Since the end of the official war, for example, sectarian militias have all been involved in the killing business, even among their own group. Al Sadr's militia has executed key players among moderate Shi'ites.

The Salvador Option may well backfire on the United States. It will unleash more killing and more mysterious mass executions and further destabilize the country. It will accelerate the Balkanization of Iraq.

PROS AND CONS OF SECTARIAN VIOLENCE

The Special Police Commando plays an important part in the Iraq's sectarian propaganda machinery. They have been supplying insurgents who confess their crimes on television. *Terrorism in the Hands of Justice* is the latest tool in the Iraqi government's slick counterinsurgency propaganda. It is broadcast six nights a week on the Iraqiya network, the national television station set up by the Pentagon.[15] According to the *Boston Globe*, camera crews are sent "wherever police commandos make a lot of arrests."[16]

The aim of the show is to demonize the insurgency. Suspects confess to participating in gay orgies, drinking alcohol, and enjoying pornography, and to offenses of rape and pedophilia, often committed inside mosques. Journalist and author A. K. Gupta reported, "[A] preacher giving a confession said he was fired for 'having sex with men in the mosque.' [. . .] The show is said to be popular, particularly among many Shi'ites and Kurds, which causes concerns that depicting Sunni Arab nationalists as 'thieving scumbags' could deepen communal strife. Political and religious leaders from the Sunni Arabs have denounced the show, calling for it to be pulled off the air. The show has explicitly promoted sectarian tensions, in one case airing the confession of a member of the Iraqi Islamic Party, a Sunni-based grouping, saying he drinks alcohol and doesn't pray."[17]

Interior Minister Falah Naqib told the *Washington Post* that the show "has shown the Iraqi people the reality of those insurgents, [that] they are criminals, killers, murderers, thieves."[18] This "reality" makes the case that the insurgency is guided and controlled by Islamist extremists, criminals who commit any type of crime, including against their own religion, and not by Iraqi nationals who in "democratic" Iraq have been plunged into a nightmare much worse than Saddam's brutal dictatorship. The "official reality" bears very little resemblance to what is actually happening in Iraq. While the U.S.-Iraqi propaganda machine claims that the insurgents are targeting civilians, killing indiscriminately, that their leaders are foreign jihadists, among whom al Zarqawi is by far the most prominent figure, official statistics belie this version of events, proving that the bulk of the attacks are directed against Coalition and Iraqi regular and irregular forces.

On 22 December 2004, the Center for Strategic and International Studies in Washington, DC, issued a report titled "The Developing Iraqi Insurgency: Status at End-2004."[19] The report states: [The U.S.] was slow to react to the growth of the Iraqi insurgency, . . . to admit it was largely domestic in character, and to admit it had significant popular support." From September 2003 to October 2004, the number of attacks on Coalition forces far exceeded any other type of attack, including al Zarqawi's suicide missions against Shi'ites. Attacks against Coalition forces, predominantly U.S. military forces, accounted for 75 percent of all attacks, versus 4.1 percent against civilian targets.

This trend did not change in the first quarter of 2005. Similar data was reported on 11 April 2005 in a *New York Times* article titled "U.S. Commanders See Possible Troop Cuts in Iraq" that included a graph categorizing resistance attacks by target. From March 2003 to March 2005, it showed that the majority of attacks were carried out against U.S. and Coalition forces. The source of the data is the U.S. defense Intelligence

Agency. Attacks conducted in the summer of 2005 confirm these data. During the first week of August, twenty-two U.S. soldiers were killed in ambushes. Sadly, these statistics have gone unnoticed because the number of civilian casualties greatly outnumbers military casualties. Clearly the damage potential of a suicide bomber is much greater if the target is a busy market rather than a military armored vehicle.

In the past, the myth of al Zarqawi was systematically used to justify a war that even the United Nations had declared illegal. Today it is used to blur the true nature of the Iraqi insurgency. This policy has greatly influenced the evolution of the resistance inside the country. To prevent the formation of a united national front against the occupying powers and the new political elites backed by them, al Zarqawi's attempts to drive a wedge between the Sunni and Shi'ite insurgent groups have been manipulated by the United States and Iraq's new political elite. They have been presented as the core of the insurgency. The proliferation of armed groups was not deliberately fostered by the Americans; rather, it emerged from the failure of Shi'ite and Sunni groups to cooperate. Instead of a united national resistance, sectarian forces have been unleashed: ethnic and pop-up militias, private clan-armies, death squads, jihadists, Islamo-nationalists, Ba'ath loyalists—the list of groups is endless.

In June 2005, the U.S. administration admitted that military victory in Iraq might not be possible, and that its representatives have attempted to enter a dialogue with some members of the Sunni insurgency. In the long run negotiation with insurgents may well be the sole option. But the real question will be with which groups to negotiate. The Balkanization of Iraq is multiplying the players, enlarging the fight, and spreading political violence. Ironically, had the insurgents in Iraq been able to unify under the banner of a nationalist secular movement, al Zarqawi would not have been able to influence events in Iraq and today both Americans and Iraqis could be facing each other across a table instead of trying to dodge bullets on yet another bloody day in "democratic Iraq."

The Next Myth

*Secretary of State Colin L. Powell has offered a $5
million reward to encourage individuals to come forward with information regarding Mustafa Setmariam Nasar. Mustafa Setmariam Nasar, also
known as Abu Mos'ab al-Suri, is an al Qaeda member and former trainer at the Derunta and al-
Ghuraba terrorist camps in Afghanistan where he
trained terrorists in poisons and chemicals. Nasar is a
Syrian with dual Spanish nationality.*
—U.S. government statement[1]

Immediately after the 7 July 2005 London bombing, the Pentagon led
the press to believe that al Zarqawi was somehow involved in the
attack. Later that month, only hours after a tourist hotel was bombed
in the Egyptian resort of Sharm el Sheikh, U.S. intelligence claimed
that Osama bin Laden had masterminded this new wave of attacks. But
although some terrorism experts in the media were happy to go along
with this story, the idea that either icon of the jihadist movement was
a prime mover in both bombings is highly improbable.

The London bombers appear to have had no direct links with the
remnants of al Qaeda's leadership nor with al Zarqawi's organization.
The former are trapped in the tribal areas of Pakistan, while al Zarqawi
himself can only operate with any degree of security in the Sunni
regions of Iraq. Yet the Bush and Blair administrations desperately

need to present al Qaeda as a conglomerate of ruthless people, headed by a leader; they want to continue to personalize the enemy. This portrayal is superficial but comforting, because it implicitly relieves the citizens of the West from the burden of understanding that adherents to a violent anti-imperialist ideology are attacking both the West and the East. To prevent Westerners from being confronted by this reality, governments have projected an image of the jihadist movement not as a political movement with deep roots in the history of the Arab Middle East and of the wider Islamic world, but as an inexplicable and exotic criminal conspiracy.

Such is the need to maintain the connections between al Zarqawi and Osama bin Laden and the latest wave of terrorist attacks that we may well see another myth launched to provide the all-important continuity.

After the London bombing, one line of investigation centered upon the possible role that Mustafa Setmariam played in the attack. Setmariam is not a new name in the jihadist universe. It has surfaced more than once in pronouncements on international terrorism by the U.S. administration. Former member of the Muslim Brotherhood, ex-mujahed in Afghanistan, ex-functionary in various ministries of the Taliban government and many more things, Mustafa Setmariam has all the attributes for becoming the new inspirational leader of the jihadists. Setmariam's whereabouts have been unknown for some years, an ideal scenario for spreading rumors about him. Some sources say that he is with al Zarqawi in Iraq,[2] others that he is in Pakistan, others that he may even be in Afghanistan. Has he really fought in Iraq together with al Zarqawi? Like the infamous Jordanian, he seems to be in many places at once.

Both the U.S. administration and Western media now accuse Setmariam of being behind the most brutal terrorist attacks of recent years—9/11,[3] 11 March 2004 and possibly the recent London bombing.[4] They also claim that he was in charge of a terrorist camp in Afghanistan specializing in chemical warfare[5] and that he is one of the founders of al Qaeda and a member of the al Zarqawi group.[6] The analysis seems to be based more upon rumor than fact, replicating the myths and legends constructed around Abu Mos'ab al Zarqawi. Some have already described Setmariam as "one of the most dangerous Islamist terrorists of the Salafist movement in the Near East," attributing to him all the terror attacks carried out by the jihadists in Europe and in the Arab world.[7]

Setmariam was born in the Syrian city of Aleppo in 1959. Like many other young people who opposed the regime of Hafez al Assad, he joined the Muslim Brotherhood as part of the Fighting Vanguard, a group which sought direct armed confrontation with the government. The Muslim Brotherhood was severely repressed by the regime in 1982, provoking an exodus of its members, several of whom took refuge in various European countries. Setmariam, like many other Islamist Syrians, moved to Jordan and then, after being expelled from the Muslim Brotherhood, went to Peshawar to participate in the anti-Soviet jihad.[8] In Peshawar he formed a small jihadist group with some Egyptians; he also wrote *The Islamic Jihadi Revolution in Syria*, which was strongly critical of the reformism of the Muslim Brotherhood.[9] Setmariam met Sheikh Abdallah Azzam, with whom he worked in 1987 and the following year, after meeting Osama bin Laden, he joined al Qaeda. He remained active inside the organization until 1992.

In the early 1990s, Setmariam settled down in Spain, married a Spanish woman and started a family. In 1995, the family moved to London where he worked for the bulletin *al Ansar*, the official publication of the Algerian GIA.[10] Around 1998, he moved to Afghanistan, where he swore an oath of allegiance to Mullah Omar. There he worked for the ministry of defense, in charge of the al Guraba training camp, before transferring to the ministry of information where he was head of the Arab department of Radio Kabul and dedicated himself to writing newspaper articles and broadcasting radio programs. He turned more and more to research and jihadist studies and eventually founded the al-Guraba Study Center "to spread jihadist belief and preach worldwide resistance."[11]

With the fall of the Taliban in December 2001, the trail of Setmariam goes cold. According to his own account, he decided to go into isolation and dedicate himself in full "to reading and writing . . . to evaluate our previous jihadist experiences . . . with a view to modernizing them. . . . During all this time, in which I have moved from one place to another, I have done no activity other than study and write . . . and I hope to conclude my research at the beginning of 2005."[12]

In response to the accusations thrown at him by the U.S. secretary of state, Setmariam denies having any connection to, or prior knowledge of, the attacks of 9/11, although his statement expresses the wish that the 9/11 planes had been loaded with weapons of mass destruction. He firmly rejects reports in the Spanish press that he was the principal planner of the attacks in Madrid on 11 March 2004, and denies any connection with them; he also denies working with Abu Mos'ab al Zarqawi, whom he says he admires but does not know.

In his writings, as a result of his research on earlier jihadi experiences, he expresses the desire that Muslims defeat the United States by resistance and guerrilla warfare so that "every Islamic country and every city [would] be transformed into a Falluja'—underlining the important reference point which that Iraqi city now forms in the jihadist mentality—because the United States cannot possibly fight in hundreds of "Fallujas" at the same time. "This is the model of worldwide Islamic resistance which we preach,"[13] he added.

Is the myth of Setmariam the next in line, another item of terror merchandise made in America to feed the nightmare scenario projected by the leaders of the West? Will he live to prove that the U.S. government's latest prophecy has been fulfilled? America's leaders and its media have helped to create and embellish the myths surrounding first Osama bin Laden and then Abu Mos'ab al Zarqawi. These myths take on a life of their own to become self-fulfilling prophecies. Our leaders have created a cadre of elusive monsters whose followers we are forced to fight. Is Setmariam out there, working to create the apocalypse of which he speaks? Will he join, or has he already joined, forces with Osama bin Laden and Abu Mos'ab al Zarqawi in order to further the assault on the West whose culture, influence, and principles they commonly despise? What we have created may be beyond our ability to subdue.

Author's Afterword

In the famous cult television show *Star Trek*, new actors replace old ones in the generational renewal of interplanetary voyagers. What remains unaltered is the script, an endless intergalactic war between good and evil. The structure of the jihadist movement—of which al Qaeda is the most famous manifestation—and of its members mutate much like the cast of *Star Trek*. From one generation to the next, the sole constant element is the drama they stage for their audience in the Middle East and beyond. Their script is the noble and wholly righteous struggle against corrupt, godless elites in the Muslim world and their Western allies.

The newest generation of jihadists does not have direct links with Osama bin Laden. Its members are not part of the old network and have very loose contacts, if any, with jihadists from previous generations. Even their "political" formation differs from the indoctrination of those who preceded them. Drawing upon the anti-imperialist propaganda of the 1970s Marxist armed groups, the new generation has more in common with these organizations than with the mujahedin of the anti-Soviet jihad. Al Qaeda is no longer the organization envisaged by Sheikh Abdallah Azzam in the 1980s. It is not the vanguard of international brigades of Arab warriors, armies traveling the world to rescue fellow Muslims from hegemonic foreign powers. Nor is it a vehicle for the armed struggle against America, the distant enemy, and Arab regimes, the near enemy, as bin Laden and Ayman al Zawahiri had envisaged. Al Qaeda has become an ideology. Both al Zarqawi and Osama bin Laden are figures of immense symbolic importance, but they can hardly be seen as operational leaders of a global movement. In the words of al Zawahiri, bin Laden is "the new Che Guevara."

For the new generation of jihadists, bin Laden is the charismatic, distant leader who inspires them as, in the 1970s, Mao inflamed the hearts of the founders of Peru's Sendero Luminoso (Shining Path). Thus, rather than speak of al Qaeda today, we should speak of "al Qaedism," a militant, new, anti-imperialist doctrine that calls for a direct violent confrontation with the West, and preaches violence against civilians because, as citizens of democratic states, they are responsible for the policies of their leaders. In the 1960s and 1970s, Marxism inspired a small segment of youth in the West, Latin America, and some parts of southeast Asia to embrace political violence. In the same way, al Qaedism today exercises, among a minority of young radical Muslims, a powerful, messianic, violent appeal.

Since 9/11, the transformation of al Qaeda into a global ideology, and the generational mutations of those who have embraced it, are the by-products of the "war on terror," the made in America myth of al Zarqawi and of the politics of fear. Without a response of this type from the West, al Qaeda would have remained a terrorist organization like many others, with one distinguishing characteristic: its transnational nature.

Al Qaeda is known to have masterminded only a handful of transnational terrorist attacks: the 1998 bombing of the U.S. embassies in Kenya and Tanzania, followed by similar attacks against U.S. interests in Sri Lanka, Uganda, and South Africa; the attack on the USS *Cole* in the port of Aden in 2000; and 9/11. A transnational attack implies a movement of people and funds across countries. According to this definition, 9/11 was the last transnational terrorist attack bearing the signature of al Qaeda. As described in this book, the organization had already begun to mutate as early as September 2001, plagued by internal opposition to bin Laden's leadership and his obsession with attacking the United States. While inspired by al Qaeda, the bombings in

Bali, Casablanca, Madrid, and London should not be viewed as being cast from the same mould.

The invasion of Afghanistan and the defeat of the Taliban accelerated the disintegration of al Qaeda, forcing its leaders to run and hide in the tribal belt between Afghanistan and Pakistan. By the end of 2001, the al Qaeda that had been—a small, highly structured, armed group with a handful of men in command and a limited number of members—no longer existed. Consequently, the financial network that had supported the organization and funded its transnational activities disappeared, not because the West succeeded in curtailing it, but because the organization it nourished had disintegrated. What remained was the conceptual nature of al Qaeda, a creed preached by bin Laden and Ayman al Zawahiri.

While the West celebrated the defeat of the Taliban regime and the "victory" over Saddam's forces of evil, this creed became al Qaedism, an anti-imperialist ideology that inspired the jihadist movement, a global reservoir of young, disenfranchised Muslims. In 2003, the creation of the myth of al Zarqawi, presented by then–Secretary of State Colin Powell as the link between al Qaeda and Saddam Hussein, strengthened al Qaedism. Though al Zarqawi was not part of the original al Qaeda and no connection existed between bin Laden and Saddam, the simple fact that on 5 February 2003, at the United Nations, Powell presented him as the new global terror leader catapulted him to fame among the jihadists who—with bin Laden trapped in the tribal belt—needed an operational leader and a symbol of heroic resistance worldwide.

The prolonged war in Iraq, the proliferation of insurgent groups, and the formation of an Iraqi resistance strengthened the anti-imperialist nature of al Qaedism and became powerful recruitment tools for potential jihadists. Many went to Iraq to join in the fight; others, mostly those who were already based in Europe, sought opportunities to attack the members of Bush's Iraq Coalition at home. It is in this context that the Madrid and London bombings took place.

These factors helped shape the new anti-imperialist ideology as a global phenomenon.

Far from pacifying the world, the war on terror and the politics of fear have boosted al Qaedism. As during the Cold War, enlarging the menace of the enemy is beneficial to its followers. In order to address terrorist violence we must deny ourselves the reassurance of myth. Al Zarqawi, like Osama bin Laden before him, is a fictitious character, a coproduction of the U.S. government and the jihadist movement. By identifying the jihad with a few individuals, we promote the dangerous fantasy that terror can be fought and defeated through military action abroad and repression at home. The "endless" war in Iraq and the London bombings seem to confirm that military intervention and antiterrorist legislation, which greatly limit the liberties of citizens, are both inadequate and even irrelevant. Yet President Bush is adamant that American soldiers remain in Iraq until the country is "pacified" and Tony Blair has promised to introduce more limitations to the fundamental principles of British democracy to combat Islamist terror at home. The life history of al Zarqawi and of many of his followers should teach us that more than war and repression, governments need to pursue prevention policies. What is needed is a policy of truth, based upon solid evidence and through that, a better understanding of the nature and motives of the jihadist movement and of its ideology, al Qaedism. This will allow us to develop a new foreign policy— one which will respect the political will of Muslims instead of pursuing the interests of the corrupted, oligarchic, ruling elites and imposing Western democracies' "political parameters." A policy of truth will also enable us to pursue a domestic strategy focused not on the present generation of jihadists, but on the next, the one being forged today, the one as yet to fall into the web of Islamist terror indoctrination, the generation that we can stop from carrying out the next wave of bombings in our cities.

The Diary of Falluja

Maaraka al-Ahzab bil Falluja (*Memoirs of Falluja*) is a diary written by Abu Anas al Shami during the first battle of Falluja. At the time Abu Mos'ab al Zarqawi was far away, and al Shami wrote to him with daily detailed reports of the battle.

Born in 1969, and a Palestinian by birth, Abu Anas al Shami was a Jordanian citizen who had lived for most of his life in Kuwait. He was also known as Omar Yusef Yumaa and was a famous Salafi preacher. In March 2003 he was arrested in Jordan for teaching his students that the Jordanian regime had transformed the country into a U.S. military base and for inciting them to join the jihad in Iraq. Once freed, he crossed over to Iraq where he joined al Zarqawi's group and became its spiritual leader, in charge of fatwas.

Al Shami's diary begins by comparing the first battle of Falluja, in April 2004, to the battle of al Ahzab, which took place at the time of the Prophet. In April 627, a combined army of Jews (some residents of Mecca) and of nomadic tribes (that had not converted to Islam) laid siege to the city of Medina, where the Prophet was living. The siege lasted fifteen days and ended in failure. The coalition army had to withdraw without inflicting any losses on the Muslims.

> God wished Falluja to be a bastion for the heroes and the mujahedin of Iraq . . . until that tranquil city became a nightmare that permitted no sleep to the Americans and a terror that made their cots tremble at the mere mention of her name and the thought of entering her. . . .

Some ten days before the events and following the orders of chief Abu Mus'ab al Zarqawi, the military council met in the city to review the situation and study recent developments. The result was painful and difficult, because we realized that after a year of jihad we still had achieved nothing on the ground. None of us had even a palm-sized lot of earth on which to reside, no place to find refuge at home in peace amongst his own. We hid during the day and came out at night like cats . . . we had all abandoned our homes, our families, to become wanderers [in foreign lands]. Homes had been assaulted, heroes expelled.

The outlook was bleak and all felt that they had failed resoundingly. A quick solution and change of plan was needed. So we decided to make Falluja a safe and impregnable refuge for Muslims and an inviolable and dangerous territory for the Americans which they would enter in fear and leave in shock, pursued and burdened with their dead and wounded.

We decided to divide the groups into brigades which would go out at night and sleep during the day, to watch the fringes of the city. . . . [T]his task was divided amongst the mujahedin, those from outside [foreigners], as well as the Iraqi mujahedin.

According to al Shami, following these changes there was a wave of enthusiasm to renew the fight against the Americans, a "longing for honor and Paradise [martyrdom]." Then the American columns advanced and the armed assault began; the sound of the mortars "announced the beginning of a new war." "Tanks and planes bombarded the city until the infidels realized that this was the most violent battle since the fall of the departed regime . . . and then began the great earthquake, the mortal blow, the legend of the age. . . Some people lit bonfires and mutilated corpses to satisfy their hearts in a display of anger which kept them from listening to reason [the lynching of four employees of Blackwater Security Consulting]. . . . It was an amazing scene which had not been repeated since the events of Somalia." Al Shami argues that Islamic law prohibits the mutilation and cremation of the dead.

Al Shami continues his tale in a style that blends apocalyptic visions with adventure. "The atmosphere was electrifying, overcast by dark clouds charged with a latent black hate, you could hear the whistling of the serpents which slithered in the dark of night to surround the mujahedin . . . the din of the war drums had closed the political horizon and the ears of the politicians were deaf to reason and to a peaceful solution." Then news circulated that the Americans had prepared a refuge for the inhabitants of Falluja to try to end the jihad: "We discussed the matter, studying the possible options . . . if we should abandon the city or remain in our positions defending the truth. We felt that this was a very important battle and the Americans were determined to make of it an exemplary punishment for all the cities." According to al Shami, the jihadist leadership decided to maintain their positions and carry on spasmodic attacks.

The writer is careful to mention the names of the mujahedin who fell in the battle of Falluja, victims of U.S. cluster bombs, such as the Yemeni Khattab whose body "exhaled the scent of musk." He also mentions deeds of heroism and comradeship like those of Thamer Mubarak al Dulaymi, a member of one of the most powerful clans of al Anbar who commanded the attack against Baqer al Hakim, and many suicide bombers. Al Dulaymi went out to gather the corpses of his companions, despite the efforts of others to prevent him, and died as he said the following words: "If it is for God, we know neither fear nor cowardice." Another who met his death was one of the mujahedin most dear to al Zarqawi, a Jordanian from the city of Salt, Nidal Arabiyyat, also known as Hamza Abu Muhammad, who had been his companion-in-arms in Afghanistan, Kurdistan, and Baghdad. An explosives specialist, Arabiyyat prepared almost all the car bombs used in the suicide attacks. According to al Shami, the death of Arabiyyat was also heroic: "The American soldiers broke into a house in which various mujahedin were staying when they were distracted (God wanted them this way so that they could fulfill their destiny [martyrdom]); . . . the mujahedin escaped and Hamza stayed back to protect them. With his pistol he finished off a good number of American soldiers but he died in a rain of bullets. The house smelled of musk and the people came to smell it, old and young wept and the spirit of the jihad spread throughout the neighborhood."

As the combat grew more and more intense, al Shami claims that some people, "the dross," began talking about the need for the mujahedin to leave Falluja as requested by the U.S. army.

Al Shami says that the non-Iraqi mujahedin preferred to live clandestinely. They were afraid that someone might denounce them, so they hid from the local population. Yet the guerrilla fight went on. Attacks carried out by smaller groups, seven or eight fighters, spread throughout the city. The groups were made up of Kuwaitis, Saudis, Egyptians, Libyans, Yemenis, and Iraqis. Some fighters came from Baghdad to support the mujahedin of Falluja. Combat actions took place everywhere; near the cemetery, al Shami describes Abul Ala al Ansari, a mujahed from Falluja, firing the first bullet "which announced the beginning of a new jihadi period in which fear disappears and where a bird confronts an elephant"—a reference to the use of a rocket propeller against a U.S. armored car.

Al Shami praises the goodness of the population of Falluja who cooperated with the mujahedin. He talks of an old lady who allowed the fighters into her house so that they could observe the enemies' movements. She quickly prepared them something to eat. These were examples of "the generosity of the Iraqis in general and of the population of Falluja in particular and the warm welcome they extend to guests."

Empty houses were used for cover by snipers. When American sharpshooters found them, they called for air cover to bomb them. "Once a group of mujahedin, about seven fighters, came out alive from the bombing of one of the houses covered in a cloud of dust, like the dead resuscitated."

Identical scenes of combat took place at all the entry points to the city. "American columns advancing and mujahedin dressed with the armor of death, playing with the vicissitudes of war, defending the community of believers and drawing with the fire of their weapons the smiling dawn of Islam."

Al Shami claims that many of the Fallujans supported the mujahedin, yet the silent majority was undecided, which made the situation a bit difficult. Al Shami decided to take action and asked the imam of al Furqan Mosque to let him preach to the people, to call them to jihad. The imam accepted. Many other imams disagreed with him and advised the people to stay in their homes between seven in the evening and seven in the morning, instead of listening to the call to jihad. Al Shami concludes that these imams are agents of the occupation.

While the fighting continued, al Zarqawi consulted al Shami and others in Falluja by letter. He wondered if he should go to Falluja "to fight with the rest. He insisted but all the brothers believed that he should not do it; we asked him not to do such a thing due to the great concern we had for his safety and to avoid the Americans becoming more and more brutal if the news should get out that he was in Falluja. But we were in daily contact with him by means of his courier, Abu Abd el Rahman, from the province of Ramadi. He went back and forth every day, either by boat, or swimming, avoiding the bullets." According to al Shami, in addition to taking al Zarqawi's letters, Abu Abd el Rahman carried arms to Falluja and supervised the passage of mujahedin into the city.

Al Shami recounts that in one of the skirmishes in which he was involved he lost his old sandals. "They were broken and destroyed. Al Zarqawi had insisted many times I should get a new pair but I did not want to because they were a gift from someone from Medina whom I greatly appreciated. I didn't want to give them up. Al Zarqawi always joked with me and said: 'I don't know how a mujahed can fight with those sandals.' . . . That day I wrote to al Zarqawi informing him that his wish had been fulfilled, I had lost my sandals. Despite the bombings we joked and laughed as if we were amongst our own, safe and sound."

Eventually U.S. troops withdrew from Falluja. To bring an end to "the revolution of Falluja," the American administration opted for negotiations between the Iraqi transitional government and the Islamist leadership. This proposal was accepted by the Islamic party. At al Zarqawi's request, al Shami did not participate in the negotiations. "Al Zarqawi wanted the heroic inhabitants of the city themselves to represent Falluja." He also thought that the absence of his group from the negotiations would deter reprisals against the population. However, al Shami participated indirectly, consulting with the delegation in secret; "there were constant messengers between us and al Zarqawi. . . . Afterwards the media described al Zarqawi's role as that of a mujahed who claimed to speak in the name of the 'patriotic Islamic resistance' [two irreconcilable concepts for al Shami] and stated that he represented a broad spectrum of mujahedin who declared acceptance of the truce." Al Shami claims that al Zarqawi's followers only represented a small group of combatants, about fifteen, all of whom had fled the combat zone. "In this way," he concludes, "the true will of the mujahedin of Falluja was distorted."

Abu Anas al Shami died in September 2004 in Baghdad during an American attack near the Abu Ghraib prison when he and his men attempted to liberate the detainees held there.

Author's Note on Sources

In recent months, several Web pages cited in this book have been obscured or are no longer online. Many others cited will disappear in the future. I have tried to provide the reader with references of the original sources, most of which came from jihadist Web sites, some of which are no longer accessible. Whenever possible, I have also provided secondary sources, from newspapers and books. I have kept a hard-copy archive of several primary sources and copies of original documents as well as translations provided by other people. The resources I have used are so voluminous it would be impractical to list them all here.

For many Arab sources I have used the FBIS (Foreign Broadcast Information Service) reports through Thomson Dialog subscription; their valuable archive is accessible at most public libraries. English translations of the transcripts of all the documentaries in Arabic I have used as sources are available through the FBIS archive.

Patrice Barrat has supplied me with an unpublished English translation of the transcript of Fouad Hussein's LBC documentary *Abu Mos'ab Zarqawi, from Herat to Baghdad* and with the unpublished transcript of the interviews for his documentary "*Zarqaoui: la Question Terroriste.*"

A source who wishes to remain anonymous gave me a translation of the "Dairy of Falluja," excerpts of which appear in the appendix.

Glossary

Anti-Soviet jihad: The war fought by the Afghans and the Muslim warriors (mujahedin) against the Soviet invasion and occupation of Afghanistan from December 1979 to February 1989. The war ended with the defeat and withdrawal of the Red Army.

Arab-Afghans: Term originally used to distinguish between Afghan and Arab Muslim fighters in the anti-Soviet jihad. It now includes all Muslims who joined the fight.

Caliph: Title of the chief Muslim civil and religious ruler who protected the integrity of the state and the faith. The caliphs were regarded as the successors of Muhammad. However, they were not prophets as Muhammad was the last prophet. The term derives from the Arab *khalifa* meaning successor. Caliph was also the honorary title adopted by the Ottoman sultans in the sixteenth century, after Sultan Selin I conquered Syria and Palestine, made Egypt a satellite of the Ottoman Empire, and was recognized as the guardian of the holy cities of Mecca and Medina.

Caliphate: The dominion or rule of the caliph.

Comintern: Acronym for Communist International, name given to the Third International, founded in Moscow in 1919. Vladimir Ilyich Lenin feared a resurgence of the Second, or Socialist, International under non-Communist leadership. The Comintern was established to claim Communist leadership of the world socialist movement.

Crusades: A series of military campaigns fought by Christian armies from Western Europe to reclaim the Holy Land from Muslim control. Towards the end of the eleventh century, Pope Urban II launched the First Crusade, which introduced the concept of a war sanctioned by divine power (the motto of the Crusaders was "*Dieu le veult,*" God wills it). Between the eleventh and thirteenth centuries there were eight crusades, and the knights who took part in them believed that they were assured of a place in heaven. For Muslims, the Crusades were a sustained military campaign to expand the territory of Christendom and eliminate Islam.

Diaspora: The term originally described the Jews living in scattered communities outside Eretz Yisrael (the Land of Israel) during and after the Babylonian Captivity (sixth century BC) and the later dispersion of the Jews by the Romans in the first and second centuries AD. In modern times the word refers to the worldwide community of Jews living outside present-day Israel. It also applies to any group of people dispersed from their country or region into other countries, such as the Palestinian Arab refugees.

Faqih: An expert in Islamic religious jurisprudence.

Fatwa: A technical term used in Islamic law to indicate a formal legal judgement or binding religious ruling made by a qualified Islamic scholar or jurist.

Fitna: Originally considered a trial or, a temptation to test the believer's faith, *fitna* now refers to periods of unrest and internal war within the Muslim community. It is often used in Islamic history with the specific historical sense of civil war.

Al Hakimiyya li-llah: The sovereignty of God.

Hizbollah: Derived from *Hizb Allah*, meaning "Party of God," the name of a major Shi'ite movement in Lebanon formed after the 1979 Iranian Revolution.

Imam: In general use, it means the leader of congregational prayers; as such it implies no ordination or special spiritual powers beyond sufficient education to carry out this function. It is also used figuratively by many Sunni Muslims to mean the leader of the Islamic community. Among Shi'ites the word takes on many complex meanings; in general, however, and particularly when capitalized, it indicates the particular descendant of the Party of Ali (see also **Shi'ite**) who is believed to have been God's designated repository of the spiritual authority inherent in that line. The identity of this individual, and the means of ascertaining his identity, have been major issues causing divisions among Shi'ites.

Islamic: Pertaining to the religion and teachings of Islam.

Islamism: Political ideology based on the legitimacy of the cause of Islam.

Islamist: Pertaining to radical and fundamentalist Islamic groups and ideology.

Jahiliyya: An Arabic word meaning "state of ignorance," usually applied to the pre-Islamic period. Today, it is used by radical groups as a term for impious rulers and societies.

Jihad: This term has often been translated as "Holy War," a concept coined in Europe in the eleventh century which refers to the Crusades and which has no equivalent in Islam. Jihad derives from the Arabic root of "striving'; therefore, a better translation would be "striving in the cause of God." There are two aspects of jihad: the greater jihad, fighting to overcome carnal desires and evil inclinations; and the lesser jihad, the armed defense of Islam against aggressors. The term has been used by different armed groups in their violent confrontations with the West; famously, Osama bin Laden called for a jihad in his fatwa against Americans, using the term as a "just war" against the oppressor.

Koran: The holy book of Muslims.

Kufr: Literally, infidelity or unbelief. The term is used to describe those who do not believe in Islam, i.e., infidels.

Martyr: Someone who is put to death or sacrifices his or her own life for a cause or religious belief.

Modern jihad: Modern interpretation of the jihad whereby it has become an instrument to fight the West. The modern jihad is an integral part of Islamist political violence.

Modern Salafism: Radical interpretation of Salafism. Strongly anti-Western movement which calls from the return to the purity of Islam.

Mufti: Religious jurist who issues judgements and opinions based on Islamic law.

Mujahedin: Plural form of the Arabic word *mujahed*, literally meaning "he who wages jihad." The term was applied to Muslims fighting the Soviet occupation of Afghanistan (1979-89), and has been translated as "holy warriors."

Mullah: A title of respect accorded to learned Muslim religious figures and jurists, from the Arabic *mawla*, master.

Muslim Brotherhood: Founded in Egypt in 1928, this association is considered the prototype for all modern Islamist movements of Sunni obedience. Present all over the world, the Muslim Brotherhood promotes a reformist Islam.

Ottoman Empire: The Muslim empire established at the end of the thirteenth century by Osman I, founder of a Turkish dynasty in northwestern Anatolia, and enlarged by his successors, known as the Ottomans, who took over the Byzantine territories of western Anatolia and southeastern Europe. At its height Ottoman power extended throughout the Middle East, parts of North Africa, and southeastern Europe, but the empire began to disintegrate in the nineteenth century and collapsed at the end of the World War I; the Anatolian heartland became the Republic of Turkey, and the outlying provinces were recognized as independent states.

Al Qaedism: A new, anti-imperialist ideology that is the product of the globalization of Osama bin Laden's anti-American message.

Salafism: A movement that takes its name from the words *al salaf al saleh*, meaning "pious ancestors." Salafists are expected to emulate the lives of the Prophet and the first three caliphs: Abu Bakr, Omar, and Othman. The Koran and Sunnah (the Prophet's words and actions) are their principal reference.

Shahid: Martyr

Sharia: The Holy Law of Islam. It contains all the rules (religious and secular) by which Muslims must live. The Sharia derives from the interpretation of the Koran and the Sunnah.

Shi'ite: A member of the smaller of the two great divisions of Islam, Shi'ism or Shia (from Shi'itet Ali, Party of Ali). The Shi'ites supported the claims of Ali, the Prophet's son-in-law, and his line to presumptive right to the caliphate and leadership of the Muslim community, and on this issue they split from the Sunnis in the first great schism within Islam in the seventh century AD. The Shi'ites, who are found especially in Iran, believe in Mehdi, an imam who will come out of hiding at the end of time to spread justice across the earth.

Shura: Meaning, variously, consultation, counsel, and consultative body, Shura generally refers to the Islamic council.

Sunnah: Literally meaning "trodden path," the Sunnah is the "customary practice" of the faithful deriving from the specific actions and sayings of the Prophet Muhammad himself.

Sunnism: The orthodox and largest section of Islam. It means "those who adhere to the Sunnah." After Muhammad's death, those followers who supported a traditional method of election based on community agreement became known as Sunnis; they were opposed by the Shi'ites.

Takfir: An accusation of apostasy.

Al Tawhid: The unity of God.

Ulema: Islamic scholars.

Umma: The community of believers which transcends national, ethnic, political, and economic differences.

Wahhabism: Name used outside Saudi Arabia to designate the official interpretation of Islam in Saudi Arabia. The faith is a puritanical concept of unitarianism (the oneness of God) preached by Mohammad ibn Abd al Wahhab (1703–92).

Zakat: The obligatory alms tax that constitutes one of the five pillars of Islam.

Bibliography

ARTICLES AND DOCUMENTARIES

Abu Mos'ab al Zarqawi, from Herat to Baghdad. Documentary by Fouad Hussein. LBC TV (Beirut), broadcast 27 and 28 November 2004, in Arabic.

Alvarez, Lizette. "Portrait of Three Suspects Emerges in Britain." *International Herald Tribune*, 15 July 2005.

Baram, Amatzia. "Post-Saddam Iraq: The Shiite Factor." Iraq Memo #15, Saban Center for Middle East Policy, 30 April 2003. www.brookings.edu.

Barnett, Anthony, Jason Burke, and Zoe Smith. "Terror Cells Regroup and Now They Target Europe." *Observer*, 11 January 2004.

Bazzi, Mohamad. "Newsday Exclusive: Where is al Zarqawi?." *Newsday*, 21 December 2004.

Bennet, James. "The Mystery of the Insurgency." *New York Times*, 15 May 2005.

Burke, Jason. "Fury at Muslim Talks in Memory of 9/11 Hijackers." *Observer*, 7 September 2003.

Campbell, Duncan. "The Ricin Ring that Never Was." *Guardian*, 14 April 2005.

"The City of al Zarqa in Jorda: Breeding Ground of Jordan's Salafi Jihad Movement." *al Hayat* (London), 17 January 2005.

Cockburn, Patrick. "Saddam's Agents 'Murdered Cleric." *Independent*, March 1999.

Colin Powell. Speech at the UN. Fox News 5 February 2003. www.foxnews.com.

Dillon, Dana R. "Insurgency Has Its Limits; Enemy Victory Is Far From Assured." *National Review*, 25 November 2003.

"The Event Program Discusses Developments, Surge in Violence in Iraq." LBC TV (Beirut), 15 May 2005 broadcast, in Arabic.

Freifeld, Daniel. "The Evolution of Salafi Thought." danfreifeld.com/salafi.htm.

Gambill. Gary, "Abu Mos'ab al Zarqawi: A Biographical Sketch." Special issue, *Terrorism Monitor* , 2, no. 24, 16 December 2004. www.jamestown.org/publications.

Garwood, Paul. "Zarqawi Stirred Violent Surge; U.S. Contends Allegedly Plotted in Syrian meeting." Associated Press, 19 May 2005.

Glover, Charles. "Smiles and Shrugs Speak Volumes About Nature of Attacks on American Troops." *Financial Times*, 25 September 2003.

Gupta, A. K. "Let a Thousand Militias Bloom." Indymedia, 21 April 2005. nyc.indymedia.org.

————. "Unraveling Iraq's Secret Militias: Ruthless U.S. Tactics are Propelling the Country Towards Civil War." *Z Magazine*. zmagsite.zmag.org/Images/gupta0505.html.

Hammadi, Khalid al-. "Al-Qa'ida organization from Inside as Reported by Abu-Jandal, Nasir al-Bahari. "Part 6 of a series of interviews with Nasir al Bahari, alias Abu-Jandal, Osama bin Laden's former personal bodyguard. *al Quds al Arabi,* 30 March 2005.

————. "Former Bin Laden 'Bodyguard' Discusses al-Qa'ida Training Methods," Part 5 of a series of interviews Nasir al Bahari, alias Abu-Jandal, Osama bin Laden's former personal bodyguard. *al Quds al Arabi,* 26 March 2005.

————."Former bin Laden 'Bodyguard' Recalls al Qa'ida Figures, Views East Africa Bombings." Part 9 of a series of interviews with Nasir al Bahari, alias Abu-Jandal, Osama bin Laden's former personal bodyguard. *al Quds al Arabi,* 31 March 2005.

Hashim, Ahmed S. "Iraq's Chaos: Why the Insurgency Won't Go Away." *Boston Review*, October–November 2004.

————. "Understanding the Roots of the Shi'a Insurgency in Iraq." *Terrorism Monitor*, 2, no.13, July 2002. www.jamestown.org/publications.

Hirsh, Michael and John Barry. "The Salvador Option, the Pentagon May Put Special Forces-led Assassination or Kidnapping Teams in Iraq." *Newsweek*, 14 January 2005.

Howard, Michael. "40,000 Iraqi Troops in Crackdown on Insurgents." *Guardian*, 27 May 2005.

————. "Kurd Chief Who Taught Mercy to Saddam's Men." *Guardian*, 27 May 2005.

"Interview with Muthanna Arit al Dari." *al Dustour* (Amman), 2 November 2004.

Iraqi, al Mashhad al-. "Maaraka al Falluja," al Jazeera, 7 November 2004. www.aljazeera.net.

Jaber, Hala and Tony Allen-Mills. "Suicide Bomber CDs Woo Martyrs to Iraq." *Sunday Times*, 22 May 2005.

Jaber, Hala, and Ali Rifat. "Suicide Bombers Stream into Iraq." *Sunday Times*, 8 May 2005.

Jaffe, Greg. "Band of Brothers: New Factor in Iraq: Irregular Brigades Fill Security Void." *Wall Street Journal*, 16 February 2005.

Joffe, Eitan, and Amir Steinhart. "Iraq: Primary Threats to Reconstruction." Interdisciplinary Center Herzliya, 30 December 2004. www.ict.org.il.

Lasseter, Tom. "Political Instability in Iraq Causes Some to Form Militias." Knight Ridder, 6 April 2005.

"LBC Talk Show Discusses Documentary on al Zarqawi, Concept of Jihad, Terrorism." LBC TV (Beirut), broadcast 28 November 2004, in Arabic.

Levitt, Matt, and Julie Sawyer. "Zarqawi's Jordanian Agenda." Special issue, *Terrorism Monitor*, 2, no. 24, 16 December 2004. www.jamestown.org/publications.

"Love among the Suicide Bombs: Iraq's Opera." *China Daily*, 21 March 2004.

Mackay, Neil. "Was it ETA or al Qaeda? The Confusion Over Who Was Behind the Madrid Bombing Obscures Intelligence Predictions of an Enhanced Terror Threat." *Sunday Herald*, 14 March 2004.

Macleod, Scott. "A Jihadist's Tale." *Time* magazine, 4 April 2005.

Maqdisi, Abu Muhammad al-. "Kashf al-litham unman wasafu bi-tanzim Bayaat al-Imam." www.tawhed.ws.

Marzuk, Moshe. "The City of Falluja: A Myth of Heroism in the Iraqi Insurgency." *Interdisciplinary Center Herzliya*, 1 December 2004. www.ict.org.il.

"Mass Resignations before Iraq Vote." CBS News, 16 January 2005.

McCarthy, Rory. "False Dawn of Peace Lost in Violent Storm." *Guardian*, 8 April 2004.

McGregor, Andrew. "Ricin Fever: Abu Mos'ab al Zarqawi in the Pankisi Gorge." Special issue, *Terrorism Monitor*, 2, no. 24, 16 December 2004. www.jamestown.org/publications.

Murphy, Brian.'Messages Hint at London Blast Recruiting." Associated Press, 16 July 2005

Murphy, Caryle, and Khalid Saffar. "Actors in the Insurgency Are Reluctant TV Stars: Terror Suspects Grilled, Mocked on Hit Iraqi Show." *Washington Post*, 5 April 2005.

Murphy, Dan. "In Fallujah's Wake, Marines Go West, U.S. and Iraqi forces have Launched Operation River Blitz, Targeting Insurgents in Cities along the Euphrates." *Christian Science Monitor*, 24 February 2005.

Parry, Robert. "Bush's Death Squads." ConsortiumNews.com, 11 January 2005. www.consortiumnews.com.

Rasan, Dhiya. "When Sadrists Confronted Saddam: Muqtada al Sadr's Uprising Recalls Revolt Triggered by the Assassination of His Father Five Years Ago." Institute for War and Peace Reporting, 14 April 2004. www.iwpr.net/index.pl?iraq_200404.html.

"Reporter Interviews al Zarqawi's neighbors, Prison-Mates." *al Sharq al Awsat*, 8 March 2004.

Ritter, Scott. "The Risk of al Zarqawi's Myth." al Jazeera, 7 January 2005.

———. "The Salvador Option." al Jazeera, 20 January 2005.

Sibaii, Hani al-. "Al-Harakat al-islamiyya al-yihadiyya: Ansar al-Islam-Yeish al-Sunna-Abu Musaab al-Zarqawi Kataib Abu Hafs." www.alshaab.com.

Sisti, Leo. "Zarqawi Segreto." *l'Espresso*, 30 September 2004.

"Tension between bin Laden, Taliban in 1996." *al Sharq al Awsat*, 10 December 2004.

"Tentacle of Terror: Ansar al Islam Goes International, Causing Tremors." *Daily Star*, 17 January 2004.

"Terrorism: Jihadist Website Describes Jihadist Movements in Iraq." English translation of Foreign Broadcast Information Service (FBIS) report, originally published as, "Ansar al Islam, Ansar al Sunnah, Abu Mus'ab al Zarqawi and Abu Hafs Brigades." Posted 14 March 2004 on al Basrah Net.

Under the Microscope. Al Jazeera Arabic Satellite TV. 1 July 2004 broadcast, in Arabic.

"Website Says al Zarqawi Wounded." al Jazeera, 24 May 2005. english.aljazeera.net.

Wedeman, Ben. "Najaf Bombing Kills Shiite leader, Followers Say." CNN.com, 30 August 2003.

Yumayli, Salman al-. "Al-Ittijahat al fikriyya wa al siyasiyya li-l-muqawama al iraqiyya." al Jazeera, 3 October 2004. www.aljazeera.net.

Zarkaoui: la Question Terroriste. Documentary by Patrice Barrat, Najat Rizk, and Ranwa Stephan. Arte TV (France and Germany), broadcast 1 March 2005 in French.

Zarqawi, Abu Mus'ab al-. "Wisaya li-l-muyahidin." www.22lajnah22.co.uk.

"Al Zarqawi 'Lone Wolf' manipulated ISI and Saudi Intelligence." *Middle East Transparent*, 10 November 2004.

BOOKS

Abderrahim Ali, Half al Irhab. *Tanzim al Qaeda min Abdallah Azzam ila Ayman al Zawahiri 1979-2003*.: Vol. I. Cairo: Dar al Mahrusa, 2004.

al Azim Ramadan, Abd. *Jamaat al takfir fi Misr.* Cairo: al Haiya al Misriyya al Amma li-l-Kitab, 1995.

Belqaziz, Abdelilah. *Al Islam wa al siyasa. Dawr al haraka al islamiyya fi sawg al majal al-siyas.* Casablanca: al Markaz al Thaqafi al Arabi, 2001.

Brisard, Jean-Charles. *Zarkaoui. Le Nouveau Visage d'Al-Qaida.* Paris: Fayard, 2005.

Burke, Jason. *Al-Qaeda: The True Story of Radical Islam.* London: Penguin, 2004.

Din Hasib, Jayr al-. *Mustqabal a Iraq. Al Ihtilal. Al Muqawama. Al tahrir wa al dimuqratiyya.* Beirut: Markaz Dirasat al Wahda al Arabiyya, 2004.

Fielding, Nick and Yosri Fouda. *Masterminds of Terror: The Truth Behind the Most Devastating Attack the World Has Ever Seen.* London: Arcade Publishing, 2003.

Gerson, Loretta, Silvia Mazzola, and Venetia Morrison. *Rome: A Guide to the Eternal City.* London: Napoleoni & Wakefield Ltd, 1999.

Hourani, Albert. *A History of the Arab Peoples.* Cambridge, Mass.: Harvard University Press, 2003.

Kohlmann, Evan F. *Al Qaida's Jihad in Europe: The Afghan Bosnian Network.* Gordonsville, Va.: Berg Publishers, 2004.

Marret, Jean-Luc. *Les Fabriques du Jihad.* Paris: Presses Universitaires de France, 2005.

Masri, Aby Khalid al-. *The Story of the Arab Afghans from the Time of Their Arrival in Afghanistan Until Their Departure with the Taliban.* Serialized in *al Sharq al Awsat,* (London) fall 2004.

Minoret, Pascal. *Sull'Orlo del Vulcano. il caso dell'Arabia Saudita.* Milan: Feltrinelli. 2004.

Napoleoni, Loretta. *Terror Incorporated.* New York: Seven Stories Press, 2005.

Qutb, Sayyed. *Maalim fi l-tariq.* Cairo: Dar al Shuruq, 1987.

Thomas, Dominique. *Les Hommes d'al Qaeda.* Paris: Éditions Michalon, 2005.

Zayyat, Montasser al-. *The Road to al Qaeda.* London: Pluto Press, 2004.

Notes

INTRODUCTION

1 Colin Powell's speech to the United Nations, 5 February 2003. See http://www.foxnews.com/story/0,2933,77676,00.html.

PROLOGUE: THE CITY OF ZARQA

1 Genesis 32:22–32
2 This event is regarded by Zionists as the biblical justification of the existence of the state of Israel. Christian fundamentalists also regard it as a proof of the existence of Greater Israel, a land which goes from Iraq to Palestine. According to their belief, Christ's second coming will be postponed until such state has been re-created.

CHAPTER 1: THE SEEDS OF RELIGIOUS RADICALISM

1 *al Arabiyya*, 13 July 2004.
2 The Banu Hassan tribe extends to Jordan, Palestine, Iraq, and even to Egypt and Sudan.
3 Jean-Charles Brisard, *Zarkaoui. Le Nouveau Visage d'Al-Qaida* (Paris: Fayard, 2005), 24.
4 Gary Gambill, "Abu Mos'ab al Zarqawi: A Biographical Sketch," in "Special Issue on Zarqawi," ed. Mahan Abedin, *Terrorism Monitor,* 2, no. 24 (16 December 2004). See www.jamestown.org/.
5 Leo Sisti, "Zarqawi Segreto," *l'Espresso*, 30 September 2004.
6 Gambill, op. cit.
7 Loretta Napoleoni, *Terror Incorporated* (New York: Seven Stories Press, 2005), chapter 5.
8 See http://encyclopedia.lockergnome.com.

9   The Muslim Brotherhood, also known as the Muslim Brethren (Jamiat al-Ikhban al-Muslimin), is an Islamic organization with a political approach towards Islam. It was founded in Egypt in 1928 as a youth organization aimed at spiritual, moral, and social reform by Hassan al Banna. The organization motto is: "Allah is our objective. The Prophet is our leader. Koran is our law. Jihad is our way. Dying in the way of Allah is our highest hope." Overall, the Brotherhood opposes secular tendencies in Islamic nations, seeks a return to the precepts of the Koran, and rejects Western influences. As an organization, it is very popular among the poor because it is active within the community, organizing social and religious groups ranging from prayer meetings and sport clubs, to charity and medical care.

The Muslim Brotherhood is considered the matrix of all modern Sunni Islamist movements and is represented all over the world. While taking an extreme stand in Egypt, the Jordanian members of the Muslim Brotherhood supported King Hussein of Jordan in his position against the PLO and against the attempts of Egyptian president Gamal Nasser to overthrow him. The Jordanian group sought changes within the Arab regimes through reforms by participating in politics. Today, the Brotherhood is considered a moderate movement.

10   See chapter two.

11   The so-called Six-Day War began on 5 June 1967 and was fought by Israel against its Arab neighbors: Egypt, Jordan, and Syria. The background to the war was the escalation of violence and mounting tension on Israel's northern and southern border, which led Egypt's president Nasser to close the Tiran Straits. Within six days the Israeli forces achieved victory and occupied Sinai, the Gaza Strip, the Golan Heights, the West Bank, and the Old City of Jerusalem.

12   In 1988, Abdallah Azzam asked bin Laden to register all the Arab mujahedin who had joined the anti-Soviet jihad. This database became an independent section of the Arab-Afghan Bureau, known as Sijl al Qaeda (Register of al Qaeda), and was under the supervision of Azzam. After Azzam's death, bin Laden took control of both the Arab-Afghan Bureau and al Qaeda.

13   Sayyed Qutb was an important theoretician of the Egyptian Muslim Brotherhood. In 1954 he was jailed after a failed assassination attempt against President Nasser. While in prison he wrote his two most important works, *In the Shade of the Koran* and *Milestone*, the latter which became the manifesto of political Islam. While in prison his popularity grew, and in 1965 he was accused and found guilty of plotting to overthrow the Nasser regime; the following year he was executed by hanging.

14   He traveled to the United States as a professor from the University of Jordan, often invited by the Association of Muslim Students.

15   The Arab-Afghan Bureau had several tasks, including unifying the Arab mujahedin in spite of their different ideologies; linking the Arab and the Islamic world with the Afghan jihad and making sure financial aid would flow to Afghanistan; distributing articles on the jihad and about the victories of the mujahedin in the

Muslim world; and training Arab volunteers for the war. See Abderrahim Ali, *Half al irhab. Tanzim al Qaeda min Abdallah Azzam ila Ayman al Zawahiri 1979–2003* (Cairo: Dar al Mahrusa, 2004) 25–26.

16 From the eighth to nineteenth century.

17 *Zarkaoui: la Question Terroriste.* Documentary by Patrice Barrat, Najat Rizk, and Ranwa Stephan. Arte TV (France and Germany), broadcast 1 March 2005. Unpublished interview by Patrice Barrat with Nadine Picaudou.

18 *Zarkaoui,* Barrat, Rizk, and Stephan, op. cit.

19 Toward the end of the nineteenth century European powers got very involved in the Middle East; in 1882 the British and French landed troops in Egypt and took control of the country. Although Egypt was not regarded as a colony, in 1914 it was officially annexed to Britain. In 1922, the British agreed to grant Egypt its independence while retaining control over many important aspects of Egyptian sovereignty.

20 Brian Murphy, "Messages hint at London blast recruiting," Associated Press, 16 July 2005. See http://news.yahoo.com/s/ap/bombings_recruiting_terror.

21 *Zarkaoui,* Barrat, Rizk and Stephan, op. cit

22 Ibid.

23 He should not be confused with Abu Qatadah, in custody in the United Kingdom at the time of writing.

CHAPTER 2: STRANGERS AMONG WARRIORS

1 Abdallah Anas, interview by the author, London, February 2005.

2 The siege of Khost (located 150 kilometers south of Kabul) is part of the legendary heroism of the mujahedin, to the point that it is considered "the conquest of conquests." Khost was under siege by the Afghans and Arab Brigades for almost eight years. The battle was led by Jalal al Din Haqqani, leader of al Hizb al Islami, and by Hikmatyar, who commanded the mujahedin; the Arab brigades fought under the leadership of Abu al Harith al Urduni. For a mujahed, having participated in the battle of Khost is a sign of prestige; this is why some people have claimed that al Zarqawi was part of the Arab-Afghan brigade. But, he actually arrived in Afghanistan after the siege of Khost had already taken place.

3 *Under the Microscope.* Al Jazeera Arabic Satellite TV. 1 July 2004 broadcast, in Arabic.

4 Ibid.

5 *Zarkaoui: la Question Terroriste.* Documentary by Patrice Barrat, Najat Rizk, and Ranwa Stephan. Arte TV (France and Germany), broadcast 1 March 2005.

6 Lizette Alvarez, "Portrait of Three Suspects Emerges in Britain," *International Herald Tribune,* 15 July 2005.

7   *Abu Mos'ab al Zarqawi, from Herat to Baghdad.* Documentary by Fouad Hussein. LBC TV (Beirut), broadcast 27 and 28 November 2004, in Arabic. Transcript by Article Z and Firehorse Films.

8   "Actually there were rivalries among al Qaeda members depending on their countries of origin. The Egyptians used to boast about being Egyptian. The Saudis, Yemenis, Sudanese, and Arab Maghreb citizens used to do the same thing sometimes. This troubled Sheikh Osama and he used to send me to them to help eliminate these regional rivalries because the enemies of God, those who have sickness in their hearts, and informants would exploit these ignorant attitudes and try to sow divisions and disagreements among al Qaeda members." Khalid al Hammadi, "Al Qaeda organization from Inside, as Reported by Abu-Jandal, Nasir Al-Bahari," part 6 of a series of interviews with Nasir al Bahari, *al Quds al Arabi*, 30 March 2005.

9   Evan F. Kohlmann, *Al Qaida's Jihad in Europe* (Oxford: Berg Publishers, 2004), 9.

10 Steven Emerson and Khalid Duran, "Interview with Abu Iman, 4 November 1993," in Kohlmann, op. cit.

11 Abderrahim Ali is an Egyptian researcher specializing in Islamic movements. He also worked as a journalist with *al-Ahali* (the most left-wing newspaper in Egypt) and is now editor of the Web page Islam Online (www.islamonline.net). He is director of the Centre for Studies on Islamism and Democracy in Cairo.

12 See chapter four for more on al Zawahiri.

13 Khalid al Hammadi "Former bin Laden 'Bodyguard' Recalls al Qaeda Figures, Views East Africa Bombings," part 9 of a series of interviews with Nasir al Bahari, *al Quds al Arabi*, 31 March 2005.

14 Abdallah Anas, interview by the author, London, February 2005.

15 Montasser al Zayyat, *The Road to al Qaeda* (London: Pluto Press, 2004).

16 Azzam insisted that the money destined for the Maktab al Khidamat had to be used within Afghanistan. See Abderrahim Ali, *Half al irhab. Tanzim al Qaeda min Abdallah Azzam ila Ayman al Zawahiri 1979–2003,* (Cairo: Dar al Mahrusa, 2004), 29.

17 Sheikh Azzam was killed, along with is two sons by a 20 kg TNT bomb while he was driving. His death remains an unsolved mystery.

18 Sheikh Omar Abd al Rahman was the spiritual guide of al Jamaa al Islamiyya, which is with al Jihad the most active radical Islamist organization in Egypt. This group used his fatwas to justify their actions. Omar Abd al Rahman issued a fatwa prior to the assassination of Sadat, in which he justified the assassination of the Pharaoh (the name given to Sadat by the radical Islamists).

19 In 1990, Sheikh Omar Abd al Rahman came to the United States for a series of lectures fully funded by Mustafa Shalabi. Once in the United States, the Blind Sheikh attempted to undermine the authority of his sponsor who refused to let him use the money of the Arab-Afghan Bureau for his own expenses. As managing director of the Arab-Afghan Bureau, Abdallah Anas was in charge of the finances of the al

Kifah Refugee Centre in Brooklyn. During a visit to Mustafa Shalabi a few months before his assassination, he confirmed that the centre could not support Sheikh Omar's expenses in the United States. Anas even went to talk to the Blind Sheikh, trying to reason with him and suggesting that he move to Peshawar. Sheikh Omar was adamant that his place was in the United States. By the time Mustafa Shalabi was killed, the Egyptians were in control of the Arab-Afghan Bureau in Peshawar, therefore making it easy for the Blind Sheikh to step into his predecessor's shoes. Abdallah Anas interview by the author, London, February 2005.

20 Loretta Napoleoni, *Terror Incorporated* (New York: Seven Stories Press, 2005), chapter 1.

21 There are several theories about the death of Abdallah Azzam, for example, that he was killed by secret agents working for the Soviets.

22 *Abu Mos'ab al Zarqawi,* Hussein, op. cit.

23 Al Maqdisi finished his secondary studies in Kuwait and studied sciences at the University of Mosul. He lived between Kuwait and the Hiyaz and learned the classic works of Ibn Taymiyya, Ibn al-Qayyem, and Muhammad ibn Abd al Wahhab.

24 Dominique Thomas, *Les Hommes d'al Qaeda* (Paris: Éditions Michalon, 2005), 87.

25 Muhammad Basil, "Al Ansaru l'Arab fi Afghanistan," Committee for Islamic Benevolence Publications, Kohlmann, op. cit.

26 Khalid al Hammadi, "Former bin Laden 'Bodyguard' Discusses al Qaeda Training Methods," part 5 of a series of interviews with Nasir al Bahari, *al Quds al Arabi,* 26 March 2005.

27 Though the term Salafi refers to Muslim predecessors and ancestors, particularly the Prophet Muhammad and his companions, Muhammad Abduh (1849–1905) was the founder and champion of the brand of modernist Islamic political thought known as *Salafiyya*. Carl Brown, *Religion and State: The Muslim Approach to Politics* (New York, Columbia University Press, 2000), 32, 97, 139.

28 Albert Hourani, *A History of the Arab Peoples* (Cambridge, Mass.: Harvard University Press, 2003).

29 Brown, op cit., 32, 96.

30 Salafism, or *Salafiyya,* centers on the concept of *al Tawhid,* which holds that God is one and the unity of God is absolute. The divine unity of God is also the unity of the umma, the community of believers. Monotheism is, therefore, the core of Islam and at the same time it represents its heartbeat. Al Tawhid demands that "people seek to become one with God," explains Muhammad Taleb, "their lives must merge into such unity, thus Islam demands from its members a multidimensional participation," in *Zarkaoui,* Barrat, Rizk, and Stephan, op. cit.

31 Sayyed Qutb, *Maalim fi l-tariq* (Cairo: Dar al Shuruq, 1987), 105.

32 Abu Bakr accused of apostasy several tribes of the Arabian Peninsula who staged an insurrection against his caliphate by refusing to pay the zakat, the religious alms-giving that is one of the five pillars of Islam. Abu Bakr utilized the concept of takfir to bar the rebellious tribes from society. Abdelilah Belqaziz, *Al Islam wa al*

siyasa. Dawr al haraka al islamiyya fi sawg al majal al-siyas (Casablanca: al Markaz al Thaqafi al Arabi, 2001), 85–98.

33   The principal root of the dispute between Sunnis and Shi'ites is the question of the origin of power, with the Shi'ites disqualifying all the caliphs except Ali and the other clans (Omeyas and Abbasis). There is also the question of the prerogatives of power; for Sunnis, the caliph is a temporal sovereign charged with protecting the religion and the law, and is fallible; for Shi'ites, the imam or the caliph, who must be a descendant of Ali, is infallible.

34   King Philip II of Spain used religion as a tool to crush the revolt of Protestant Flanders.

35   Pascal Minoret, *Sull'Orlo del Vulcano, il caso dell'Arabia Saudita* (Milan: Feltrinelli, 2004), chapter 2.

36   *Zarkaoui,* Barrat, Rizk, and Stephan op. cit.

CHAPTER 3: THE IMPRISONMENT

1   For a full account of al Gharib and al Maqdisi's propaganda activity see the testimony of Abu al Montassir in Fouad Hussein, *Al Zarqawi . . . The Second Generation of al Qaeda,* serialized in fifteen parts in *al Quds al Arabi,* June 2005.

2   "Al Hayat Inquiry: The City of al Zarqa in Jordan—Breeding Ground of Jordan's Salafi Jihad Movement," *al Hayat* (London), 17 January 2005.

3   *Under the Microscope.* Al Jazeera Arabic Satellite TV. 1 July 2004 broadcast, in Arabic.

4   *Al Hayat* (London), 8 February 2005.

5   Al Maqdisi did not support suicide missions, he even issued a *fatwa* which prohibited them. See Hussein, *al Zarqawi,* op cit.

6   "Reporter Interviews al Zarqawi's neighbors, Prison-Mates," *al Sharq al Awsat,* 8 March 2004.

7   According to al Zarqawi's attorney, Muhammad al Duaik, he was "not very intelligent." See *al Hayat* (London), 14 July 2004; see also, Leo Sisti, "Zarqawi Segreto," *l'Espresso,* 30 September 2004.

8   "Reporter Interviews al Zarqawi's neighbors, Prison-Mates," op. cit.

9   Abu Muhammad al Maqdisi, *Kashf al-litham unman wasafu bi-tanzim Bayaat al-Imam.* See www.tawhed.ws.

10   *Abu Mos'ab al Zarqawi, from Herat to Baghdad.* Documentary by Fouad Hussein. LBC TV (Beirut), broadcast 27 and 28 November 2004, in Arabic. Transcript by Article Z and Firehorse Films.

11   Michael Howard, "Kurd Chief Who Taught Mercy to Saddam's Men," *Guardian,* 27 May 2005.

12   Ibid.

13   "Reporter Interviews al Zarqawi's neighbors, Prison-Mates," op. cit.

14   *Zarkaoui: la Question Terroriste.* Documentary by Patrice Barrat, Najat Rizk, and Ranwa Stephan. Arte TV (France and Germany), broadcast 1 March 2005.

15 *Abu Mos'ab al Zarqawi,* Hussein, op. cit.

16 Abdallah Anas, interview by the author, London, February 2005.

17 *Zarkaoui,* Barrat, Rizk and Stephan, op. cit

18 *Abu Mos'ab al Zarqawi,* Hussein, op. cit.

19 *Zarkaoui,* Barrat, Rizk, and Stephan, op. cit.

20 He was sentenced to death, later converted to twenty-five years' imprisonment, for having thrown a bomb at a car to protest the signing of the Oslo Agreement.

21 *Al Hayat* (London), 14 December 2004.

22 "Reporter Interviews al Zarqawi's neighbors, Prison-Mates," op. cit.

23 Ibid.

24 "Al Hayat Inquiry: The City of al Zarqa in Jordan," op. cit.

25 Sisti, "Zarqawi Segreto," op. cit.

26 "Special Issue on Zarqawi," ed. Mahan Abedin, *Terrorism Monitor,* 2, no. 24 (16 December 2004). See www.jamestown.org/terrorism/news/article.php?issue-id=3179.

27 *Abu Mos'ab al Zarqawi,* Hussein, op. cit.

28 "Special Issue on Zarqawi," ed. Abedin, op. cit.

29 *Under the Microscope,* op.cit.

30 "Reporter Interviews al Zarqawi's neighbors, Prison-Mates," op. cit.

31 *Abu Mos'ab al Zarqawi,* Hussein, op. cit.

32 Ibid.

33 *Al Hayat* (London), 14 July 2004.

34 Ibid.

35 *Abu Mos'ab al Zarqawi,* Hussein, op. cit.

36 Ibid.

37 "Al Hayat Inquiry: The City of al Zarqa in Jordan," op. cit.

38 *Al Hayat* (London), 14 July 2004.

39 *Zarkaoui,* Barrat, Rizk, and Stephan, op. cit.

40 "Reporter Interviews al Zarqawi's neighbors, Prison-Mates," op. cit.

41 Ibid.

42 *Under the Microscope,* op.cit.

43 "Al Hayat Inquiry: The City of al Zarqa in Jordan," op. cit.

44 *Under the Microscope,* op.cit.

45 Sisti, "Zarqawi Segreto," op. cit.

46 *Abu Mos'ab al Zarqawi,* Hussein, op. cit.

47 Fouad Hussein was imprisoned in 1996 after the so-called "Bread Revolt" (caused by the rise in the price of several products, including bread), for having criticized the behavior of the prime minister, Abdelkarim al Karabiti, in *al Aswaq,* the newspaper he wrote for. *Abu Mos'ab al Zarqawi,* Hussein, op. cit.

48 *Abu Mos'ab al Zarqawi,* Hussein, op. cit.

49 *Zarkaoui,* Barrat, Rizk, and Stephan, op. cit.

CHAPTER 4: THE ROAD TO 9/11

1   Khalid al Hammadi "Former bin Laden 'Bodyguard' Recalls al Qaeda Figures, Views East Africa Bombings," part 9 of a series of interviews with Nasir al Bahari, *al Quds al Arabi*, 31 March 2005.

2   *Abu Mos'ab al Zarqawi, from Herat to Baghdad.* Documentary by Fouad Hussein. LBC TV (Beirut), broadcast 27 and 28 November 2004, in Arabic. Transcript by Article Z and Firehorse Films.

3   Montasser al Zayyat, *The Road to al Qaeda* (London: Pluto Press, 2004), 62.

4   *Zarkaoui: la Question Terroriste*, documentary by Patrice Barrat, Najat Rizk, and Ranwa Stephan. Arte TV (France and Germany), broadcast 1 March 2005. Unpublished interview by Patrice Barrat with Nadine Picaudou.

5   Ibid.

6   "The word martyr derives from Greek and means 'witness.' Christ was the first martyr, 'the witness of the Christian faith,' as he was called in the Apocalypse of John." Loretta Gerson, Silvia Mazzola, and Venetia Morrison, *Rome, A Guide to the Eternal City* (London: Napoleoni & Wakefield Ltd, 1999), 50.

7   Abdallah Anas, interview by the author, London, February 2005.

8   Gerson, Mazzola, Morrison, *Rome*, op. cit.

9   Thus, their heroic sacrifices are reminiscent of the Italian *carbonari*, politically motivated heroes, like Pietro Micca,who willingly died in the struggle to achieve independence from Austria in the nineteenth century.

10 It is legitimized by a fatwa issued by the Saudi religious leader Abd al Aziz Ben Saleh al Yarbuu. This Saudi sheikh, who has influenced al Qaeda, is known for his condemnation of the United States. He considers America a source of evil and moral corruption and the main enemy because it launched a war against Islam. Al Yarbuu issued a fatwa in which he explained that the current relations between Islam and the West will lead to a total war against the infidels. Al Yarbuu, like other Saudi scholars (Ali al Judayr and Abderrahman al Sadis, for instance), has also issued fatwas to justify the jihad against the United States as well as to justify the Madrid bombing of 11 March 2004.

11 In al Yarbuu's book *al Mukhtar fi hukm al intihar jawf ifsha al asrar* [Summary of the Meaning of Suicide to Avoid Revealing Secrets], quoted in Abderrahim Ali, *Half al irhab. Tanzim al Qaeda min Abdallah Azzam ila Ayman al Zawahiri 1979–2003* (Cairo: Dar al Mahrusa, 2004), 3: 55. He concludes that it is legal for imprisoned Muslims to commit suicide in order to avoid revealing secrets that could damage other Muslims or the community of believers. There is no precedent in Islamic literature for this statement, so he uses analogies with nonreligious situations. He refers, for instance, to circumstances in which someone is thrown into the sea to lighten the weight of a boat which otherwise would sink, killing everybody on board, or when the enemy uses a group of Muslims as a human shield. In these circumstances, he argues, it is legal to kill Muslims to safeguard the umma. In the book he presents ten differ-

ent situations that he considers similar to the suicide of an imprisoned Muslim and which entitle someone who commits suicide to the status of martyr.

12 Al Zawahiri presents his argument in *Wuyub al-yihad wa-fadl al-shahada* [Obligation of the Jihad and Excellence of Martyrdom], a document edited and produced by his group, al Jihad. The document became the strategic manifesto of Islamist terror. Ali, *Half al irhab*, op.cit.

13 Ibid.

14 Loretta Napoleoni, *Terror Incorporated* (New York: Seven Stories Press, 2005), chapter 8.

15 Fouad Hussein, *Al Zarqawi . . . The Second Generation of al Qaeda*, serialized in fifteen parts in *al Quds al Arabi*, June 2005.

16 Paul Garwood, "Zarqawi Stirred Violent Surge, U.S. Contends Allegedly Plotted in Syrian Meeting," Associated Press, 19 May 2005.

17 "Love among the Suicide Bombs: Iraq's Opera," *China Daily*, 21 March 2004.

18 Hala Jaber and Tony Allen-Mills, "Suicide Bomber CDs Woo Martyrs to Iraq," *Sunday Times*, 22 May 2005.

19 *The Event*, LBC TV (Beirut), broadcast 15 May 2005.

20 Jaber and Allen-Mills, "Suicide Bomber CDs," op. cit.

21 Ibid.

22 Hala Jaber and Ali Rifat, "Suicide Bombers Stream into Iraq," *Sunday Times*, 8 May 2005.

23 British authorities have deliberately avoided admitting that the 7 July London bombers were suicide bombers to avoid spreading more fear among the population. However, terrorist experts are adamant that the attack was carried out by suicide bombers. See Elaine Sciolino and Don Van Natta Jr., "Bombings in London: July 7 Blasts; Police Debate if London Plotters Were Suicide Bombers, or Dupes," *New York Times*, 27 July 2005.

24 *Zarkaoui*, Barrat, Rizk, and Stephan, op. cit.

25 Ibid.

26 The first Russian campaign against the Chechens ended with the defeat of the Russian forces in 1996. Khattab emerged as the new leader from the power struggle which followed the death of General Jawhar Dudayev.

27 Khattab, who belonged to the Salafi jihadist stream, was poisoned in April 2002. He had fought the Soviets in Afghanistan as well as with the Muslim opposition in Tajikistan during the civil war (1992–94). He helped the Azeri Muslims during the conflict in Nagorno Karabah (1988–94) and arrived in Chechnya during the first war (1994–96). The Russian authorities blamed him for the terrorist attacks in Russia in August and September 1999.

28 For a full profile of Khattab, see www.ummah.com/forum/archive/ index.php/t-5383.html.

29 *Al Sharq al Awsat* (London), 9–10 April 2004.

30 *Zarkaoui*, Barrat, Rizk, and Stephan, op. cit.

31 Peter Ern interview, CNN, March 1998. See anusha.com/oamaint.htm.

32 Abu Whalid al Masri, *The Story of the Arab Afghans from the Time of Their Arrival in Afghanistan Until Their Departure with the Taliban, serialized* in *al Sharq al Awsat* (London), fall 2004.

33 ———, *The Story of the Arab-Afghans,* part 2 "Views Efforts to Acquire WMD," 9 December 2004.

34 ———, *The Story of the Arab-Afghans,* part 3, "Tension between bin Laden, Taliban in 1996," 10 December 2004.

35 Ibid.

36 al Masri, *The Story of the Arab-Afghans,* part 2, op. cit.

CHAPTER 5: RETURN TO AFGHANISTAN

1 *Under the Microscope,* al Jazeera Arabic Satellite TV, broadcast 1 July 2004.

2 Leo Sisti, "Zarqawi Segreto," *l'Espresso,* 30 September 2004.

3 *Under the Microscope,* op. cit.

4 *Abu Mos'ab al Zarqawi, from Herat to Baghdad.* Documentary by Fouad Hussein. LBC TV (Beirut), broadcast 27 and 28 November 2004, in Arabic. Transcript by Article Z and Firehorse Films.

5 *Zarkaoui, la Question Terroriste,* documentary by Patrice Barrat, Najat Rizk, and Ranwa Stephan, Arte TV (France and Germany), broadcast 1 March 2005.Unpublished original script.

6 *Al Arabiyya,* 13 July 2004

7 *Zarkaoui,* Barrat, Rizk, and Stephan, op. cit.

8 According to the Libyan Nuuman Ben Uthman, in *al Hayat,* 8 November 2004.

9 *Zarkaoui,* Barrat, Rizk, and Stephan, op. cit.

10 Muhammad Makawi, an Egyptian, was born in 1963. He belonged to al Jihad and was considered one of the top leaders of al Qaeda, in charge of military and security matters. He is believed to have been responsible for the terrorist attacks against the U.S. embassies in Kenya and Tanzania in August 1998.

11 *Zarkaoui,* Barrat, Rizk, and Stephan, op. cit.

12 "Al Zarqawi 'Lone Wolf' Manipulated ISI and Saudi Intelligence," *Middle East Transparent,* 10 November 2004. See www.metransparent.com/texts/.

13 The idea of setting up a camp in Herat was linked to the presence of a few hundred mujahedin from Syria, Jordan, Lebanon, and Palestine who preferred to keep independent of al Qaeda due to slight ideological differences. Mullah Omar offered them an area near Herat on the condition that al Zarqawi was in charge of the leadership. See *al Hayat,* 15 February 2004.

14 *Zarkaoui,* Barrat, Rizk, and Stephan, op. cit.

15 Ibid.

16 Ibid.

17 Ibid.

18 *Under the Microscope,* op. cit.

19 Ibid.

20 Ibid.

21 Abu Baseer issued a fatwa from London in August 2003 calling on Muslims to fight against the British and American troops, even if doing so would help a "bad Muslim" like Saddam Hussein. Jason Burke, "Fury at Muslim Talks in Memory of 9/11 Hijackers," *Observer,* 7 September 2003.

22 Dr. Hani al Sibaii, "al-Harakat al-islamiyya al-yihadiyya: Ansar al-Islam-Yeish al-Sunna- Abu Musaab al-Zarqawi- Kataib Abu Hafs," [Ansar al Islam, Ansar al Sunnah, Abu Mus'ab al Zarqawi, and Abu Hafs Brigades] posted 14 March 2004 on al Basrah Net. For the www.alshaab.com, see also Foreign Broadcast Information Service (FBIS) English translation see "Terrorism: Jihadist Web Site Describes Jihadist Movements in Iraq," from Thompson Dialog.

23 Shell-states are the result of the process through which armed organizations assemble the socioeconomic infrastructure (taxation, employment, services, etc.) of a state that has no political structure (no territory, no self-determination). Loretta Napoleoni, *Terror Incorporated* (New York: Seven Stories Press, 2005).

24 al Sibaii, op. cit.

25 *Under the Microscope,* op. cit.

26 al Sibaii, op. cit.

27 "Terrorism: Jihadist Web Site Describes Jihadist Movements in Iraq,"op. cit.

28 Ibid. Mullah Krekar had the status of political refugee in Norway since 1991. He was arrested by the authorities in March 2003 and charged with taking part in terrorist activities, but was subsequently cleared.

29 *Zarkaoui,* Barrat, Rizk, and Stephan, op. cit.

30 Ibid.

31 Ibid.

32 *Abu Mos'ab al Zarqawi,* Hussein, op. cit.

33 Ibid.

34 Ibid.

35 *Zarkaoui,* Barrat, Rizk, and Stephan, op. cit.

36 Ibid.

37 Ibid.

38 Ibid.

CHAPTER 6: THE MYTH OF ABU MOS'AB AL ZARQAWI

1 *Under the Microscope,* al Jazeera Arabic Satellite TV, broadcast 1 July 2004.

2 Proof of al Zarqawi's involvement in the Millennium Plot is all based on the confessions of the perpetrators; to date no hard evidence has been produced. How were such confessions extracted? The use of torture in Arab prisons is widespread, hence several people cast doubts on the validity of these confessions and accusations.

The involvement of al Zarqawi in the plot also seems unlikely when put in the context of his plans to leave Jordan after being released from al Suwaqah prison. "He had always wanted to leave Jordan because he couldn't tolerate it here any more, he wanted to support Islam from within an environment which was considered friendly to Islam. In those days other nations were considered better for this than other Arab nations," explains Jarrah El Qaddah. In 1999, al Zarqawi was still dreaming of joining Khattab, to go to Chechnya and fight the Russians. *Zarkaoui: la Question Terroriste,* documentary by Patrice Barrat, Najat Rizk, and Ranwa Stephan. Arte TV (France and Germany), broadcast 1 March 2005.

3   "Abu-Zubaydah played no role in the al Qaeda organization. He was arrested in Pakistan, as I heard later. He had a guesthouse in the Pakistani capital Islamabad and he used to receive and give accommodation to Arab mujahedin. His only job was to serve the mujahedin and he was not affiliated with the al Qaeda organization or other organizations. I remember that the al Qaeda organization coordinated with him to receive the sick or the wounded from the Arab brothers and treat them in Pakistan, or to complete security papers and ensure transportation and communication and means of movement. He used to offer these services in exchange for material benefits. This house or guesthouse was opened for commercial use." See Khalid al Hammadi "Former bin Laden 'Bodyguard' Recalls al Qaeda Figures, Views East Africa Bombings," part 9 of a series of interviews with Nasir al Bahari, *al Quds al Arabi,* 31 March 2005.

4   *Al Sharq al Awsat,* 29 November 2001

5   "Killing of Israeli in Amman Related to Violence: Israeli Official," *People's Daily,* 8 August 2001.

6   *Zarkaoui,* Barrat, Rizk, and Stephan, op. cit.

7   *Abu Mos'ab al Zarqawi, from Herat to Baghdad,* documentary by Fouad Hussein, LBC TV (Beirut), broadcast 27 and 28 November 2004, in Arabic. Transcript by Article Z and Firehorse Films. See also *Under the Microscope,* op. cit.

8   *Zarkaoui,* Barrat, Rizk, and Stephan, op. cit.

9   Ibid.

10   *Abu Mos'ab al Zarqawi,* Hussein, op. cit.

11   Colin Powell's speech to the United Nations, 5 February 2003. See http://www.foxnews.com/story/0,2933,77676,00.html

12   Dr. Hani al Sibaii, "al-Harakat al-islamiyya al-yihadiyya: Ansar al-Islam-Yeish al-Sunna- Abu Musaab al-Zarqawi- Kataib Abu Hafs" [Ansar al Islam, Ansar al Sunnah, Abu Mus'ab al Zarqawi and Abu Hafs Brigades,] posted 14 March 2004 on al Basrah Net. For the www.alshaab.com; see also Foreign Broadcast Information Service (FBIS) English translation see "Terrorism: Jihadist Web site Describes Jihadist Movements in Iraq," from Thompson Dialog.

13   Andrew McGregor, "Ricin Fever: Abu Mos'ab al Zarqawi in the Pankisi Gorge" in "Special Issue on Zarqawi," ed. Mahan Abedin, *Terrorism Monitor,* 2, no. 24 (16 December 2004). See www.jamestown.org/publications.

14 Duncan Campbell, "The Ricin Ring that Never Was," *Guardian*, 14 April 2005.

15 Duncan Campbell, interview by the author, London, February 2005.

16 Colin Powell's speech to the United Nations, 5 February 2003. See http://www.foxnews.com/story/0,2933,77676,00.html.

17 *Under the Microscope*, op. cit.

18 Ibid.

19 Ibid.

CHAPTER 7: FACTS AND FICTION ABOUT AL ZARQAWI'S INTERNATIONAL NETWORK

1   Abdallah Anas, interview by the author, London, February 2005.

2   *Under the Microscope,* al Jazeera Arabic Satellite TV, 1 July 2004 broadcast, in Arabic.

3   *Abu Mos'ab al Zarqawi, from Herat to Baghdad,* documentary by Fouad Hussein, LBC TV (Beirut), broadcast 27 and 28 November 2004, in Arabic. Transcript by Article Z and Firehorse Films.

4   Jordan National Television, 26 April 2004 broadcast. See www.arabic.cnn.com.

5   Al Jayyusi is one of the young Jordanians who supposedly trained in the camp of Herat with al Zarqawi. The Jordanian authorities accused him of being the leader of the cell that plotted to attack the U.S. embassy in Jordan in 2004.

6   *Under the Microscope*, op. cit.

7   *Zarkaoui: la Question Terroriste*, documentary by Patrice Barrat, Najat Rizk, and Ranwa Stephan. Arte TV (France and Germany), broadcast 1 March 2005.

8   www.assabeel.net (n1 539, 2 May 2004)

9   For this interpretation see Gary Gambill, "Abu Mos'ab al Zarqawi: A Biographical Sketch" in "Special Issue on Zarqawi," ed. Mahan Abedin, *Terrorism Monitor*, 2, no. 24 (16 December 2004). See www.jamestown.org/terrorism/news/article.php?issue_id=3179.

10 Former mujahed, interview with the author, London, February 2005

11 Matt Levitt and Julie Sawyer, "Zarqawi's Jordanian Agenda" in "Special Issue on Zarqawi," ed. Mahan Abedin, *Terrorism Monitor*, 2, no. 24 (16 December 2004).

12 Waddah Sharara in *al Hayat*, 8 February 2005, points out that, as was the case previously with other Islamist and nationalist groups, al Zarqawi combines the preparation of his Jordanian cells with the supervision of the European cells, e.g. the al Tawhid cell in Germany. It is claimed that members of his group contacted the famous cell in Hamburg which planned the 9/11 attacks and another cell in Milan; it is also believed that his men contacted French jihadists in Paris and Lyon, and Moroccans in Madrid. See Jean-Charles Brisard, *Zarkaoui. Le nouveau visage d'Al-Qaida* (Paris: Fayard, 2005).

13 *Al Hayat*, 8 February 2005.

14 The first one was in Germany, the al Tawhid cell that many claim had relations with the 11 September al Qaeda cell in Hamburg. The other European cells were located in Italy, France, and Spain. *Zarkaoui,* Brisard, op. cit.

15 *Zarkaoui,* Barrat, Rizk, and Stephan, op. cit.

16 Neil Mackay, "Was it ETA or al Qaeda? The Confusion Over Who Was Behind the Madrid Bombing Obscures Intelligence Predictions of an Enhanced Terror Threat," *Sunday Herald,* 14 March 2004.

17 Anthony Barnett, Jason Burke, and Zoe Smith, "Terror Cells Regroup and Now They Target Europe," *Observer,* 11 January 2004.

18 "Tentacle of Terror: Ansar al-Islam Goes International, Causing Tremors," *Daily Star,* 17 January 2004.

19 Ibid.

20 Barnett, Burke, and Smith, "Terror Cells Regroup," op. cit.

21 Scott Macleod, "A Jihadist's Tale," *Time* magazine, 4 April 2005.

22 *Al Sharq al Awsat,* 13 March 2005.

23 See www.petra.gov.jo./nepras/2004/Apr/26/191114500.htm.

24 *Zarkaoui,* Barrat, Rizk, and Stephan, op. cit.

25 Ibid.

26 *Al Sharq al Awsat,* 24–25 February 2005.

27 *Al Sharq al Awsat,* 8 February 2005. The Ba'ath party is an Arab nationalist party which believes in the unity of all Arabs; there were Ba'ath parties in various Arab countries including Iraq, Syria, Yemen, and Sudan.

28 *Al Sharq al Awsat,* 16 February 2005.

29 *Zarkaoui,* Barrat, Rizk, and Stephan, op. cit.

30 See www.info.state.gov.

31 *Zarkaoui,* Barrat, Rizk, and Stephan, op. cit.

32 Loretta Napoleoni, *Terror Incorporated* (New York: Seven Stories Press, 2005).

CHAPTER 8: INSURGENT IRAQ

1 Patrick Cockburn, "Saddam's Agents 'Murdered Cleric,'" *Independent,* March 1999. See http://www.geocities.com/BourbonStreet/Quarter/1803/mmsalsadr.html.

2 Dhiya Rasan, "When Sadrists Confronted Saddam: Muqtada al Sadr's Uprising Recalls Revolt Triggered by the Assassination of His Father Five Years Ago," Institute for War and Peace Reporting, 14 April 2004; see www.iwpr.net/index.pl?iraq_200404.html.

3 Moqtada al Sadr was born in 1973. After his father's assassination, Moqtada remained under house arrest for a while. He is a disciple of the Iranian Shi'ite authority Ayatollah Kazem al Jayry, and studied with him in the Iranian holy city of Qom.

4 Ahmed S. Hashim, "Understanding the Roots of the Shi'a Insurgency in Iraq," *Terrorism Monitor,* 2, no.13 (July 2002); see www.jamestown.org/publications.

5 Al Sadr never obtained the *mujtahid*, the ability to produce legislation based upon the analysis of the Koran and the life of the prophet. The mujtahid is granted to religious students who have studied these sources.

6 Eitan Joffe and Amir Steinhart, "Iraq—Primary Threats to Reconstruction," International Policy Institute for Counter-Terrorism, 30 December 2004; see www.ict.org.il.

7 Ibid.

8 Hashim, "Understanding the Roots," op. cit.

9 Ahmed S. Hashim, "Iraq's Chaos: Why the Insurgency Won't Go Away," *Boston Review*, October–November 2004.

10 Amatzia Baram, "Post-Saddam Iraq: The Shiite Factor," *Iraq Memo #15*, 30 April 2003; see http://www.brookings.edu/views/oped/fellows/baram20030430.htm.

11 These tribunals replaced the previous ones of Saddam Hussein.

12 Baghdad, Basra, Mosul, Hilla, Diwaniyya, and Baaquba.

13 Jayr al Din Hasib, *Mustqabal a Iraq. Al Ihtilal. Al Muqawama. Al tahrir wa al dimuqratiyya* (Beirut: Markaz Dirasat al Wahda al Arabiyya, 2004), 168.

14 Quoted in Rory McCarthy, "False Dawn of Peace Lost in Violent Storm," *Guardian*, 8 April 2004.

15 Norwegian journalist, interview by the author, London, February 2005.

16 Ahmed S. Hashim, "Iraq's Chaos," op. cit.

17 Ibid.

CHAPTER 9: THE NEW MONGOLS

1 Quoted in Charles Glover, "Smiles and Shrugs Speak Volumes about Nature of Attacks on American Troops," *Financial Times*, 25 September 2003.

2 Saad al Fagih, interview by the author, London, February 2005.

3 *Bashaer*, no. 26, 27 December 2004. For more information on the concept of Americans as the new Mongols see also "Iraqi Vice President: 'Thousands of Suicide Attackers Will Fight Against US,'" *Der Spiegel*, 1 February 2003; Sam Hamod, "The New Mongols," al Jazeera, 19 November 2004.

4 Ibid.

5 On 28 April 2003, Saddam Hussein declared that Bush had entered Baghdad with the help of Alqami; see *al Quds al Arabi*, 30 April 2003.

6 Abu Mos'ab al Zarqawi, *Wisaya li-l-Mujahedin*, www.22lajnah22.co.uk; see also FBIS archives, Thompson Dialog.

7 Nick Fielding, interview by the author, London, February 2005.

8 *Zarkaoui: la Question Terroriste*, documentary by Patrice Barrat, Najat Rizk, and Ranwa Stephan. Arte TV (France and Germany), broadcast 1 March 2005.

9 Ibid.

10 Talk-show discussion of *Abu Mos'ab al Zarqawi, from Herat to Baghdad* (documentary by Fouad Hussein, LBC TV, broadcast 27 and 28 November 2004), LBC TV (Beirut), 28 November 2004.

11 *Al Sharq al Awsat*, 7 August 2004.

12 *Zarkaoui*, Barrat, Rizk, and Stephan, op. cit.

13 Talk-show discussion of *Abu Mos'ab al Zarqawi*, op. cit.

14 In April 2005 the United States abnegated any responsibility for the killing of Calipari.

15 *Al Sharq al Awsat*, 29 March 2005.

16 *Al Sharq al Awsat*, 13 March 2005.

17 *Al Sharq al Awsat*, 29 March 2005.

18 One of the demands made in return for Berg's life was the freeing of Iraqi women prisoners.

19 al Zarqawi, *Wisaya li-l-mujahedin*, op. cit.

20 In March 624, about three hundred Muslims led by the Prophet himself defeated the army of Mecca in the area of Badr; see *al Quds al Arabi* (London), 12 May 2004.

21 *Al Sharq al Awsat*, 29 March 2005.

22 Fatwas justifying the execution of hostages and prisoners are also issued by the Saudi Ulema. Yusuf al Ayyiri is a theorist of the Salafi jihadist groups and the author of *Hidaya al hiyari fi yawaz qatl al asara* [Guide for the Bewildered on the Legitimacy of Killing Prisoners], and Abu al Bara al Najdi wrote *Isaad al ajyar fi ihyá sunna nahr al kuffar* [The Happiness and the Advantages of Revitalizing the Tradition of Slaughtering Infidels]. Al Ayyiri answers those who consider it unacceptable to cut the throats of prisoners and those who prefer to respect the international treaties on the treatment of prisoners. Primarily his document is a legal justification for the slaughtering of hostages and prisoners, but he adds that it is acceptable to free them for money. He also includes as prisoners of war civil hostages not taken on the battlefield and even those who are seized unarmed.

Abu al Bara al Najdi attacks those who reject the view that the mujahedin who cut the throat of infidels are "applying God's law and the Tradition of the Prophet, and [acting] in revenge of the oppressed Muslim brothers." In this short book he cites evidence of the lawfulness of such actions extracted from the Koran, the Tradition of the Prophet, and the sayings of the ulema. "God has ordered us to sow panic among the enemy by any legal means until they fear us and stop thinking about killing our brothers and raping our sisters. Slaughtering the infidel who makes war frightens the enemy . . . and provokes his retreat and his defeat."

23 Such as the Egyptian group al Takfir wa al Hijra of Shukri Mustafa. In July 1977 this group had kidnapped the ex-minister of Awqaf (religious endowment), Sheikh Muhammad al Dhahabi, who had been very critical of its thinking. Al Takfir demanded the liberation of some of its members and a ransom for al Dhahabi. The kidnapping ended with his murder. See Abd al Azim Ramadan, *Jamaat al takfir fi Misr* (Cairo: al Haiya al Misriyya al Amma li-l-Kitab, 1995), 111–16.

24 The Movement of National Islamic Resistance fights against the Coalition forces' occupation with the aim of building an independent state; see Salman al Yumayli, um' "al-Ittijahat al fikriyya wa al siyasiyya li-l-maqawama al imqiyya," al Jazeera, 3 October 2004, www.aljazeera.net.

25 *Al Sharq al Awsat*, 20 March 2005.

CHAPTER 10: THE IRAQI JIHAD

1 *Zarkaoui: la Question Terroriste*, documentary by Patrice Barrat, Najat Rizk, and Ranwa Stephan. Arte TV (France and Germany), broadcast 1 March 2005.

2 "Najaf Bombing Kills Shi'ite Leader, Followers Say Iraqi Officials: At Least 125 Dead, 142 Wounded," *al Hayat*, 12 February 2004.

3 Al Tawhid wa al Jihad was a transitional group, formed in April–May 2004 by the merging of small jihadist groups. It lasted until the end of the year when al Zarqawi became the representative of al Qaeda in Iraq.

4 Author's personal archive. See also Fouad Hussein, *Al Zarqawi . . . The Second Generation of al Qaeda,* serialized in fifteen parts in *al Quds al Arabi,* June 2005.

5 Ahmed S. Hashim, "Iraq's Chaos: Why the Insurgency Won't Go Away," *Boston Review*, October–November 2004.

6 Former mujahed who has access to the Iraqi Sunni umma, interview by the author, London, February 2005.

7 Hashim, "Iraq's Chaos," op. cit.

8 Saad al Fagih, interview by the author, London, February 2005.

9 Hashim, "Iraq's Chaos," op. cit.

10 *Al Sharq al Awsat*, 27 August 2004.

11 Communication of al Zarqawi, *Ila ummati al galiyya,* 5 April 2004, author's personal archive. See also Fouad Hussein, *Al Zarqawi . . . The Second Generation of al Qaeda,* serialized in 15 parts in *al Quds al Arabi,* June 2005.

CHAPTER 11: SLIPPING INTO CIVIL WAR

1 Moshe Marzuk, "The City of Falluja, a Myth of Heroism in the Iraqi Insurgency," International Policy Institute for Counter-Terrorism, 1 December 2004; see www.ict.org.il.

2 Ibid.

3 Michael Howard, "40,000 Iraqi Troops Crackdown on Insurgents," *Guardian*, 27 May 2005.

4 Scott Ritter, "The Risk of al Zarqawi's Myth," al Jazeera, 7 January 2005.

5 Dana R. Dillon, "Insurgency Has Its Limits; Enemy Victory Is Far From Assured," *National Review*, 25 November 2003. See http://www.nationalreview.com.

6 "Interview with Muthanna Arit al Dari," *al Dustour* (Amman), 2 November 2004.

7 *Al Sharq al Awsat*, 10 February 2005.

8   Communication of al Zarqawi, "Ila ummati al galiyya," 5 April 2004, author's personal archive. See also Fouad Hussein, *Al Zarqawi . . . The Second Generation of al Qaeda,* serialized in fifteen parts in *al Quds al Arabi,* June 2005.

9   Declaration of Hatem Karim al Fallahi (member of the mediating delegation of the Falluja population), "Maaraka al Falluja," al Jazeera, 7 November 2004.

10 Osama bin Laden,"Communication to the Great Iraqi People and to our Glorious Arab Community Regarding the Battle for the Liberation of Iraq and the Heroic Battle of Falluja,"; see www.al-moharer.net.

11 Al Mashhad al Iraqi, "Maaraka al Falluja," al Jazeera, 7 November 2004. www.aljazeera.net.

12 *Al Sharq al Awsat,* 6 June 2004.

13 According to Abdullah Anas, who fought with the legendary Masood for seven years, there were no more that three thousand Arabs in Afghanistan at any given time.

14 Bin Laden, "Communication to the Great Iraqi People," op. cit.

15 The Iraqi minister of the interior, Fallah al Naquib, declared that al Zarqawi managed to escape one hour before the Iraqi security forces arrived at the end of January 2005, and added that he had managed to elude them several times previously, despite the existence of a special security unit to pursue the leaders of armed groups. In May 2003 Islamic sources in London claimed he had been captured in Falluja, after having opened fire on American soldiers during a protest demonstration carried out by the population; see *al Sharq al Awsat,* 1 May 2003. Almost one year later, a communiqué distributed in Falluja claimed that al Zarqawi had died in an allied air raid against the camps of Ansar al Islam in Sulaymaniyya (Iraqi Kurdistan) in April 2003.

16 Osama bin Laden, "Message to the Iraqi Muslims in Particular and in General to the Community of Believers," *Dhirwat al-Sinam* (virtual magazine of the group Qaida al-Yihad fi bilad al-Rafidayn), no.1 (muharram 1426), 27 December 2004. See also the author's personal archive.

17 Ibid.

18 Khalid al Hammadi , "Former bin Laden 'Bodyguard' Discusses al Qaeda Stance on Saudi, Iraqi Affairs," part 8 of a series of interviews with Nasir al Bahari, *al Quds al Arabi,* 31 March 2005.

CHAPTER 12: THE TRUE NATURE OF THE IRAQI INSURGENCY

1   "Website Says al Zarqawi Wounded," al Jazeera, 24 May 2005; see english.aljazeera.net.

2   Mohamad Bazzi, "Newsday Exclusive: Where is al Zarqawi?," *Newsday,* 21 December 2004.

3   Ibid.

4   James Bennet, "The Mystery of the Insurgency," *New York Times,* 15 May 2005.

5   *The Event*, LBC TV (Beirut), 15 May 2005 broadcast; English translation of transcript by FBIS.

6   Ibid.

7   Scott Ritter, "The Risks of the al Zarqawi Myth," al Jazeera, 14 December 2004.

8   Bennet, "The Mystery of the Insurgency," op. cit.

9   Tom Lasseter, "Political Instability in Iraq Causes Some to Form Militias," Knight Ridder, 6 April 2005.

10   *The Event*, op. cit.

11   "On the question of whether the invasion liberated Iraq or humiliated it, again we see that this region shows more sympathy with the American administration, as 49% of Shi'ites declare that the war was a liberating one, while only 27% say it humiliated their nation. Among Shi'ites outside of this region, the support levels were significantly lower (34%). While many Shi'ites were supportive of the invasion, many more are unsatisfied with the occupation. Support for the Shi'ite Islamist cleric Moqtada al Sadr, who has led the fighting against the US forces in Najaf, one of the holiest cities for Shi'ites, has increased dramatically over the passing month." Eitan Joffe and Amir Steinhart, "Iraq—Primary Threats to Reconstruction," International Policy Institute for Counter-Terrorism, 30 December 2004.

12   Ibid.

13   Greg Jaffe, "Bands of Brothers—New Factor in Iraq: Irregular Brigades Fill Security Void," *Wall Street Journal*, 16 February, 2005.

14   Lasseter, "Political Instability," op. cit.

15   Ibid.

16   A. K. Gupta, "Let a Thousand Militias Bloom," Indymedia, 21 April 2005; see nyc.indymedia.org/feature/display/148554/index.php.

17   Joffe and Steinhart, "Iraq," op. cit. "The Sunni region is a source of great resistance to the American occupation. This region alone has been responsible for over half of the coalition casualties in Iraq from hostile causes. In the main cities of this region alone—Falluja, Ramadi, Tikrit, and Sammara—over 170 American casualties occurred, nearly 20% of all hostile coalition casualties in Iraq since the beginning of the war. Of all regions, it appears that the Sunni areas have been impacted most heavily by violence during the recent war and the occupation that followed. Survey shows that out of the 22% of Iraqi households which have been directly affected by violence over the past year, over 33% came from the Sunni region and another 33% from Baghdad which also includes many Sunni Arabs."

18   "Website Says al Zarqawi Wounded," al Jazeera, op. cit.

CHAPTER 13: THE BALKANIZATION OF IRAQ

1   Mohamad Bazzi, "Newsday Exclusive: Where Is al Zarqawi?," *Newsday*, 21 December 2004.

2   Dan Murphy, "In Fallujah's Wake, Marines Go West, U.S. and Iraqi Forces Have Launched Operation River Blitz, Targeting Insurgents in Cities along the Euphrates," *Christian Science Monitor*, 24 February 2005.

3   "Mass Resignations Before Iraq Vote," CBS News, 16 January 2005.

4   Greg Jaffe, "Bands of Brothers—New Factor in Iraq: Irregular Brigades Fill Security Void," *Wall Street Journal*, 16 February 2005.

5   A. K. Gupta, "Unraveling Iraq's Secret Militias: Ruthless U.S. Tactics are Propelling the Country Toward Civil War," *Z Magazine*. See zmagsite.zmag.org/Images/gupta0505.html.

6   Milan Rai, interview by the author, London, February 2005. See also Milan Rai, *Regime Unchanged: Why the War on Iraq Changed Nothing*, (London: Pluto Press, 2003).

7   Jaffe, "Bands of Brothers," op. cit.

8   Gupta, "Unraveling Iraq's Secret Militias," op. cit

9   Michael Hirsh and John Barry, "The Salvador Option: The Pentagon May Put Special Forces-Led Assassination or Kidnapping Teams in Iraq," *Newsweek*, 8 January 2005; see www.msnbc.msn.com/id/6802629/site/newsweek/.

10 Scott Ritter, "The Salvador Option," al Jazeera, 20 January 2005.

11 Hirsh and Barry, "The Salvador Option," op. cit.

12 Ibid.

13 Robert Parry, "Bush's Death Squads," ConsortiumNews.com, 11 January 2005.

14 Hirsh and Barry, "The Salvador Option," op. cit.

15 Ibid.

16 Thanassis Cambis, "Fight for Minds Uses a TV Show as Battleground," *Boston Globe*, 18 March 2005.

17 Gupta, "Unraveling Iraq's Secret Militias," op. cit. Gupta wrote in *ZMagazine* that the program is now run by the Australian-based Harris Corporation (a major U.S. government contractor that gave 96 percent of its political funding, more than $260,000, to Republicans in 2004).

18 Caryle Murphy and Khalid Saffar, "Actors in the Insurgency Are Reluctant TV Stars: Terror Suspects Grilled, Mocked on Hit Iraqi Show," *Washington Post*, 5 April 2005. See www.washingtonpost.com.

19 See www.csis.org/features/iraq_deviraqinsurgency.pdf.

EPILOGUE

1   See www.usinfo.state.gov, posted 18 November 2004.

2   "Setmariam Nasar is now believed to be in Iraq fighting alongside Jordan-born terrorist chief Abu Musab al Zarqawi, said Brisard, the French investigator, who works for lawyers representing 9/11victims in the United States," Associated Press, 10 March 2005.

3   Spain's leading antiterrorism judge, Baltasar Garzon, said in an indictment
    handed down in September 2003 against thirty-five al Qaeda suspects—includ-
    ing Osama bin Laden and Setmariam—that the Tarragona meeting was used to
    decide last-minute details of the attacks on the World Trade Center and the Pen-
    tagon, including the exact date. See www.usatoday.com/ news/world/2004-11-28-
    spain-911.

4   "The man is believed to be a lieutenant of Mustafa Setmariam, a fugitive with dual
    Syrian and Spanish nationality who is considered a key figure in the March 11 back-
    pack bombings that targeted the Madrid commuter rail network, the newspaper
    ABC said, citing information from the FBI." See ibid.

5   "[Setmariam Nasar], a Spanish citizen by marriage, formerly directed and taught
    at terrorist training camps in Afghanistan, where he met with Osama bin Laden,
    and is known to be an expert in the use of poisons." See www.tkb.org/
    KeyLeader.jsp?memID=6065.

6   "Mustafa Setmariam is currently the 'number two' and ideologue of the terror-
    ist network of Abu Mus'ab al Zarqawi, the head of al Qaeda operating in Iraq,"
    For complete article see "Spanish Daily Examines Role of Two Spanish Terror-
    ists in al Qaeda," Department of Homeland Security, 21 March 2005. See home-
    landsecurotyusnet/spanish_daily_examines_role_of_t.htm.

7   Jean-Charles Brisard, *Zarkaoui, Le nouveau visage d'Al-Qaida* (Paris: Fayard,
    2005), 248–9.

8   *Al Hayat*, 14 January 1996

9   Ibid.

10 *Al Hayat* regarded Setmariam Nassar (Abu Musab al Suri) as the leader of the
    Islamic Armed Group and responsible for the fatwas issued by this group in
    which the assassination of the leader of the Islamic Salvation Front was author-
    ized (30 March 1995, 12 January 1996, 14 January 1996). Setmariam denied this
    accusation (*al Hayat*, 17 January 1996) and won a lawsuit by which the journal
    had to publish an apology to Setmariam (*al Hayat*, 20 April 1997).

11 Omar Abd al Hakim (Abu Musab al Suri), "Raddan ala iilan wizarat al Kharijiyya
    al Amrikiyya" [Answer to the Announcement of the U.S. Secretary of State],
    December 2004, author's personal archive.

12 Ibid.

13 Ibid.

Chronology

OCTOBER 1966: Ahmad Fadel al Khalayash is born in the Ma'sum district of Zarqa, Jordan.

JUNE 1967: On 5 June, the so-called Six Day War between Israel and its Arab neighbors—Egypt, Jordan and Syria—begins. After the Israeli victory, Israel occupies the Sinai, the Gaza Strip, the Golan Heights, the West Bank, and the Old City of Jerusalem.

1967: The exodus of Palestinians begins from the Occupied Territories. Among them is Issam Muhammad Taher al Barqawi, better known as Abu Muhammad al Maqdisi, who takes refuge in Zarqa with his family before moving on to Kuwait. He will become al Zarqawi's future mentor.

1968–1969: The military wing of the PLO clashes repeatedly with Jordanian authorities.

SEPTEMBER 1970: King Hussein of Jordan quashes an attempt by Palestinian groups, mainly the PLO, to overturn his monarchy, and expels the PLO from Jordanian refugee camps housing Palestinians displaced by the Israeli occupation. The event becomes known as Black September.

1971: Sheikh Abdallah Azzam moves to Jordan.

DECEMBER 1979: The Soviet Union invades Afghanistan and what will become known as the anti-Soviet Jihad begins.

1980: The Jordanian government expels Sheikh Abdallah Azzam by military decree.

1981: Sheikh Abdallah Azzam moves to Pakistan and then on to Afghanistan where he soon becomes the spiritual guide of the mujahedin.

1982: Beirut, Lebanon, is shelled during the Israeli occupation.

1984: Sheikh Abdallah Azzam founds the Maktab al Khidamat, the Arab-Afghan Bureau, to coordinate the flow of Arab fighters to Afghanistan to participate in the anti-Soviet Jihad.

1984: Al Zarqawi's father, Fadil Nazzal, dies.

1987: Al Zarqawi is sentenced to two months in prison on a violence-crime conviction.

1988: Sheikh Abdallah Azzam asks Osama bin Laden to produce a register of all Arab mujahedin who participated in the anti-Soviet Jihad. The database is known as Sijl al Qaeda (Register of al Qaeda).

1988: Al Zarqawi marries his first wife, a cousin, Intisar Baqr al Umari.

1988: The siege of Khost, Afghanistan ends and the Soviets withdraw from the city in defeat.

FEBRUARY 1989: The Soviets complete their withdrawal of troops from Afghanistan.

SPRING 1989: Al Zarqawi arrives in Pakistan, from where he moves to Khost.

NOVEMBER 1989: Sheikh Abdallah Azzam is assassinated. Osama bin Laden and Ayman al Zawahiri take control of al Qaeda and transform it into an international terrorist organization.

1989–1990: Al Zarqawi meets and befriends Saleh al Hami, a mujahed, correspondent for a jihadist magazine.

1990: Ayman al Zawahiri develops the concept of suicide missions as terrorist technique for use against the enemy.

1991: Al Hami marries one of al Zarqawi's sisters in Pakistan.

1991: Al Zarqawi begins frequenting the Zayd Bin Mosque in Peshawar.

1991: Al Zarqawi meets al Maqdisi, who becomes his mentor, and begins his religious indoctrination to modern Salafism.

MARCH 1991: Mustafa Shalabi, a supporter of Azzam, is assassinated in New York.

OCTOBER 1991: The Jordanian government backs a Middle East peace conference held in Madrid.

1992: Al Zarqawi begins military training in the Sada camp in Afghanistan.

FEBRUARY 1993: Ramzi Youssef and his accomplices attempt to topple the World Trade Centre in New York.

SEPTEMBER 1993: Israel and the PLO sign the Oslo Peace Agreement in Washington.

AUTUMN 1993: Al Zarqawi and al Maqdisi return to Zarqa.

1994: Al Maqdisi issues a fatwa legitimizing recourse to armed attacks, including the use of explosives, against the Israeli army in Palestine. Al Zarqawi and al Maqdisi form al Tawhid, a jihadist organization.

MARCH 1994: Al Zarqawi and al Madisi are arrested, along with associates, for having established the illegal cell al Tawhid (called Bayaat al Imam by the Jordanian authorities). They are imprisoned in al Suwaqah prison.

OCTOBER 1994: The Jordanian government signs a peace agreement with Israel and a new wave of political violence descends on Jordan.

1995: Al Qaeda bombs the Egyptian embassy in Islamabad, Pakistan.

JUNE 1996: Al Qaeda attacks the Khobar Towers in Dhahran, Saudi Arabia, killing nineteen U.S. soldiers, in what was to date the deadliest attack on Americans in the Middle East since 1983.

NOVEMBER 1996: Al Zarqawi and al Maqdisi are sentenced to fifteen years in prison by the Jordanian courts. They are incarcerated in al Suwaqah and then in Jafar prison.

1996: The first Chechen war ends with the defeat of the Russians. Tamer Sakeh Suwaylam, better known as al Khattab, becomes the leader of the jihadists in Chechnya.

JULY 1997: The Egyptian wing of the Islamic Jihad kills four police officers and fifty-eight tourists in Luxor, Egypt.

1998: Osama bin Laden and Ayman al Zawahiri form the International Front for Jihad Against the Jews and the Crusaders.

AUGUST 1998: Al Qaeda bombs the U.S. embassies in Kenya and Tanzania.

1999: The second Chechen war begins.

1999: Jordanian authorities foil the Millennium Plot.

MAY 1999: King Abdallah of Jordan grants an amnesty in honor of his coronation; al Zarqawi is released from prison.

FALL 1999: Al Zarqawi travels to Pakistan with his mother.

2000: Al Zarqawi is imprisoned in Pakistan for holding an expired visa. When released, he moves to Afghanistan. He settles in Lougar and forms a small group of Jordanians and Palestinians.

2000: Al Zarqawi meets Osama bin Laden in Kandahar.

SEPTEMBER 2000: The Jordanian authorities sentenced to death eight of the twenty-eight men charged with the Millennium Plot. Al Zarqawi's participation is not mentioned.

OCTOBER 2000: Al Qaeda attacks the USS *Cole* in the harbor of Aden, Yemen.

2000–2001: Al Zarqawi establishes a training camp near Herat, on the Afghan border with Iran, for Jordanian, Palestinian, and Syrian fighters.

2000–2001: A group of jihadists from the Jordanian city of Salt settles in Iraqi Kurdistan and forms Yund al Islam, the Army of Islam.

AUGUST 2001: Yitzhak Snir, a fifty-one-year-old Israeli diamond dealer is assassinated in Jordan. The Honourables of Jordan, a previously unknown organization, claims responsibility for the murder.

SEPTEMBER 2001: Al Qaeda attacks the United States.

SEPTEMBER 2001: Al Zarqawi leaves the camp in Herat with a caravan headed for Kandahar.

OCTOBER 2001: Coalition forces begin bombing Afghanistan.

NOVEMBER 2001: Kurdish secret service officials alert the United States that al Zarqawi has crossed over to Kurdish Iraq and that he is al Qaeda's man in Iraq.

NOVEMBER 2001: In the second Millennium Plot trial, al Zarqawi's name is included in the list of people accused of participation.

DECEMBER 2001: Ansar al Islam is formed in Iraqi Kurdistan as members of Yund al Islam merge with other Jihadist groups.

2002: Al Zarqawi participates in the battle of Tora Bora. After the defeat, he crosses Iran and from there reaches Iraqi Kurdistan.

FEBRUARY 2002: Al Zarqawi is sentenced *in absentia* to fifteen years in prison for participating in the Millennium Plot.

OCTOBER 2002: Laurence Foley, an American diplomat, is assassinated in Amman. The Jordanian authorities accuse al Zarqawi of his murder and also of the assassination of Yitzhak Snir.

OCTOBER 2002: Jemaah Islamiyah carries out an attack against a night club in Bali, killing more than two hundred people.

FEBRUARY 2003: U.S. Secretary of State Colin Powell, during his speech to the United Nations Security Council, describes al Zarqawi as the link between al Qaeda and Saddam Hussein's regime.

MARCH 2003: Coalition forces launch a military intervention in Iraq.

APRIL 2003: Residents of Sadr City in Baghdad take up arms against Coalition forces under the leadership of a young Shi'ite cleric Moqtada al Sadr.

MAY 2003: In the Sunni triangle, Sunni residents take up arms against Coalition forces.

JUNE 2003: Moqtada al Sadr forms his own militia, Jeish al Mahdi.

AUGUST 2003: A car bomb explodes at the United Nations' headquarters in Baghdad, killing the head of the delegation and several other members. A few days later, Yassin Jarrad, father of al Zarqawi's second wife, detonates a suicide car bomb at the Imam Ali Mosque in Najaf, killing 125 people, including the Ayatollah Muhammad Baqer al Hakim, spiritual leader of the Shi'ite religious organization Supreme Council of the Islamic Revolution (SCIRI). Al Zarqawi claims responsibility for both attacks.

AUGUST 2003: An attack on the Jordanian embassy in Iraq, leaving fourteen dead and forty wounded, is attributed to al Zarqawi.

DECEMBER 2003: Saddam Hussein is captured by Coalition forces.

JANUARY 2004: In a letter seized by the United States government and attributed to al Zarqawi, the author takes credit for most of the actions carried out against Coalition forces since March 2003.

MARCH 2004: A series of coordinated bombings of the commuter rail system kills 191 in Madrid on March 11. Weeks later Islamic suspects implicated in another failed train bombing blow themselves up.

MARCH 2004: Coalition forces stage first assault on Falluja in an effort to quell resistance to the Coalition occupation. Four Blackwater Security consultants are lynched in Falluja.

APRIL 2004: The Jordanian authorities foil an attack against the U.S. embassy in Amman. Al Zarqawi claims responsibility for the attempted attack. A few days later the Honourables of Jordan claims responsibility for the assassinations of Lawrence Foley and Yitzhak Snir. The message is accompanied by the bullet shells that had been fired at the two victims.

APRIL 2004: More than 250 are killed as U.S. forces launch the siege of Falluja.

APRIL 2004: Al Zarqawi is sentenced to death by hanging by the Jordanian Security Court for his participation in the murder of Laurence Foley.

APRIL 2004: Nicholas Berg is taken hostage by al Zarqawi and executed the following month.

OCTOBER 2004: Osama bin Laden designates al Zarqawi the representative of al Qaeda in Iraq.

NOVEMBER 2004: Coalition forces stage a second major assault on Falluja.

JANUARY 2005: Iraqi legislative elections take place, as Sunni groups call for a boycott, and the party of Ibrahim al Jaafari emerges as the winner.

FEBRUARY 2005: A wave of suicide attacks against Shi'ites hits Iraq.

FEBRUARY 2005: Al Qaeda in Iraq claims responsibility for the attack against a rocket attacks against a U.S. military base against Falluja.

MARCH 2005: Al Zarqawi releases several videos claiming responsibility for various attacks against U.S. forces and Shi'ites in Iraq.

APRIL 2005: A British court acquits four of five defendants in the ricin ring trial. It emerged that no traces of ricin had even been found.

APRIL 2005: Al Zarqawi claims responsibility for suicide attack in al Qa'im and an attack on the west wing of Abu Ghraib prison.

MAY 2005: Rumors of al Zarqawi's injury and death are quashed as al Zarqawi's reassures Osama bin Laden that he alive and well.

JUNE 2005: Al Zarqawi's group claimed responsibility for suicide attacks in six Iraqi cities that killed more than one hundred people and wounded more than three hundred.

JULY 2005: Suicide bombers attack London's transit system during rush hour; more than fifty people are killed. Two weeks later another attack fails as bombs are not properly detonated.

JULY 2005: Egyptian resorts in Taba and Sharm el Sheihk are hit by suicide attacks.

AUGUST 2005: Al Qaeda in Iraq issues a statement declaring that the insurgency will "destroy the American empire."

AUGUST 2005: Al Zarqawi claims responsibility for the Aqaba and Eliat attack against U.S. warship.

AUGUST 2005: Nearly one thousand Shi'ites on pilgrimage are killed in Iraq as a stampede occurs when the crowd panics in response to the rumored presence of a suicide bomber in their midst.

SEPTEMBER 2005: Al Zarqawi claims responsibility for a wave of suicide attacks that kill more than one hundred Shi'ites in Iraq. He states that the attacks are the work of the Abu al Bara bin Malik Brigade, which "specialize[s]" in suicide bomb attacks. He remarks that the attack was part of the "all out war against Shi'ites."

SEPTEMBER 2005: Iraq is in the grip of civil war.

Index

LORETTA NAPOLEONI, a former Fulbright scholar at Johns Hopkins University's Paul H. Nitze School of Advanced International Studies and Rotary Scholar at the London School of Economics, is an expert on international terrorism. Her work appears regularly in many journals and publications, including several European newspapers. As chairman of the countering terrorism financing group for the Club de Madrid, Loretta Napoleoni brought heads of state from around the world together to create a new strategy for combating the financing of terror networks. She has written novels and guidebooks in Italian, and translated and edited books on terrorism. Her most recent novel, *Dossier Baghdad,* is a financial thriller set during the Gulf War. She was among the few people to interview the Red Brigades in Italy after three decades of silence. She is author of *Terror Incorporated* (Seven Stories Press, May 2005).

JASON BURKE is a leading expert on Islamic extremism and chief reporter for the *Observer* (UK). He is author of *Al Qaeda: Casting a Shadow of Terrorism.* He lives in Paris.

NICK FIELDING is a senior reporter at the *Sunday Times* (London), where he specializes in covering stories on terrorism and intelligence issues. He is coauthor of *Masterminds of Terror.* He lives in Oxfordshire.